KILLING THE MESSENGER

Killing the Messenger is a highly readable survey of the current political and legal wars over social media platforms. The book carefully parses attacks against social media coming from both the political left and right to demonstrate how most of these critiques are overblown or without empirical support. The work analyzes regulations directed at social media in the United States and European Union, including efforts to amend Section 230 of the Communications Decency Act. It argues that many of these proposals not only raise serious free-speech concerns but also likely have unintended and perverse public policy consequences. *Killing the Messenger* concludes by identifying specific regulations of social media that are justified by serious, demonstrated harms and that can be implemented without jeopardizing the profoundly democratizing impact social media platforms have had on public discourse. This title is also available as open access on Cambridge Core.

Ashutosh Bhagwat is a Distinguished Professor and the Boochever and Bird Endowed Chair at the University of California, Davis School of Law. Professor Bhagwat is the author of *Our Democratic First Amendment* (2020) and *The Myth of Rights* (2010). He is also a member of the American Law Institute.

Killing the Messenger

THE WAR ON SOCIAL MEDIA

ASHUTOSH BHAGWAT
University of California, Davis

Shaftesbury Road, Cambridge CB2 8EA, United Kingdom

One Liberty Plaza, 20th Floor, New York, NY 10006, USA

477 Williamstown Road, Port Melbourne, VIC 3207, Australia

314–321, 3rd Floor, Plot 3, Splendor Forum, Jasola District Centre,
New Delhi – 110025, India

103 Penang Road, #05–06/07, Visioncrest Commercial, Singapore 238467

Cambridge University Press is part of Cambridge University Press & Assessment,
a department of the University of Cambridge.

We share the University's mission to contribute to society through the pursuit of
education, learning and research at the highest international levels of excellence.

www.cambridge.org
Information on this title: www.cambridge.org/9781009547659

DOI: 10.1017/9781009547703

© Ashutosh Bhagwat 2025

This publication is in copyright. Subject to statutory exception and to the provisions
of relevant collective licensing agreements, with the exception of the Creative Commons
version the link for which is provided below, no reproduction of any part may take
place without the written permission of Cambridge University Press & Assessment.

An online version of this work is published at doi.org/10.1017/9781009547703 under a
Creative Commons Open Access license CC-BY-NC 4.0 which permits re-use,
distribution and reproduction in any medium for non-commercial purposes providing
appropriate credit to the original work is given and any changes made are indicated.
To view a copy of this license visit https://creativecommons.org/licenses/by-nc/4.0

When citing this work, please include a reference to the DOI 10.1017/9781009547703

First published 2025

A catalogue record for this publication is available from the British Library

Library of Congress Cataloging-in-Publication Data
NAMES: Bhagwat, Ashutosh, author.
TITLE: Killing the messenger : the war on social media / Ashutosh Bhagwat,
University of California, Davis
DESCRIPTION: Cambridge, United Kingdom ; New York, NY : Cambridge
University Press, 2025. | Includes bibliographical references and index. |
IDENTIFIERS: LCCN 2025011542 | ISBN 9781009547680 (hardback) | ISBN 9781009547703 (ebook)
SUBJECTS: LCSH: Social media – Law and legislation. | Online social
networks – Law and legislation. | Social media – Government policy. |
Public policy (Law) | Privacy, Right of. | Big data. | Freedom of speech.
CLASSIFICATION: LCC K4345 .B44 2025 | DDC 343.09/944–dc23/eng/20250317
LC record available at https://lccn.loc.gov/2025011542

ISBN 978-1-009-54768-0 Hardback
ISBN 978-1-009-54765-9 Paperback

Cambridge University Press & Assessment has no responsibility for the persistence
or accuracy of URLs for external or third-party internet websites referred to in this
publication and does not guarantee that any content on such websites is, or will
remain, accurate or appropriate.

For EU product safety concerns, contact us at Calle de José Abascal, 56, 1°, 28003 Madrid,
Spain, or email eugpsr@cambridge.org

Contents

Acknowledgments		*page* vii
	Introduction: Social Media as the Mirror of Our Times	1
1	The Conservative War: Social Media as Censors	9
2	The Progressive War: Social Media as Enablers	26
3	The Data War: Social Media Kills Privacy	51
4	Social Media Platforms as Common Carriers	62
5	Social Media as the New Gatekeepers	92
6	Making Social Media Pay for Its Sins: Repealing or Amending Section 230	118
7	Privacy, Big Data, and Free Speech	146
8	Some Ways Forward	164
	Conclusion: Embracing the Unknown	191
Index		195

Acknowledgments

As my thoughts about the role of social media in society have evolved and sharpened over the past five years over which I wrote this book, I benefited from conversations, feedback, and guidance from a huge number of people, all of whom I cannot possibly name here. But thanks are due in particular to Enrique Armijo, Jane Bambauer, Joseph Blocher, Alan Chen, Erin Carroll, Chris Elmendorf, Greg Magarian, Helen Norton, Alex Tsesis, and Jim Weinstein for guidance, feedback, and excellent conversations which deeply shaped this book. Special thanks to Eugene Volokh not only for feedback throughout the time I wrote this book but also for inviting me to become an Executive Editor for a new journal he created, *The Journal of Free Speech Law*, which has provided a key venue for me to work out my thoughts on the subject of social media. Thanks also to Jose Ayala-Artiga and Christine Hanon for exemplary research assistance that helped shape this project. Thanks to my colleagues at the UC Davis School of Law and to Deans Afra Afsharipour, Jessica Berg, Kevin Johnson, and Donna Shestowsky for their support and kindness, and for creating an almost perfect environment in which to do creative work. Finally, thanks to my family – Shannon, Uma, and Declan – for tolerating me even when writing made me close to unbearable.

This book is dedicated to them and to my broader family, including the family we have chosen over the years (you know who you are). You are the people who make everything that I do not only possible but worth doing.

Portions of this book, before revisions, appeared in the following articles and chapters. I would like to thank the journals and editors I have worked with over the years for helping to make my work better.

The New Gatekeepers?: Social Media and the "Search for Truth," 3 J. Free Speech L. 41 (2023), *reprinted in* Media and Society After Technological Disruption (Kyle Langvardt and Justin (Gus) Hurwitz, eds., 2024)

Why Social Media Platforms Are Not Common Carriers, 2 J. Free Speech L. 127 (2022)

Do Platforms Have Editorial Rights?, 1 J. Free Speech L. 97 (2021)

The Law of Facebook, 54 U.C. Davis L. Rev. 2353 (2021)

Introduction

Social Media as the Mirror of Our Times

Looking around the media landscape in recent years, social media is seemingly always in the news; and the news is grim. Politicians and traditional journalists, in particular, appear to loath social media, attributing to it most if not all of the ills of our time. Conservative politicians such as Senator Josh Hawley,[1] Governor Ron DeSantis,[2] and Governor Greg Abbott,[3] as well as their journalistic counterparts at Fox News and the *Wall Street Journal*, attack social media for its alleged bias against conservative speakers and messages. Progressive politicians such as Senator Elizabeth Warren,[4] Senator Amy Klobuchar,[5] and former Speaker Nancy Pelosi,[6] along with their counterparts at the *New York Times* and *Washington Post*, attack social media for failing to block harmful speech such as COVID disinformation, electoral manipulation, and hate speech. Others (notably the left-leaning Brookings Institute) have argued that social media lies at the roots of our increasing political polarization[7] (interestingly, conservatives appear less concerned about polarization).

---

[1] Jane Coaston, *A Republican Senator Wants the Government to Police Twitter for Political Bias*, Vox (June 26, 2019, 3:30 PM), www.vox.com/2019/6/26/18691528/section-230-josh-hawley-conservatism-twitter-facebook.

[2] NetChoice, LLC v. Att'y Gen., Fla., 34 F.4th 1196, 1205 (11th Cir. 2022).

[3] NetChoice, LLC v. Paxton, 1:21-CV-840-RP, 2021 WL 5755120, at *1 (W.D. Tex. Dec. 1, 2021).

[4] Cecelia Kang and Thomas Kaplan, *Warren Dares Facebook with Intentionally False Political Ad*, N.Y. Times (Oct. 12, 2019), www.nytimes.com/2019/10/12/technology/elizabeth-warren-facebook-ad.html.

[5] *See, e.g.*, Health Misinformation Act of 2021 (S.2448), www.congress.gov/bill/117th-congress/senate-bill/2448/text#.

[6] *Pelosi Slams Facebook for Not Taking Down Doctored Video that Makes Her Look Drunk or Impaired*, CBS News (May 30, 2019), www.cbsnews.com/news/pelosi-slams-facebook-for-not-taking-down-doctored-video-that-makes-her-look-drunk-or-impaired/.

[7] Paul Berrett, Justin Hendrix, and Grant Sims, *How Tech Platforms Fuel U.S. Political Polarization and What Government Can Do about It*, Brookings (Sept. 27, 2021), www.brookings.edu/blog/techtank/2021/09/27/how-tech-platforms-fuel-u-s-political-polarization-and-what-government-can-do-about-it/.

And politicians and journalists of all stripes attack social media for failing to adequately protect children, as well as personal privacy. Many of these critics seem to be saying that we would be better off as a society without social media, or at best with a highly mutated and truncated version of it.

This book will examine these and other attacks on social media in some detail, and argue that while criticisms of social media certainly have some basis, they are vastly overstated, sometimes to the point of becoming caricatures. Social media, it is certainly true, is a very new and also highly disruptive communications technology. The same was true of other radically new forms of communication, from the printing press to broadcasting to cable television. But critics of social media tend to attribute almost magical properties to the technology, suggesting that its very existence has fundamentally undermined a previously functional and happy society. This is nonsense.

The truth is that the societal ills that critics attribute to social media clearly predate the technology, and while perhaps they have been exacerbated by social media, in fact no one really knows if that is true.[8] What is clear is that these social problems were already getting worse even before social media burst in on the scene, and probably would have continued to do so without the modern communications revolution. Consider political polarization. If one reads contemporary newspapers, one could easily come to believe that polarization did not exist before the explosion of social media after about 2010. But in fact, it is quite clear that at least as far back as the 1990s, as illustrated by Newt Gingrich's Contract with America and the impeachment of President Bill Clinton, political polarization was a major force in our society. Furthermore, there are good reasons to think that the most important accelerant for that polarization has not been social media but rather Fox News – which was launched in 1996.[9] Fox News, it should be noted, was enabled not by the internet but by the last communications revolution, the explosion in subscriptions to cable television. That is what made cable-only channels such as Fox News, targeted to specific audiences (in this case conservatives), financially profitable. But again, Fox News did not *create* political polarization, it merely benefited from it, and to some degree exacerbated it.

Conservative complaints about liberal bias in social media are similarly deceptive. Regardless of whether this bias exists or not (a question taken up in

---

[8] For a good summary of why empirical research has not given definitive answers regarding harms associated with social media, *see* Gideon Lewis-Kraus, *How Harmful Is Social Media?*, THE NEW YORKER (June 3, 2022), www.newyorker.com/culture/annals-of-inquiry/we-know-less-about-social-media-than-we-think.

[9] *See, e.g.,* Gregory J. Martin and Ali Yurukoglu, *Bias in Cable News: Persuasion and Polarization*, 107 AM. ECON. REV. 2565 (2017).

Chapter 1), the idea that "wokeness" is a particular feature of social media is simply not true. Anti-woke warriors such as Governor Ron DeSantis of Florida regularly accuse almost every major institution in this country, including academia,[10] large corporations,[11] teachers, and civil servants, of being "woke" and biased against the political right. Indeed, that is the whole point of his recent legislative efforts such as his "Don't Say Gay" bill,[12] and seeking to strip Disney of special legal protections.[13] The short of it is that even if, as seems likely, employees and founders of tech firms tend to lean left politically (the two most important tech hubs are, after all, the Bay Area and Seattle), that simply reflects the broader sphere of elite institutions staffed by highly educated people.[14] In other words, this alleged "bias" is not a social media, or even a tech, phenomenon. Furthermore, prominent examples such Peter Thiel and Elon Musk demonstrate that too much should not be made of this – even if somewhat under-represented, conservatives are certainly present in the tech and social media firmament, and in the case of Musk one of them now controls perhaps the most important social media platform for political discourse.

Finally, consider the swath of publicity generated in the fall of 2021 by the disclosure of an internal Facebook study finding that Instagram usage worsened body image issues among teenage girls (the study was leaked by whistleblower Frances Haugen).[15] The results of the study, and Facebook's failure to respond to the findings, is potentially troubling, though as further discussed in Chapter 2, serious questions remain about the actual nature and extent of the problem. Regardless of that, the reports published at the time come close to suggesting that Instagram created this problem, or suddenly made it a serious issue. But this idea – that teenage girls in our society did not suffer from serious body image issues before Instagram's release in 2010 – is beyond ridiculous. Body image

---

[10] Stephanie Saul, Patricia Mazzei and Trip Gabriel, *DeSantis Takes on the Education Establishment, and Builds His Brand*, N.Y. TIMES (Jan. 31, 2023), www.nytimes.com/2023/01/31/us/governor-desantis-higher-education-chris-rufo.html.

[11] Katie Glueck and Frances Robles, *Punishing Disney, DeSantis Signals a Lasting G.O.P. Brawl with Business*, N.Y. TIMES (April 22, 2022), www.nytimes.com/2022/04/22/us/politics/desantis-disney-florida.html.

[12] Jaclyn Diaz, *Florida's Governor Signs Controversial Law Opponents Dubbed "Don't Say Gay,"* NPR (March 28, 2022), www.npr.org/2022/03/28/1089221657/dont-say-gay-florida-desantis.

[13] Mike Schneider, *Settlement Reached in Lawsuit between Disney and Florida Gov. Ron DeSantis' Allies*, AP NEWS (March 27, 2024), https://apnews.com/article/disney-florida-ron-desantis-settlement-91040178ad4708939e621dd57bc5e494.

[14] Nate Cohn, *How Educational Differences Are Widening America's Political Rift*, N.Y. TIMES (Sept. 8, 2021), www.nytimes.com/2021/09/08/us/politics/how-college-graduates-vote.html.

[15] Georgia Wells, Jeff Horwitz, and Deepa Seetharaman, *Facebook Knows Instagram Is Toxic for Teen Girls, Company Documents Show*, WALL STREET JOURNAL (Sept. 14, 2021), www.wsj.com/articles/facebook-knows-instagram-is-toxic-for-teen-girls-company-documents-show-11631620739.

issues (and related problems such as eating disorders) have been a severe, if seriously under-addressed, problem in our society for decades. Long before social media, these problems were stoked by the fashion industry (and the body types of the models they chose to employ), magazines, and of course Hollywood. Again, is it possible that social media (and Instagram in particular) have made the problem worse? Of course it is; but given the long-standing severity of this issue, it seems difficult to believe that social media is responsible for most of it.

Nor should any of this be a surprise. Social media, after all, is very new. The first true social media site, MySpace, did not launch until 2003, and the two first modern platforms, Facebook and Twitter/X, did not become available to the general public until 2006[16] (Instagram, as noted earlier, did not launch until 2010[17]). Furthermore, early in their existence social media were relatively niche services. Only with the widespread use of smart phones after about 2010 (the very first iPhone was not released until 2007[18]) did social media become a significant force in society. Yet the story told by social media critics is that somehow, in the merely six years from 2010 to 2016 (with its extraordinarily divisive presidential election), social media had turned American society topsy turvy and created an entire bevy of fundamental, new societal problems. That is very hard to believe, given the pace at which social transformations typically occur.

In fact, the current palpitations over social media must be understood in the context of a long, historical trend of panic in the face of new communications and media technologies. The invention of the printing press around 1440 by Johannes Gutenberg triggered concerns among contemporary rulers, and the Catholic Church, about the possibility that widespread access to printed works would foment dissent. And certainly, in the case of the Church the concerns were legitimate given the crucial role of the printing press in the Protestant Reformation (Martin Luther is often described as the first best-selling author). These concerns in turn triggered responses such as the licensing of the press by the English King Henry VIII in 1538,[19] and the adoption

---

[16] *Meta: Who We Are, Company History*, https://about.meta.com/company-info/; Jonathan Vanian, *Twitter Is Now Owned by Elon Musk: Here's a Brief History from the App's Founding in 2006 to the Present*, CNBC (Oct. 29, 2022), www.cnbc.com/2022/10/29/a-brief-history-of-twitter-from-its-founding-in-2006-to-musk-takeover.html. After purchasing Twitter in 2022, Elon Musk renamed the platform "X" on July 23, 2023. For clarity and simplicity, that platform will be called "Twitter/X" throughout the book.

[17] Gareth Evans, *Instagram: The Dog That Launched a Social Media Giant*, BBC NEWS (Sept. 25, 2018), www.bbc.com/news/technology-45640386.

[18] www.apple.com/newsroom/2007/01/09Apple-Reinvents-the-Phone-with-iPhone/.

[19] Michael I. Meyerson, *The Neglected History of the Prior Restraint Doctrine: Rediscovering the Link between the First Amendment and the Separation of Powers*, 34 IND. L. REV. 295, 298 (2001).

by the Catholic Church of the Index of Prohibited Books (*Index Librorum Prohibitum*) in 1559.[20]

When motion pictures came around, the reaction was similarly panicked. Justice Antonin Scalia of the United States Supreme Court, in an opinion striking down a California law banning the sale of violent video games to minors, quotes a *New York Times* article from the early motion picture era expressing concerns that motion pictures will "turn the thoughts of the easily influenced to paths which sometimes lead to prison."[21] Indeed, these concerns were so widespread that the Supreme Court at first refused to extend *any* First Amendment protections to movies;[22] indeed, it did not reverse course until 1952![23] And as Justice Scalia also notes in the violent video game case, similar hysterical fears were raised about dime novels, radio dramas, and comic books.[24]

Turning to more recent times, consider the internet. Despite the enormous expressive and commercial potential of this new technology, Congress's first reaction to the internet was to pass a law (quickly invalidated by the Supreme Court) banning indecent or "patently offensive" materials on the internet, if they were accessible by minors.[25] Given the nature of the internet, especially in its early days, this law covered almost all online content. And it should be noted that the ill-defined terms "indecent" or "patently offensive" cover material that is, in the main, entirely legal and protected as to adults, and goes far beyond pornography (however defined). The effect of this law, then, would have been to reduce the entire internet to a level appropriate for children, an obviously terrible outcome; yet Congress adopted this silly provision by an overwhelming vote, driven by anxiety over the societal implications of the internet as a new medium of communication.

The current panic over social media, then, looks very familiar (and one suspects will look equally overblown in a few decades). Coming back now to specific concerns raised by social media, one might ask in closing where to draw the line between legitimate concerns about this new technology (which surely exist) and existential panic. Addressing that question is, in a nutshell, the theme and goal of this book. But to take a first cut at the answer now, it is worth considering how exactly social media has changed the social and

---

[20] Lucien Febvre and Martin Henri-Jean, THE COMING OF THE BOOK: THE IMPACT OF PRINTING 1450–1800, at 244 (1976).
[21] Brown v. Entertainment Merchants Ass'n, 564 U.S. 786, 797 (2011).
[22] Mutual Film Corp. v. Industrial Comm'n of Ohio, 236 U.S. 242 (1915).
[23] Joseph Burstyn, Inc. v. Wilson, 343 U.S. 495 (1952).
[24] *Brown*, 564 U.S. at 797–98.
[25] Reno v. American Civil Liberties Union, 521 U.S. 844 (1997).

communicative landscape. One short answer, as Professor Eugene Volokh of UCLA predicted decades ago, is cheap speech.[26] The internet in general, but social media in particular, has radically decreased the cost of speech to ordinary people who, in the pre-internet age, had no practical way to reach large audiences at a reasonable cost. Relatedly, social media has democratized speech, eliminating the monopoly that traditional media and political elites had over the content of public discourse. Another way of putting this point is that social media has eliminated gatekeepers. During most of the twentieth century these gatekeepers, the traditional institutional media (newspapers, radio stations, and most importantly the Big Three television broadcast networks), had almost complete control over what speakers and content reached mass audiences (this is the topic of Chapter 5). Today, in contrast, cacophony prevails.

That these changes have occurred is obvious. That they have important consequences is also obvious. And that some of those consequences are negative is also surely true. Human beings being what we are, some people have inevitably misused the new power of communication they possess by doing things like defaming their enemies, lying about all sorts of things, spreading hatred of vulnerable groups, doxing vulnerable individuals, up to such grotesque things as posting nonconsensual intimate images (including "revenge porn") and incitements to violence. All technology can be misused, and social media is surely no exception.

But to focus solely on such negative consequences is to miss the big picture. In many ways, the elimination of elite gatekeepers is a highly positive development in that it empowers ordinary people to decide for themselves what matters. In other words, it is in many ways a good thing that the universe of speech available to all of us has exploded thanks to social media and other internet-enabled phenomenon such as Substack. It is also a good thing that ordinary people can potentially have a real voice in public discourse, and reach mass audiences when they have something to say without convincing a gatekeeper that what they are saying is worthwhile. Gatekeepers inevitably have their own, self-serving agendas, and there are upsides to being free of them. No longer can media elites – who often were entangled with political elites – decide what citizens should and should not know, such as whether political leaders have committed personal improprieties (consider JFK's adultery) or worse. It is also true that social media grants people a level of interaction with the wider world, including with friends and relatives in faraway places, that never existed before – I for one have had more contact with my

---

[26] Eugene Volokh, *Speech and What It Will Do*, 104 YALE L.J. 1805 (1995).

cousins in India in the past decade than in my entire life before put together, all thanks to social media. In short, democratizing speech, like democracy in general, empowers ordinary people, both as citizens and in their personal lives. And this should generally be seen as a valuable development, to be embraced rather than feared.

Given these fairly obvious points, it may seem strange that so much of the commentary over social media is so negative. But then consider the source of the commentary: It is precisely those media and political elites, the gatekeepers and dominant voices of the earlier age, who have been most harmed and disempowered by this technological revolution. Their negativity, then, should come as no surprise. The more interesting question is why criticisms of social media resonate so much with the rest of us, who have on the whole gained rather than lost power and access thanks to social media. The answer must lie, I would suggest, in the general malaise and divisiveness that our broader society has suffered in recent decades. Our current problems – such as political polarization, deaths of despair,[27] economic stagnation in the heartland and among the working class, and a general decline in sociability and community[28] – are very real, and they have been building for decades. And since 2020 they have been amplified by the COVID pandemic and attendant lock downs (and opportunistic political reactions to the same, on both sides of the political aisle). But importantly, while social media may play some role in amplifying some of these problems (such as polarization and the decline in social contacts), their roots lie elsewhere, and some issues such as economic stagnation and deaths of despair surely have little or nothing to do with social media or the internet.

Nonetheless, many people, including some extremely serious and well-respected public intellectuals,[29] associate the rise of social media with some or most of these ills. The reason that is so, one suspects, is that social media is the place where these problems are displayed to most people. As former Justice Anthony M. Kennedy of the US Supreme Court put it in a case involving regulation of social media, "the most important place ... for the exchange of views, today ... is cyberspace – the 'vast democratic forums of the Internet' in general, ... and social media in particular."[30] In other words, social media is today, for most ordinary people, their primary source of news and information.

---

[27] ANNE CASE and ANGUS DEATON, DEATHS OF DESPAIR AND THE FUTURE OF CAPITALISM (2020).
[28] ROBERT D. PUTNAM, BOWLING ALONE: THE COLLAPSE AND REVIVAL OF AMERICAN COMMUNITY (2000).
[29] Jonathan Haidt, *Why the Past 10 Years of American Life Have Been Uniquely Stupid*, THE ATLANTIC (April 11, 2022), www.theatlantic.com/magazine/archive/2022/05/social-media-democracy-trust-babel/629369/.
[30] Packingham v. North Carolina, 137 S. Ct. 1730, 1735 (2017) (*quoting* Reno, 521 U.S., at 868).

So, because today teenage girls are most likely to view unreasonably perfect body shapes on Instagram, we attribute the problem to Instagram. And because today, vociferous political statements are most likely to be spread via Twitter/X, ditto.

But this association is an attribution error. The problems that contemporary commentators are fixated on long predate the rise of social media, and have at best been modestly amplified by it. The truth is that the supposed ills of social media are in fact the ills of our broader culture. It is just that the pervasiveness of social media makes it the primary mirror in which we see ourselves; and apparently, we do not much like what we see.

1

The Conservative War

Social Media as Censors

For many years, conservative politicians and journalists have complained that the major social media and other tech platforms are biased against conservative speech and speakers. And while these criticisms are not new, they have become much louder and more insistent following the deplatforming of President Trump by the major social media platforms, following the attack on the US Capitol on January 6, 2021. What is the nature of these critiques, to what extent are they legitimate, and what ultimately lies behind them? These are the questions this chapter explores.

As a starting point, it is important to recognize that while their volume has increased since 2021, conservative claims of alleged political bias on the part of social media are not new. As far back as the 2016 presidential campaign, conservative commentators began accusing Facebook of a left-leaning bias in its selection of "trending" news articles.[1] These claims were rooted in conservatives' (probably accurate) perception that the employees and management of the major social media firms, who are mainly residents of the San Francisco Bay Area, tend to lean politically to the left. Whatever the legitimacy of these claims (a question addressed later), the irony of this, of course, is that then-candidate Donald Trump was *far* more effective at deploying social media, especially Twitter/X, to his political advantage than his Democratic rival in the presidential election, Hilary Clinton (though, to be fair, he was also more effective than his Republican rivals in the primary elections).

After Trump's election, the loudest attacks on social media shifted to their data privacy practices, especially after the Cambridge Analytica scandal of 2018. That scandal arose when in the lead-up to the 2016 presidential

---

[1] John Herrman and Mike Isaac, Conservatives Accuse Facebook of Political Bias, N.Y. TIMES (May 9, 2016), www.nytimes.com/2016/05/10/technology/conservatives-accuse-facebook-of-political-bias.html.

election Cambridge Analytica, a political firm tied to Republican donors and to Stephen Bannon (who later became a senior adviser to President Trump), harvested private data on over 50 million Facebook users. The data was gathered by a Cambridge University scientist on the pretense that they were engaged in academic research, and then it was used by Cambridge Analytica to construct profiles of voters, which were in turn used by the firm to provide services to the 2016 presidential campaigns of Senator Ted Cruz and then Donald Trump.[2] The fact that Facebook, albeit inadvertently, aided the Trump campaign in this fashion, as well as in other ways (notably by failing to block Russian manipulation of the election[3]), did not, however, have any impact on ongoing conservative claims of bias against them.

For example, during Mark Zuckerberg's testimony before Congress in July 2020, Republican members of Congress repeatedly accused Facebook of disproportionately targeting conservative content for blocking, echoing long-standing similar claims made by a number of prominent Republican political leaders.[4] Soon thereafter, in early August, Facebook deleted a post by President Trump's campaign linking to a video in which Trump had said that children were "virtually immune" from COVID-19, on the grounds that the post violated its policies against COVID misinformation (soon after this Twitter/X blocked the Trump campaign's account for linking to the same video).[5] In response, the White House deputy national press secretary accused Facebook and other Silicon Valley firms of "flagrant bias against this president, where the rules are only enforced in one direction."[6]

Indeed, throughout the COVID-19 pandemic, conservative politicians and commentators attacked social media firms for blocking, or labeling as misinformation, what they perceived to be conservative views on the disease. One example is social media platforms' response to the claim, heavily pushed by

---

[2] Kevin Granville, *Facebook and Cambridge Analytica: What You Need to Know as Fallout Widens*, N.Y. TIMES (MARCH 19, 2018), www.nytimes.com/2018/03/19/technology/facebook-cambridge-analytica-explained.html.

[3] Mike Isaac and Daisuke Wakabayashi, *Russian Influence Reached 126 Million through Facebook Alone*, N.Y. TIMES (Oct. 30, 2017), www.nytimes.com/2017/10/30/technology/facebook-google-russia.html.

[4] David McCabe and Cecelia Kang, *Lawmakers from Both Sides Take Aim at Big Tech Executives*, N.Y. TIMES (July 29, 2020), www.nytimes.com/live/2020/07/29/technology/tech-ceos-hearing-testimony#republicans-focused-on-bias-concerns-about-platforms.

[5] Cecilia Kang and Sheera Frenkel, *Facebook Removes Trump Campaign's Misleading Coronavirus Video*, N.Y. TIMES (Aug. 5, 2020), www.nytimes.com/2020/08/05/technology/trump-facebook-coronavirus-video.html.

[6] Ibid.

senior Trump Administration officials,[7] that COVID-19 originated from an accidental leak from a lab in Wuhan, China. Facebook originally decided to remove claims, though it later rescinded that decision;[8] and Twitter/X originally labeled such claims as misinformation.[9] When some, but not all, US government agencies expressed "low confidence" support for the lab-leak theory, conservative politicians and journalists claimed vindication and sharply attacked Facebook and Twitter/X for their earlier policies.[10] Similarly, when President Trump began publicly claiming that the antimalarial drug hydroxychloroquine was effective in treating COVID-19,[11] Facebook and Twitter/X began blocking such claims as medical misinformation[12] (they were probably correct to do so,[13] though definitive proof remains elusive). Conservative politicians duly attacked social media for their "censorship."[14] Senator Ted Cruz of Texas, a prominent Republican, indeed went so far as to criticize both the Biden Administration and "Big Tech" for allegedly coordinating actions to block misinformation about COVID-19 vaccines.[15] And ultimately, a group of Republican politicians and activists, led by Missouri's Attorney General, sued the Biden Administration on the theory that its efforts to pressure the

[7] Erin Banco and Daniel Lippman, *Top Trump Officials Pushed the COVID-19 Lab-Leak Theory. Investigators Had Doubts*, POLITICO (June 15, 2021), www.politico.com/news/2021/06/15/wuhan-lab-trump-officials-covid-494700.

[8] Guy Rosen, *An Update on Our Work to Keep People Informed and Limit Misinformation about COVID-19*, META (April 16, 2020, updated Feb. 8, 2021 and May 26, 2021), https://about.fb.com/news/2020/04/covid-19-misinfo-update/#removing-more-false-claims.

[9] Amanda Seitz, *Twitter to Label Disputed COVID-19 Tweets*, AP NEWS (May 11, 2020), https://apnews.com/article/virus-outbreak-health-us-news-ap-top-news-technology-c8a542e2f22004c0c06cbbe1e1b58a52.

[10] Cristiano Lima, *New Report on COVID-19 Origin Puts Social Media in GOP's Crosshairs*, WASHINGTON POST (Feb. 27, 2023), www.washingtonpost.com/politics/2023/02/27/new-report-covid-19-origin-puts-social-media-gops-crosshairs/.

[11] Andrew Solender, *All the Times Trump Has Promoted Hydroxychloroquine*, FORBES (May 22, 2020), www.forbes.com/sites/andrewsolender/2020/05/22/all-the-times-trump-promoted-hydroxychloroquine/?sh=fd1982046432.

[12] Christopher Giles, Shayan Sararizadeh, and Jack Goodman, *Hydroxychloroquine: Why a Video Promoted by Trump Was Pulled on Social Media*, BBC (July 28, 2020), www.bbc.com/news/53559938.

[13] Katie Thomas, *F.D.A. Revokes Emergency Approval of Malaria Drugs Promoted by Trump*, N.Y. TIMES (June 15, 2020), www.nytimes.com/2020/06/15/health/fda-hydroxychloroquine-malaria.html.

[14] Natalie Allison, *Tennessee Doctor in U.S. Senate Race Slams Fauci, Defends Use of Disproved COVID-19 Cure*, THE TENNESSEAN (Aug. 3, 2020), www.tennessean.com/story/news/politics/2020/08/03/tennessee-senate-race-dr-manny-sethi-bill-hagerty-slam-fauci-argue-hydroxychloroquine-censorship/5574329002/.

[15] Danielle Wallace, *Cruz Accuses Biden of Being "In Bed" with Big Tech Amid Vaccine Misinformation Controversy*, FOX NEWS (July 18, 2021), www.foxnews.com/politics/cruz-biden-big-tech-in-bed-vaccine-controversy.

platforms regarding COVID misinformation violated the First Amendment. The claimants originally won a resounding victory in the (very conservative) United States Court of Appeals for the Fifth Circuit.[16] Their lawsuit, however, was ultimately dismissed by the US Supreme Court on grounds that effectively rejected the claim that the Biden Administration was responsible for the platforms' misinformation policies.[17]

While the COVID-19 pandemic (and responses to it) sharply stimulated the conservative war on social media and claims of political bias, it was only a beginning. The event that unquestionably took it to a new level (and, as we shall see, even brought some Supreme Court Justices into the mix) was the deplatforming of President Donald Trump by the major platforms in January of 2021. The background here is of course familiar. After losing reelection in the November 2020 presidential election, President Trump (supported by conservative news outlets such as Fox News and Breibart) began aggressively disseminating unsupported charges of widespread election fraud, claiming that he had in fact won the election. On January 6, 2021, Congress was scheduled to convene to count electoral votes, as required by the Twelfth Amendment to the US Constitution. On the same day, President Trump called for a rally of his supporters outside the White House. After President Trump addressed the rally, his supporters began moving toward the Capitol. Eventually, some of those supporters began to break through police barricades and physically attack Capitol police officers, and then broke into the Capitol itself. Hours of violence and mayhem followed, during which time President Trump continued to Tweet claims of election fraud, though he also did call for his supporters to remain peaceful. Eventually law enforcement was able to secure the Capitol, after which Trump uploaded posts onto social media which seemed to express support for the rioters. These posts were, shortly thereafter, taken down by Facebook and Twitter/X, and President Trump's accounts were temporarily suspended. Ultimately, Congress reconvened, and certified Joe Biden's election as President (though only after a number of Republican members of Congress challenged the election results).[18]

Horrific as the events of that day were, for our purposes the key point is that social media platforms' suspension of President Trump originally occurred on January 6 itself, immediately in the wake of the attack on the Capitol. And

---

[16] Missouri v. Biden, 83 F.4th 641 (5th Cir. 2023).
[17] Murthy v. Missouri, 144 S. Ct. 1972 (2024).
[18] Kat Lonsdorf, Courtney Dorning, Amy Isackson, Mary Louise Kelly, and Ailsa Chang, *A Timeline of How the Jan. 6 Attack Unfolded – Including Who Said What and When*, NPR (June 9, 2022), www.npr.org/2022/01/05/1069977469/a-timeline-of-how-the-jan-6-attack-unfolded-including-who-said-what-and-when.

originally, those suspensions were temporary, in response to the seemingly continuing risk of violence. Soon thereafter, however, citing concerns about violence leading up to Biden's inauguration on January 21, Facebook and Twitter/X made Trump's deplatforming permanent.[19] Twitter/X ultimately reinstated Trump's account after Elon Musk's purchase of the platform in late 2022,[20] and Facebook reduced its suspension to two years, in conformity with a recommendation by the Facebook Oversight Board[21] (Trump was duly reinstated in January of 2023[22]).

The primary conservative response to these events was a deluge of criticism alleging that the major tech platforms were intentionally silencing conservative speakers up to and including the sitting President of the United States. Donald Trump, Jr., the President's son, described the actions (on Twitter/X, ironically) as Orwellian.[23] Similarly, then-Representative Devin Nunes, a prominent Trump supporter who later left Congress to run Trump's new social media platform Truth Social, sent a letter to colleagues in the House of Representatives on January 12, 2021, stating that "Big Tech has launched an overwhelming offensive to deprive Americans of our freedom to communicate with each other," with the goal of "transforming our digital space into a left-wing monoculture in which conservatives are harassed, ostracized, banned, deplatformed, and threatened with an array of other punishments."[24]

Nor did the attacks originate only in Washington, DC. Republican Governor Ron DeSantis of Florida, in particular, has made criticisms of social media bias a central part of his "War on Woke," inducing the Florida legislature to pass legislation (titled S.B. 7072) that restricts social media platforms' power to moderate content on their platforms or remove users.[25] While the provisions of the Florida law are complex, their primary thrust was to ban

---

[19] Dylan Byers, *How Facebook and Twitter Decided to Take Down Trump's Accounts*, NBC News (Jan. 14, 2021), www.nbcnews.com/tech/tech-news/how-facebook-twitter-decided-take-down-trump-s-accounts-n1254317.

[20] Ryan Mac and Kellen Browning, *Elon Musk Reinstates Trump's Twitter Account*, N.Y. Times (Nov. 19, 2022), www.nytimes.com/2022/11/19/technology/trump-twitter-musk.html.

[21] Elizabeth Dwoskin, *Trump Is Suspended from Facebook for 2 Years and Can't Return Until "Risk to Public Safety Is Receded*," Washington Post (June 4, 2021), www.washingtonpost.com/technology/2021/06/03/trump-facebook-oversight-board/.

[22] Nick Clegg, *Ending Suspension of Trump's Accounts with New Guardrails to Deter Repeat Offenses*, Meta (Jan. 25, 2023), https://about.fb.com/news/2023/01/trump-facebook-instagram-account-suspension/.

[23] Donald Trump Jr. (@DonaldJTrumpJr), X (Jan. 8, 2021, 4:10 PM), https://twitter.com/donaldjtrumpjr/status/1347697226466828288.

[24] Paul Gosar (@DrPaulGosar), X (Jan. 12, 2021, 12:33 PM), https://twitter.com/DrPaulGosar/status/1349092033491853316 (displaying Letter from Devin Nunes, Member of Congress, to House Colleagues (Jan. 12, 2021).

[25] Fla. State. §§ 106.072, 501.2041.

platforms from deplatforming candidates for political office (a rather obviously self-serving provision by the Florida legislature), limiting the visibility of posts *about* political candidates, and limiting "journalistic enterprises." The legislature justified these steps by describing social media platforms as being equivalent to "public utilities" or "common carriers." When he signed the bill, Governor DeSantis explained that its purpose was to ensure that "Big Tech" does not "discriminate in favor of the dominant Silicon Valley ideology," or against conservative voices.[26] When challenged in court, major portions of the Florida law were struck down by both a federal district court and the regional federal court of appeals (the Eleventh Circuit).[27] How the Supreme Court ultimately resolved the case will be taken up in detail in Chapter 4 (spoiler alert: The Supreme Court failed for technical reasons to finally resolve the case but strongly endorsed the Eleventh Circuit's basic legal reasoning).

Not to be outdone by his fellow conservative, Republican Governor Greg Abbott of Texas soon followed suit. In particular, Abbott began making public statements regarding the need to adopt legislation that would prevent platforms from "silenc[ing] conservative speech and ideas."[28] And at Abbott's urging (after a first, unsuccessful attempt), in September of 2021 a special session of the Texas legislature enacted HB 20. Like the Florida law, HB 20 insists that "social media platforms function as common carriers."[29] And like Florida, the Texas law limited social media content moderation policies. But in its impact on social media content moderation, Texas went well beyond Florida. Rather than merely protecting politicians and journalists, HB 20 forbids *all* censorship by social media platforms based on "the viewpoint of the user or another person," "the viewpoint represented in the user's expression," or "a user's geographic location" within Texas.[30] In practice, then, the effects of HB 20 were intended to be enormously broad, effectively depriving social media firms of any meaningful editorial control over the platforms that they own. When this law was challenged in federal court, the regional federal court of appeals covering Texas (the Fifth Circuit) *upheld* HB 20, reversing a lower court decision and adopting reasoning that was essentially the opposite of the Eleventh Circuit's.[31] But as we shall see in Chapter 4, the Supreme Court, on

---

[26] NetChoice, LLC v. Att'y Gen., Fla., 34 F.4th 1196, 1205 (11th Cir. 2022).
[27] Ibid.
[28] Greg Abbott (@GregAbbott_TX), X (March 4, 2021, 8:52 PM), https://twitter.com/GregAbbott_TX/status/1367699473703579652.
[29] Tex. H.B. No. 20, 87th Leg., 2nd Sess. § 1(4) (2021).
[30] Tex. Civ. Prac. & Rem. Code § 143A.002(a)(1)–(3).
[31] NetChoice v. Paxton, 49 F.4th 439 (5th Cir. 2022).

review, flatly rejected the Fifth Circuit's legal reasoning as inconsistent with precedent and basic First Amendment principles.

That conservative politicians would want to invoke a "War on Woke" or a "War on Big Tech" to energize their base is hardly surprising. What is striking, however, is where the legal inspiration for their actions originated. It was Justice Clarence Thomas of the United States Supreme Court. A few months after President Biden took office on January 21, 2021, the Supreme Court dismissed a First Amendment case brought against President Trump based on his actions blocking certain users from posting on his Twitter/X account (the case was dismissed because Trump was no longer President, so no longer subject to the First Amendment). Justice Thomas agreed with the Court's action, but then went on to write a lengthy screed (I say screed because the opinion had little or nothing to do with the case under review) raising concerns about social media's power over free speech, and advocating legislative action regulating social media platforms as either "common carriers" or "places of public accommodation."[32] His arguments were primarily historical and legal, but they were clearly motivated (he said as much) by the seeming anomaly that the First Amendment arguably prevented President Trump from controlling his Twitter/X account but did not prevent Twitter/X from entirely deplatforming Trump. Justice Thomas is of course a famously conservative member of the Supreme Court, and also one of its most overtly partisan members (his wife was prominently involved in efforts to overturn the 2020 presidential election[33]). As such, his publicly stated views on this matter provide an important window into how broadly distrust of social media, and belief in its political bias, pervaded conservative circles in the aftermath of the January 6 attack and President Trump's subsequent deplatforming.

In short, conservatives apparently strongly dislike and distrust the major social media platforms. But are they justified in doing so? That question is almost impossible to definitively resolve, and in truth the answer generally lies in the eyes of the beholder. What is relatively clear is that prior to Elon Musk's purchase of Twitter/X in late 2022,[34] there was little empirical or other strong evidence supporting conservative claims of social media bias

---

[32] Biden v. Knight First Amend. Inst. at Columbia Univ., 141 S. Ct. 1220 (2021) (Thomas, J., concurring).
[33] *Ginni Thomas, Justice Clarence Thomas' Wife, Exchanged Texts with Mark Meadows about Efforts to Overturn the 2020 Election*, CBS NEWS (March 24, 2022), www.cbsnews.com/news/ginni-thomas-clarence-wife-mark-meadows-texts-2020-election-overturn/.
[34] Kate Conger and Lauren Hirsch, *Elon Musk Completes $44 Billion Deal to Own Twitter*, N.Y. TIMES (Oct. 27, 2022), www.nytimes.com/2022/10/27/technology/elon-musk-twitter-deal-complete.html.

(though to be fair, there was also no conclusive evidence refuting them).[35] Indeed, press reports suggest the contrary, that social media platforms historically bent over backward to permit conservative content to remain online,[36] and an internal Twitter/X study suggests that its recommendation algorithms also favored conservative content (except, apparently, in Germany).[37]

After his takeover, however, Musk released a selection of internal documents – the so-called Twitter Files – which purported to support conservative claims of bias.[38] These documents consisted of communications among Twitter/X employees regarding some of their most important content-moderation decisions, including the deplatforming of President Trump. The small group of (carefully chosen) journalists to whom Musk released the material, including notably Matt Taibbi and Bari Weiss, duly argued that the files demonstrated a left-leaning bias on the part of Twitter/X in its content moderation decisions, just as Elon Musk had claimed.[39] Unsurprisingly, conservative media outlets such as Fox News took up the call, treating the Twitter Files revelations as a major scandal undermining the legitimacy of the major social media platforms, especially Twitter/X.[40] Other major media outlets such as CNN and NPR, however, expressed skepticism that the Twitter Files contained any significant new revelations or demonstrated bias, suggesting instead that the files "have largely not contained any revelatory information. So far, the files have failed to do much

---

[35] Alison Durkee, *Are Social Media Companies Biased against Conservatives? There's No Solid Evidence, Report Concludes*, FORBES (Feb. 1, 2021), www.forbes.com/sites/alisondurkee/2021/02/01/are-social-media-companies-biased-against-conservatives-theres-no-solid-evidence-report-concludes/.

[36] Michel Martin and Will Jarvis, *Far-Right Misinformation Is Thriving on Facebook. A New Study Shows Just How Much*, NPR (March 6, 2021), www.npr.org/2021/03/06/974394783/far-right-misinformation-is-thriving-on-facebook-a-new-study-shows-just-how-much; Bobby Allyn, *Facebook Keeps Data Secret, Letting Conservative Bias Claims Persist*, NPR (Oct. 5, 2020), www.npr.org/2020/10/05/918520692/facebook-keeps-data-secret-letting-conservative-bias-claims-persist.

[37] Luca Bell, *Examining Algorithmic Amplification of Political Content on Twitter*, X BLOG (Oct. 21, 2021), https://blog.twitter.com/en_us/topics/company/2021/rml-politicalcontent.

[38] Shannon Bond, *Elon Musk Is Using the Twitter Files to Discredit Foes and Push Conspiracy Theories*, NPR (Dec. 14, 2022), www.npr.org/2022/12/14/1142666067/elon-musk-is-using-the-twitter-files-to-discredit-foes-and-push-conspiracy-theories.

[39] Matt Taibbi (@mtaibbi), *1. Thread: THE TWITTER FILES*, X (Dec. 2, 2022, 3:34 PM), https://twitter.com/mtaibbi/status/1598822959866683394; Bari Weiss, *Our Reporting at Twitter*, THE FREE PRESS (Dec. 15, 2022), www.thefp.com/p/why-we-went-to-twitter.

[40] Joseph A. Wulfsohn, *What Elon Musk's Twitter Files Have Uncovered about the Tech Giant So Far*, FOX NEWS (Jan. 22, 2023), www.foxnews.com/media/what-elon-musks-twitter-files-uncovered-about-tech-giant.

outside highlighting exactly how messy content moderation can be."[41] In other words, nothing to see here folks.

So who is right? Gerard Baker, a conservative former *Wall Street Journal* editor-in-chief, may have had it right when he suggested that while the Twitter Files do not reveal any intentional misbehavior or bias on the part of Twitter/X decisionmakers (apart from a lack of transparency or honesty), it does reveal a form of groupthink as a result of the fact that the staff of Twitter/X (based in San Francisco) overwhelmingly share a particular, progressive worldview which does not partake of doubt. The result, Baker argues, is a *good-faith* willingness on the part of Twitter/X employees to suppress content with which they disagree, labeling it illegitimate misinformation.[42] Given empirical evidence provided by Taibbi (and cited by Weiss) that Twitter/X's workforce is between 97 percent and 99 percent Democratic (based on campaign contributions at least),[43] that story is an eminently plausible one that also does not rely on conspiracy theories (much to Musk's disappointment, one imagines) or identifying "bad guys."

There is, however, another possible, and not even inconsistent, explanation for why it is that high-profile content moderation seems to disfavor conservative over progressive voices. Let us start by considering what kind of content it is that the major social media platforms – we will focus on Facebook and Twitter/X here, though the others are not so different – prohibit. These rules are laid out in Facebook's Community Standards[44] and in the Twitter/X Rules.[45] Most fundamentally, both sets of standards/rules, for obvious and generally noncontroversial reasons, prohibit incitement of violence, including speech that has a serious possibility of leading to violence. Twitter/X also prohibits glorifying violence, and although Facebook's Community Standards do not explicitly do the same, their prohibition on implicit calls for violence can easily be read to prohibit such glorification. Indeed, it was President Trump's claimed violation of precisely these rules that lead to his deplatforming by both Twitter/X and Facebook. But the truth is that, in today's world, calls for violence and glorification of violence are *far* more likely to emerge from

---

[41] Oliver Darcy, *Why News Organizations Are Largely Skeptical of Elon Musk's "Twitter Files" Theater*, CNN BUSINESS (Dec. 12, 2022), www.cnn.com/2022/12/12/media/twitter-files-reliable-sources/index.html; Bond, *supra* n. 38.

[42] Gerard Baker, *Elon Musk's Twitter Files Revelations Are Instructive but Not Surprising*, WALL STREET JOURNAL (Dec. 12, 2022), www.wsj.com/articles/twitter-files-revelations-are-instructive-but-not-surprising-media-cultural-elites-misinformation-disagreement-musk-11670856198.

[43] Matt Taibbi (@mtaibbi), X (Dec. 2, 2022, 4:02 PM), https://twitter.com/mtaibbi/status/1598829996264390656.

[44] *Meta Community Standards*, https://transparency.meta.com/policies/community-standards/.

[45] *The X Rules*, https://help.x.com/en/rules-and-policies/x-rules.

the political right than the political left (in the 1960s and 1970s it would have been the opposite, with the radical left far more likely to call for violence). Of course, most mainstream conservatives do not call for or support political violence. But more radical elements of the political right such as the Proud Boys and the Oathkeepers quite explicitly do endorse violence[46] – and some of the more extreme Republican members of Congress, such as Marjorie Taylor Greene and Matt Gaetz, are not all that far apart from that position.[47] Given these facts, it is hardly surprising that conservative figures are more likely to violate content moderation rules regarding violence than progressives.

Facebook and Twitter/X also prohibit hate speech (or what Twitter/X calls hateful conduct), which Facebook defines as direct attacks on people on the basis of their "race, ethnicity, national origin, disability, religious affiliation, caste, sexual orientation, sex, gender identity and serious disease"[48] (Twitter/X's rules are similar and encompass attacks "on the basis of race, ethnicity, national origin, caste, sexual orientation, gender, gender identity, religious affiliation, age, disability, or serious disease"[49]). The question one might ask oneself is who, today, is most likely to violate these rules. The answer is not always conservatives – people on the left certainly can and do engage in such attacks (notably based on religious affiliation, but also sometimes race). But it is also true that with the unfortunate, possible exception of antisemitism, it is not generally a part of mainstream progressive ideology to condemn individuals on the basis of such characteristics, while hostility to or exclusion of individuals based on sexual orientation and gender identity most certainly are embraced by elements of the mainstream political right – as illustrated by the fact that the official platform of the Texas Republican Party, adopted in 2024, flatly opposes "the teaching of sex education, sexual health, or sexual choice

---

[46] Matthew Kriner and Jon Lewis, *Pride & Prejudice: The Violent Evolution of the Proud Boys*, COMBATING TERRORISM CENTER AT WEST POINT, CTS SENTINEL (July/August 2021), https://ctc.westpoint.edu/pride-prejudice-the-violent-evolution-of-the-proud-boys/; Lindsay Whitehurst, *Pro-Trump Oath Keepers Sought "Violent Overthrow" of Government on Jan. 6, Prosecutors Tell Court*, PBS NEWS (Nov. 18, 2022), www.pbs.org/newshour/politics/pro-trump-oath-keepers-sought-violent-overthrow-of-government-on-jan-6-prosecutors-tell-court.

[47] Andrew Kaczynski and Em Steck, *Marjorie Taylor Greene Confronted over Old Social Media Posts Advocating Violence against Democrats in Court Testimony*, CNN POLITICS (April 23, 2022), www.cnn.com/2022/04/22/politics/marjorie-taylor-greene-social-media-posts-violence/index.html; Kate Conger, *Twitter Places Warning on Congressman's Tweet for Glorifying Vioence*, N.Y. TIMES (June 1, 2020), www.nytimes.com/2020/06/01/technology/twitter-matt-gaetz-warning.html.

[48] *Meta Community Standards: Hateful Conduct*, https://transparency.fb.com/policies/community-standards/hate-speech/.

[49] *X Help Center: Hateful Conduct*, https://help.twitter.com/en/rules-and-policies/hateful-conduct-policy.

or identity in any public school in any grade whatsoever,"[50] and one speaker at the 2023 Conservative Political Action Conference (CPAC) convention (historically the most prominent conservative political convention) stated that "transgenderism must be eradicated from public life entirely."[51]

It is thus again unsurprising that the major social media platforms' hate speech policies are far more likely to impact conservative than progressive speakers. Is it nonetheless possible that employees of social media enforce their rules more strictly against conservative than progressive users, perhaps even inadvertently? For example, is it possible that a Twitter/X employee was more likely, prior to the platform's purchase by Elon Musk, to label an attack based on sexual orientation as hate speech than to label one as such based on an individual being an Evangelical Christian?[52] Of course it is. But the problem is that simple statistics showing that more conservatives than progressives run afoul of hate speech policies – assuming such statistics exist – cannot demonstrate the existence of bias on the part of platforms, either conscious or unconscious.

Finally, consider one more example of a widely followed content moderation policy: bans on particular forms of dis- and misinformation, especially related to the COVID-19 pandemic. Facebook continues to enforce such a rule,[53] and Twitter/X did so until Elon Musk's purchase of the company in late 2022.[54] In enforcing their rules, both platforms inevitably relied on outside health policy experts in determining what constituted misinformation, according to the prevailing scientific consensus. But as with hate speech, while COVID misinformation flowed from across the political spectrum, the tendency of political figures on the right to endorse such things as vaccine skepticism, or unproven treatments such as hydroxychloroquine and ivermectin, unsurprisingly lead to greater enforcement of this policy against conservative speakers. Of course, the reality is that enforcement of the anti-misinformation policy was spotty and sometimes grossly wrong – as most

[50] 2024 *Platform and Resolutions of the Republican Party of Texas*, https://texasgop.org/platform/.
[51] Gustaf Kilander, *CPAC Speaker Sparks Alarm with Call for Transgenderism to Be "Eradicated,"* INDEPENDENT (March 4, 2023), www.independent.co.uk/news/world/americas/us-politics/cpac-transgenderism-daily-wire-michael-knowles-b2294252.html.
[52] The problem of antisemitism and sometimes bigoted descriptions of Jewish individuals as "Zionists" pose a more difficult problem, because of ongoing disagreements about where criticisms of the policies of the State of Israel become effectively a form of hate speech.
[53] *Meta Community Standards: Misinformation*, https://transparency.fb.com/policies/community-standards/misinformation/.
[54] David Klepper, *Twitter Ends Enforcement of COVID Misinformation Policy*, AP (Nov. 29, 2022), https://apnews.com/article/twitter-ends-covid-misinformation-policy-cc232c9ce0f193c505bbc63bf57ecad6.

obviously was true of the decision to label the theory that COVID-19 originated from a lab leak in Wuhan, China as misinformation early in the pandemic. But as with the incitement and hate speech policies, the fact that the misinformation policy disproportionately affected conservatives proves nothing regarding alleged bias.

Indeed, a very recent study published in the leading scientific journal *Nature* provides strong empirical support for this explanation.[55] Focusing on data regarding politically active Twitter/X users during the 2020 US presidential election, the authors of the study concluded that while pro-Trump conservative users were indeed more likely to be suspended than pro-Biden/liberal users, conservative users were also far more likely to link to what the authors call "low-quality news sites." And strikingly, this result held even when *Republican* laypeople evaluated the quality of the relevant news. Furthermore, when the authors examined a broader set of datasets examining Twitter/X and Facebook users from 2016 to 2023 across sixteen different countries, the same results emerged. Of course, these empirical results do not rule out the possibility of platform bias, especially because the study did not examine reasons provided for individual suspensions; but it does raise doubts about such claims when they are based (as they generally are) only on anecdotal observations of platform actions against conservatives.

Furthermore, whatever the evidence (or lack thereof) of anti-conservative bias in the past, there is every reason to believe that, going forward, this issue has largely disappeared. Most obviously, Elon Musk's purchase of Twitter/X in late 2022 has resulted in that platform, if anything, adopting an anti-progressive bias (as illustrated by its banning of the terms "cis" and "cisgender" in 2023[56]). More fundamentally, one of the coauthors of the *Nature* study, Professor David G. Rand of MIT, points out that in the current (late 2024) political environment, platforms are receiving far more public attacks for their alleged anti-conservative bias than for spreading misinformation, making it likely that moving forward (especially after Donald Trump's victory in the 2024 presidential election), social media platforms will lean over backward to avoid blocking conservative content.[57] And indeed, in an August 2024 letter from Mark Zuckerberg, the CEO of Meta (which owns both the Facebook and Instagram, as well as

---

[55] Mohsen Mosleh, Qi Yang, Tauhid Zaman, Gordon Pennycook, and David G. Rand, *Difference in Misinformation Sharing Can Lead to Politically Asymmetric Sanctions*, NATURE (Oct. 2, 2024), www.nature.com/articles/s41586-024-07942-8.

[56] Kim Elsesser, *Elon Musk Deems "Cis" a Twitter Slur – Here's Why It's Is So Polarizing* FORBES (July 2, 2023), www.forbes.com/sites/kimelsesser/2023/07/02/elon-musk-deems-cis-a-twitter-slurheres-why-its-is-so-polarizing/.

[57] Will Oremus, *Why Conservatives Get Suspended More than Liberals on Social Media*, WASHINGTON POST (Oct. 3, 2024), www.washingtonpost.com/politics/2024/10/03/nature-study-social-media-liberal-bias-censorship/.

the related Threads, platforms), to Representative Jim Jordan, the Republican chair of the House Judiciary Committee, Zuckerberg apologized for yielding to pressures from the Biden Administration to block alleged COVID-19 disinformation. And in the same letter, Zuckerberg strongly suggested that moving forward, Meta platforms will work hard to avoid complying with such political pressure, as well as reducing the extent to which they demote content labeled as misinformation.[58] Given that Zuckerberg and Musk, between themselves, fully control Facebook, Instagram, and Twitter/X, concerns about anti-conservative bias on the major social media platforms seem, going forward, to be baseless.

Stepping back from the uncertainties surrounding whether claims of past anti-conservative bias on the part of platforms have any validity (my own suspicion is that they do, but that the extent of such bias is vastly exaggerated), it is worth considering the underlying assumptions and bases of the public and legislative attacks on social media from conservative circles. At first cut, the reasoning behind the conservative attack seems straightforward. Social media has become the primary source of news and information, and the primary site for political debate and discourse, in this country and abroad since social media's explosion in the early 2010s. Indeed, especially for younger people social media is often their *sole* source of news and political information. Furthermore, the social media industry is dominated by a handful of platforms, controlled by a handful of individuals – Mark Zuckerberg alone, with his control over both the Facebook and Instagram platforms, can impose his will on the availability of information, and access to discourse, for a huge percentage of the global population of all ages. If this kind of power is used to bias the debate in favor of particular viewpoints or perspectives, as conservatives claim is the case, then that will have a profoundly distorting effect on political discourse, and ultimately on democracy itself. It is therefore, this argument goes, perfectly legitimate for states like Florida and Texas to step in and prevent such abuses of power.

But now let us take a step back and consider the implications of this position for another very important, and in many ways more dominant, source of news and public discourse: Fox News. Fox News has for years been the most-watched cable network of any kind in the country – in particular, it is far ahead of its primary news competitors, MSNBC and CNN.[59] Fox News is also the most important source of news and political commentary for Republicans,

---

[58] Will Oremus, *Zuckerberg Expresses Regrets over Covid Misinformation Crackdown*, Washington Post (Aug. 27, 2024), www.washingtonpost.com/technology/2024/08/27/meta-zuckerberg-covid-misinformation-jordan-white-house/.

[59] Carlie Porterfield, *Fox News Dominates Cable Ratings for Seventh Consecutive Year— And Gained Viewers while Competitors Plummeted*, Forbes (Dec. 15, 2022), www.forbes.com/sites/carlieporterfield/2022/12/15/fox-news-dominates-yearly-cable-ratings-for-seventh-consecutive-year/?sh=131c68c144dc.

especially for older Republicans (which matters because older people are more likely to vote).[60] As a consequence of the broad support, trust, and loyalty that Fox News enjoys with conservatives, its coverage has a significant (and from the point of view of progressives deleterious) impact on national politics.[61] And, of course, Fox News's coverage and commentary famously takes a highly conservative slant, to the point sometimes of knowingly spreading falsehoods such as claims that the 2020 presidential election was stolen through electoral fraud, in order to please their conservative audience.[62] In short, the conservative bias of Fox News has at least as important an impact on public discourse in the United States as the alleged anti-conservative bias of social media platforms, and almost certainly a far greater one.

So do conservatives, or does anyone, believe that progressive commentators should have a right to appear on Fox News, and be given equal treatment compared to conservative commentators such as Tucker Carlson or Laura Ingraham? Of course not. Most people, whether conservative or progressive, surely agree that Fox News, as a media outlet, has a right to hold and spread its own chosen political opinions using its privately owned platform. Indeed, the right to such editorial discretion and control lies at the core of the freedoms protected by the Press Clause of the First Amendment to the US Constitution; and it also follows from the property rights Fox News holds over its assets. And exactly the same is true of other forms of media such as newspapers – the *Wall Street Journal*'s editorial pages are famously conservative, while the *New York Times* and *Washington Post* pages lean progressive – and radio stations such as those who host right-wing talk radio shows (think of Rush Limbaugh, Mark Levin, and Ben Shapiro).

To be clear, the right to such editorial slant was not always the law. During the heyday of *broadcast* (not cable) television and radio, beginning in 1949, the Federal Communications Commission (FCC), an agency of the US government, enforced a set of rules called the Fairness Doctrine which required broadcasters to report news evenly. And in the 1960s the Supreme Court upheld the Fairness Doctrine against a First Amendment challenge.[63] But

---

[60] John Gramlich, 5 *Facts about Fox News*, Pew Research Center (April 8, 2020), www.pewresearch.org/fact-tank/2020/04/08/five-facts-about-fox-news/.

[61] Phillip Bump, *The Unique, Damaging Role Fox News Plays in American Media*, Washington Post (April 4, 2022), www.washingtonpost.com/politics/2022/04/04/unique-damaging-role-fox-news-plays-american-media/.

[62] Alison Durkee, *New Fox News Documents Show Tucker Carlson, Murdoch and More Disputing 2020 Election Fraud—Here Are Their Most Explosive Comments*, Forbes (March 8, 2023), www.forbes.com/sites/alisondurkee/2023/03/08/sidney-powell-is-lying-new-fox-news-dominion-documents-show-tucker-carlson-murdoch-and-more-disputing-2020-election-fraud-here-are-their-wildest-comments/?sh=1fea6bfe6a59.

[63] Red Lion Broadcasting Co. v. FCC, 395 U.S. 367 (1969).

the FCC repealed the Fairness Doctrine in 1987 (thereby enabling the rise of right-wing talk radio), and even when it was in place, the Fairness Doctrine was strictly limited to the broadcasting industry – the Supreme Court explicitly rejected efforts by the State of Florida to impose similar requirements on newspapers.[64]

The obvious question that arises, of course, is that if Fox News has a right to adopt a political slant, and so do newspapers and radio stations, why don't Facebook or Twitter/X have the same rights, either under the First Amendment or as a matter of fairness? And from a more traditionally conservative perspective, one might ask why social media companies should not have the right to use their private property as they choose, and exclude from their property whomever and whatever they want. After all, President or not, Donald Trump has no right to invade my living room, or use my backyard, to hold a rally. And it should be noted that in a recent case pitting property rights against the free speech interests of labor organizers, the conservative majority of the US Supreme Court ruled resoundingly in favor of protecting property rights.[65] So why, according to conservatives such as Justice Clarence Thomas (and his colleagues Justices Samuel Alito and Neil Gorsuch), are social media platforms differently situated?

To be fair, there are important differences between social media platforms and traditional media outlets such as Fox News and the *New York Times*. Most obviously, the latter primarily distribute content that they themselves have created or, in the case of advertisements and op eds, chosen; social media platforms, in contrast, obviously distribute primarily user-generated, third-party content. Because of this, the Florida and Texas legislatures argued (inspired by Justice Thomas) that social media are more like telephone companies than newspapers; and historically, telephone companies were regulated as common carriers, meaning that they had to serve all customers in a nondiscriminatory fashion. In other words, common carriers such as telephone companies (and railroads and inns and ferries) did not have a right to exclude customers or content of which they disapproved. And this was true regardless of the First Amendment, or the fact that the relevant firms were privately owned.

The conservative efforts to regulate social media thus are not without any plausible legal basis. But they are ultimately wrong. The full explanation for why the common carrier label is not a good fit for social media platforms will have to wait until Chapter 4, but at the outset it is important to note that common carrier status is very much the exception in our legal tradition – normally

---

[64] Miami Herald Publishing Co. v. Tornillo, 418 U.S. 241 (1974).
[65] Cedar Point Nursery v. Hassid, 594 U.S. 139 (2021).

the assumption is that private actors can choose with whom to do business, subject (in modern times) to narrow antidiscrimination laws. And such labels were never applied to media outlets possessing First Amendment rights – which, as I will argue in Chapter 4, social media platforms do possess. Indeed, even at the height of the Fairness Doctrine era, the Supreme Court explicitly rejected an argument that television broadcast stations should be treated as common carriers.[66]

Ultimately, then, what conservative attacks on social media amount to is a claim that, unlike most owners of private property, social media firms for some reason have moral, and eventually legal, obligations to permit conservative speakers to access and use the platforms' private property. On its face, such a claim is extraordinary. After all, in our political dialogue it is normally conservatives who defend the sacrosanctity of private property rights, fiercely resisting attempts to regulate such property via, for example, environmental regulation (no matter how strong the economic case is for such regulation). Aside from the common carrier argument, perhaps the conservative claim of a right to access platform private property might be justified if a there was a single social media platform possessing an absolute monopoly power to control public discourse; but no such monopoly exists. After all, there are several major social media platforms (Facebook, Twitter/X, Instagram, YouTube, and TikTok at a minimum) as well as numerous smaller platforms such as Gab, Parler, Telegram, and Reddit. Furthermore, the very fact that Donald Trump was able to create his own social media platform – Truth Social – from scratch following his deplatforming demonstrates that no single platform constitutes a bottleneck (or in the antitrust legal jargon, an "essential facility") for public discourse.

Ultimately, then, one comes to suspect that the enormous conservative deviation from their general values where social media is concerned is simply a product of self-interest, not any form of principle (much the same is true of progressives, it might be added, as the next chapter will demonstrate). This suspicion tends to find support in the fact that during the lead-up to the 2024 presidential election, Elon Musk used his control over the Twitter/X platform to systematically favor conservative messages, without a peep of concern or protest from conservative crusaders for platform neutrality.[67]

---

[66] CBS v. Democratic National Committee, 412 U.S. 94 (1973).
[67] Zeynup Tufekci, *Republicans Hate Tech's Influence on Politics. Unless It Comes from Elon Musk*, WASHINGTON POST (Oct. 9, 2024), www.nytimes.com/live/2024/10/08/opinion/thepoint.

In short, conservatives want to spread specific messages to their political base, and the large platforms are a cheap (indeed, free) and convenient tool for doing so. And if platform owners will not play ball, conservatives are happy to impose political pressure and legal obligations, cloaked in the name of free speech, to make them do so. Because after all, the ultimate stakes here are very high.

2

The Progressive War

Social Media as Enablers

If conservative criticisms of social media ultimately come down to the claim that social media platforms, through their content moderation practices, suppress too much speech, progressive claims come down to the assertion that platforms do not suppress enough harmful speech. Both sets of criticisms are, to some extent, sincere. And just as there is some basis for conservative unhappiness with platforms, so too there is some legitimacy to progressive claims. But the fact that both sets of polar-opposite criticisms can co-exist tells us something both about the extraordinary difficulty of achieving Goldilocks-style "just right" content moderation and about our broader social tendency to attribute fundamental dysfunctions rooted in our culture to social media.

2.1 POLITICAL MANIPULATION

Let us begin by laying out the basic elements of the progressive case. One specific area where platforms have been especially criticized is in their seeming inability to block misinformation, disinformation, and other forms of online political manipulation. These concerns first became prominent during the 2016 presidential election. After Donald Trump's victory in that close-fought election, evidence emerged that a number of actors, both foreign and domestic, engaged in a variety of forms of political manipulation on social media platforms, many (though not all) with the goal of benefiting the Trump campaign.[1] The tools used to manipulate voters in 2016 ranged from outright

---

[1] Robert Yablon, *Political Advertising, Digital Platforms, and the Democratic Deficiencies of Self-Regulation*, 104 MINN. L. REV. HEADNOTES 13, 14 and n.5 (2020) (citing Nathaniel Persily, *Can Democracy Survive the Internet?*, 28 J. DEMOCRACY 63, 67–71 (2017); Abby K. Wood and Ann M. Ravel, *Fool Me Once: Regulating "Fake News" and Other Online Advertising*, 91 S. CAL. L. REV. 1223, 1229–34 (2018)).

disinformation – "fake news" – to more subtle attempts to increase social divisions on hot button political issues by using bots and other devices to spread stories quickly.[2] And while the actual impact of all of this on the election results is unknowable (though probably fairly small), it is no surprise that commentators and politicians on the political left were upset by these revelations.

Most prominent and controversial, and to this day disputed by Donald Trump and his supporters,[3] was evidence that the government of Russia engaged in a massive disinformation and manipulation campaign on social media during the 2016 election cycle, with the goal of benefiting Trump's campaign at the expense of both his Republican rivals during the primary season and his ultimate Democratic opponent Hilary Clinton.[4] One prominent example of such manipulation concerns the Internet Research Agency, a (now closed) Russian company owned by Yevgeny Prigozhin, then an ally of Russian President Vladimir Putin (Prigozhin later led the Wagner Group uprising against Putin's government, and then died in a "mysterious" airplane crash). During the 2016 election, the Internet Research Agency reportedly spread stories using fake accounts, claiming to be American, that supported candidate Trump's attacks on various individuals and government institutions. In addition, and most strikingly, evidence came to light that Russian manipulation was especially targeted at particular segments of African American voters, a demographic that tilts heavily Democratic, seeking to discourage the targets from voting for Hilary Clinton.[5] These tactics, which exploited real and existing racial tensions and grievances such as concerns about President Bill Clinton's record on race issues during his presidency, sought to convince voters to refrain from voting during the general election, or to support the Green Party candidate Jill Stein. Revelations such as these inevitably outraged political progressives. One concern of these critics was of course the political impact of the Russian actions. But more fundamentally, these actions, in seeking to suppress the African American vote, were deeply racist and as such come with a long and troubling historical pedigree.

In the wake of revelations about especially the Russian election interference, the major platforms took substantial steps to try and limit future

---

[2] Wood and Ravel, *supra* n. 1, at 1229–32.
[3] Julie Hirschfeld Davis, *Trump, at Putin's Side, Questions U.S. Intelligence on 2016 Election*, N.Y. TIMES (July 16, 2018), www.nytimes.com/2018/07/16/world/europe/trump-putin-election-intelligence.html.
[4] *Ibid.*; *see also* Derek E. Bambauer, *Information Hacking*, 2020 UTAH L. REV. 987, 987–94 (summarizing various Russia-backed disinformation campaigns in 2016).
[5] Scott Shane and Sheera Frenkel, *Russian 2016 Influence Operation Targeted African-Americans on Social Media*, N.Y. TIMES (Dec. 17, 2018), www.nytimes.com/2018/12/17/us/politics/russia-2016-influence-campaign.html.

manipulation.[6] Nonetheless, the US intelligence community documented strong evidence that Russia continued, in the 2020 election, to seek to benefit President Trump's reelection campaign in a number of ways, including via the spread of misinformation.[7] Such reports again, inevitably, triggered sharp complaints from Democratic political leaders, albeit perhaps not as sharp as in the wake of the 2016 election because of Democratic candidate Joe Biden's ultimate victory in the presidential election.

2.2 MISINFORMATION AND THE COVID-19 PANDEMIC

If election manipulation was the original trigger for progressive concerns about online disinformation and manipulation, the COVID-19 pandemic led to their apex.

As everyone knows, COVID-19, which was first detected in the Chinese city of Wuhan in December of 2019, was declared a global pandemic by the World Health Organization in March of 2020 (specifically, March 11). The ensuing stay-at-home orders, business closures, and other unprecedented measures created massive social and economic disruptions, the long-term effects of which are likely to be felt for decades. Conspiracy theories, a variety of unsupported factual claims, and some level of outright lies about the coronavirus causing the pandemic began to spread on social media almost immediately after the Wuhan outbreak, well before the WHO's March declaration. These included claims that the virus was deliberately engineered and released, and (my favorite for sheer wackiness) that 5G cellular networks helped create or spread the virus.[8]

Along with misinformation about the source and spread of COVID-19, early in the pandemic controversial stories spread about potential treatments for the virus. Most dangerously, a nontrivial number of individuals, some inspired by off-hand comments by President Trump in April of 2020, ingested bleach or other disinfectants as purported cures for COVID; the results were predictably tragic.[9] Less dangerous, though as noted in Chapter 1 also probably wrong,

---

[6] Ashutosh Bhagwat, *The Law of Facebook*, 54 U.C. DAVIS L. REV. 2353, 2363–65 (2021).

[7] Julian E. Barnes, *Russian Interference in 2020 Included Influencing Trump Associates, Report Says*, N.Y. TIMES (March 16, 2021), www.nytimes.com/2021/03/16/us/politics/election-interference-russia-2020-assessment.html.

[8] Josh Taylor, *Bat Soup, Dodgy Cures and "Diseasology": The Spread of Coronavirus Disinformation*, THE GUARDIAN (Jan. 30, 2020), www.theguardian.com/world/2020/jan/31/bat-soup-dodgy-cures-and-diseasology-the-spread-of-coronavirus-bunkum.

[9] Nicholas Reimann, *Some Americans Are Tragically Still Drinking Bleach as a Coronavirus "Cure"*, FORBES (Aug. 24, 2020), www.forbes.com/sites/nicholasreimann/2020/08/24/some-americans-are-tragically-still-drinking-bleach-as-a-coronavirus-cure/?sh=110fb41b6748.

were claims by President Trump beginning in May of 2020 that hydroxychloroquine, a malaria drug, was effective in treating COVID-19.[10] Then, in the summer of 2021 a number of prominent conservative media personalities (mainly associated with Fox News) began endorsing a story that had developed in certain social media circles (notably on the far-right platform Gab) that the drug ivermectin, a deworming medication primarily used for horses, could cure COVID-19[11] (the Food and Drug Administration (FDA), the US government agency responsible for regulating drug safety, prior to the second Trump Administration firmly opposed the use of ivermectin,[12] and later research suggests that ivermectin is not effective in treating the disease[13]).

For our purposes, what is important and interesting about COVID-19 mis- and disinformation was not so much the existence of the phenomenon, but rather the response of the major platforms to it, and the political dynamic that emerged from all of this. As for the platforms, very early in the pandemic, misinformation was rife across all social media platforms. Indeed, given the lack of information about or scientific understanding of the virus, it was often impossible in the early days to distinguish misinformation from guesswork, whether factually based or not. As an example of such shoddy, but no doubt sincerely intended, guesswork, consider the prediction in March of 2020 by well-known and respected law professor Richard Epstein (with whom I studied, full disclosure) that the total number of COVID deaths in the United States would be approximately 5,000 (increased from his original estimate of 500).[14] Given that as of April of 2023 the Centers for Disease Control and the World Health Organization both report over 1 million COVID deaths in the United States (a possibility that Epstein pooh-poohed in his essay), Epstein was obviously dead wrong. Furthermore, if his and other sanguine estimates led people to ignore safety warnings, they might have cost lives. But, given the

---

[10] Andrew Solender, *All the Times Trump Has Promoted Hydroxychloroquine*, FORBES (May 22, 2020), www.forbes.com/sites/andrewsolender/2020/05/22/all-the-times-trump-promoted-hydroxychloroquine/?sh=fd1982046432; Katie Thomas, *F.D.A. Revokes Emergency Approval of Malaria Drugs Promoted by Trump*, N.Y. TIMES (June 15, 2020), www.nytimes.com/2020/06/15/health/fda-hydroxchloroquine-malaria.html.
[11] Oliver Darcy, *Right-Wing Media Pushed a Deworming Drug to Treat COVID-19 that the FDA Says Is Unsafe for Humans*, CNN (Aug. 23, 2021), www.cnn.com/2021/08/23/media/right-wing-media-ivermectin/index.html.
[12] The link to the relevant page on the FDA website appears to have been disabled by officials in the second Trump Administration (as of April 2025).
[13] Susanna Naggie et al., *Effect of Ivermectin vs Pacebo on Time to Sustained Recovery in Outpatients with Mild to Moderate COVID-10: A Randomized Clinical Trial*, JAMA NETWORK (Oct. 21, 2022), https://jamanetwork.com/journals/jama/fullarticle/2797483.
[14] Richard A. Epstein, *Coronavirus Perspective*, HOOVER INSTITUTE (March 16, 2020), www.hoover.org/research/coronavirus-pandemic.

lack of information about COVID-19 available in March of 2020, such claims cannot be described as mis- or disinformation.

Claims regarding the origins of the virus, as well as claims to have discovered "miracle cures," were also, given the lack of data, extremely hard to evaluate or refute early in the pandemic (though even in the early days, it was surely clear that drinking bleach was a very bad idea, and that 5G networks did not create the virus). As such, the failure of platforms (and news organizations) to filter trustworthy from non-trustworthy information is understandable. Nonetheless, because of the risks associated with COVID misinformation, the major platforms began collaborating with outside experts to identify, label, and sometimes remove content determined to be misinformation. Facebook's and Twitter/X's first efforts in this direction, focused in particular on misinformation likely to lead to material harm, were adopted in January of 2020, but expanded significantly in later months, as more scientific consensus emerged regarding COVID.[15] YouTube adopted a similar policy in May of 2020,[16] and as of April of 2023 Meta (the owner of Facebook and Instagram) and Google (the owner of YouTube) continued to enforce their policies. Twitter/X, however, stopped enforcing its policy in November of 2022, in the wake of Elon Musk's purchase of the platform.[17]

The adoption of anti-misinformation policies did not, of course, eliminate the spread of falsehoods and conspiracies about COVID. For one thing, enforcement of misinformation policies was inevitably imperfect. A big part of the reason for this is that the sheer scale of social media makes perfect content moderation impossible, especially because the major platforms operate in many different languages. But in addition, the state of knowledge and the scientific consensus regarding COVID changed, making the accuracy or inaccuracy of some arguable claims (such as the efficacy of hydroxychloroquine as a COVID treatment) only clear over time. Indeed, in some cases it turned out that uncertainty led the major platforms to over-suppress, such as with the theory that the COVID-19 virus leaked from a research lab in Wuhan, China, a theory which was originally labeled misinformation but which later (in Facebook's case in May of 2021[18]) was permitted, in light of the ongoing uncertainty about the origins of the virus.

---

[15] Guy Rosen, *An Update on Our Work to Keep People Informed and Limit Misinformation about COVID-19*, META NEWSROOM (April 16, 2020), https://about.fb.com/news/2020/04/covid-19-misinfo-update/. The relevant Twitter/X link has been disabled as of April 2025.
[16] *YouTube Help: Medical Misinformation Policy*, https://support.google.com/youtube/answer/9891785?hl=en.
[17] Associated Press, *Twitter Will No Longer Enforce Its COVID Misinformation Policy*, NPR (Nov. 29, 2022), www.npr.org/2022/11/29/1139822833/twitter-covid-misinformation-policy-not-enforced.
[18] Rosen, *supra* n. 15.

In addition to the imperfections of content moderation on the major platforms, however, another important avenue for the spread of misinformation was the fact that smaller platforms such as Gab and Parler failed to adopt content moderation policies similar to those on the major platforms. As a consequence, these platforms became important avenues of misinformation, especially about vaccines, for individuals (admittedly a self-selecting minority) who frequented such sites.[19] Combined with the continuing spread of vaccine skepticism on more traditional media such as Fox News,[20] it seems clear that COVID misinformation contributed, to some significant but unknowable extent, to reduced rates of vaccination against COVID within the United States and elsewhere, thereby increasing sickness and mortality.

These events inevitably drew a sharp, critical response directed at the major social media platforms (and to a lesser extent, minor ones). What is striking, however, is that the attacks on social media platforms for permitting the spread of COVID misinformation (or more accurately, for not doing enough to prevent such spread) came almost exclusively from the political left. This is because public discussion of COVID origins and cures had, from the beginning, a sharp political divide. On the progressive left, however, the message was clear. In the summer of 2021 the Biden Administration, led by Surgeon General Vivek Murthy, strongly urged tech companies to fight vaccine misinformation, and President Biden went as far, in a press conference, as to accuse platforms of "killing people."[21] These and similar actions ultimately led to a lawsuit against the Biden Administration claiming that their pressure campaign violated the First Amendment. This lawsuit, though it met with initial success in the ultra-conservative United States Court of Appeals for the Fifth Circuit,[22] was ultimately dismissed by the US Supreme Court.[23]

Nor were congressional leaders from the Democratic Party silent on the matter. Tech-savvy members such as Senators Amy Klobuchar and Mark Warner cheered the Biden Administration's efforts. Separately, Senator

---

[19] Sheryl Gay Stolberg, *A Lasting Legacy of Covid: Far-Right Platforms Spreading Health Myths*, N.Y. TIMES (Nov. 22, 2022), www.nytimes.com/2022/11/22/us/politics/covid-misinformation-gab.html.

[20] Tiffany Hsu, *Despite Outbreaks among Unvaccinated, Fox News Hosts Smear Shots*, N.Y. TIMES (July 11, 2021), www.nytimes.com/2021/07/11/business/media/vaccines-fox-news-hosts.html.

[21] Rebecca Klar, *Feds Step Up Pressure on Social Media Over False COVID-19 Claims*, THE HILL (July 18, 2021), https://thehill.com/policy/technology/563470-administration-puts-new-pressure-on-social-media-to-curb-covid-19/.

[22] Missouri v. Biden, 83 F.4th 641 (5th Cir. 2023).

[23] Murthy v. Missouri, 144 S. Ct. 1972 (2024).

Klobuchar (who represents Minnesota) and Senator Ben Ray Lujan of New Mexico introduced legislation that would have imposed liability on platforms if they became vehicles for the spread of medical misinformation (specifically, the legislation would have stripped tech companies of the immunity they normally enjoy under Section 230 of the Communications Decency Act for third party content posted on their platforms – Section 230 is discussed in more detail in Chapter 6).[24] Senator Elizabeth Warren of Massachusetts similarly issued strong and sharply critical comments about the role of tech platforms in spreading misinformation, albeit she did not focus on medical misinformation specifically.[25] And more generally, Democratic politicians throughout the country urged social media platforms to curb COVID misinformation – indeed, the Democratic leadership in California went so far as to pass legislation that would have caused disciplinary sanctions to be imposed on doctors who spread COVID disinformation (defined as "false information that is contradicted by contemporary scientific consensus contrary to the standard of care").[26]

Finally, the message of traditionally left-leaning news outlets such as the *New York Times* and *Washington Post* was largely the same as that of progressive politicians. News stories largely supported the narrative of Big Tech incompetence and conservative involvement in the spread of misinformation, and editorials regularly flayed the major platforms for their inaction. On the mainstream political and journalistic left, it would seem that a wide consensus exists regarding the failure of social media platforms to control the spread of medical misinformation, and their moral (and perhaps legal) obligation to cure those failures.

In short, on the subject of social media platforms' efforts to control medical misinformation during the COVID-19 pandemic, progressives and conservatives have taken polar-opposite positions. Progressives have consistently, and sharply, criticized such efforts as inadequate, and expressed concerns about lost lives. Conservatives, on the other hand (as discussed in Chapter 1), have criticized them as excessive and have consistently expressed concerns about threats to liberty, going so far as to sue the Biden Administration over their

---

[24] *News Releases: Klobuchar, Luján Introduce Legislation to Hold Digital Platforms Accountable for Vaccine and Other Health-Related Misinformation* (July 22, 2021), www.klobuchar.senate.gov/public/index.cfm/2021/7/klobuchar-luj-n-introduce-legislation-to-hold-digital-platforms-accountable-for-vaccine-and-other-health-related-misinformation.

[25] *Fighting Digital Disinformation*, https://elizabethwarren.com/plans/fighting-digital-disinformation.

[26] Brendan Pierson, *California Law Aiming to Curb COVID Misinformation Blocked By Judge*, REUTERS (Jan. 26, 2023), www.reuters.com/business/healthcare-pharmaceuticals/california-law-aiming-curb-covid-misinformation-blocked-by-judge-2023-01-26/.

efforts to pressure the platforms on these issues. As we shall see next, COVID is far from the only subject on which such a stark dichotomy has emerged.

2.3 MOB HARASSMENT, DOXING, AND THREATS

One of the most persistent, concerning, and impactful forms of online misbehavior is mob attacks on individuals, often via social media platforms. The forms of such mass harassment vary. One common form of harassment is doxing, whereby private information about individuals is released online, including such things as phone numbers, home addresses, and intimate images (often called "revenge porn," or – more accurately – nonconsensual pornography[27]). Threats of violence are also quite common, and especially likely to be directed at women. One particularly well-publicized example of this was the thoroughly awful "Gamergate" events in 2013–14, during which a succession of women involved in, or writing about, the video game industry were targeted by (overwhelmingly male) online mobs with horrifying threats of violence (and in particular, of rape, illustrating the heavily misogynistic nature of such attacks). These threats were sometimes accompanied by doxing of personal information such as home addresses. In one instance a women named Brianna Wu, who had cofounded an indie game studio, was targeted simply for tweeting jokes about these events, and as a result of resulting threats had to flee her home.[28]

In a pathbreaking 2009 article,[29] law professor Danielle Keats Citron extensively documented the scale of such attacks, particularly on women and African Americans. In the article, Citron noted evidence that such attacks, or the threat of them, significantly reduced female participation in online forums and also imposed severe privacy harms on victims. The reputation of the targets of such campaigns can also be shattered, because online threats and doxing are often accompanied by vicious falsehoods about victims – a good example being a 2007 incident in which anonymous posters used the social networking site AutoAdmit, which focused on law school admissions, to post threats and lies about a number of female law students, mainly at the Yale Law School.[30]

---

[27] Asia A. Eaton, Holly Jacobs, and Yanet Fuvalcaba, *Cyber Civil Rights Initiative: 2017 Nationwide Online Study of Nonconsensual Porn Victimization and Perpetration, A Summary Report* (June 2017), https://cybercivilrights.org/wp-content/uploads/2017/06/CCRI-2017-Research-Report.pdf.
[28] Caitlin Dewey, *The Only Guide to Gamergate You Will Ever Need to Read*, WASHINGTON POST (Oct. 14, 2014), www.washingtonpost.com/news/the-intersect/wp/2014/10/14/the-only-guide-to-gamergate-you-will-ever-need-to-read/.
[29] Danielle Keats Citron, *Cyber Civil Rights*, 89 B.U. L. REV. 61 (2009).
[30] Ibid. at 71–75.

It should be noted, moreover, that the Citron article and the incidents it recounts predated or occurred in the very early years of the major social media platforms, before they exploded around 2010. Since then, social media platforms have, unsurprisingly, become a major conduit for online harassment. In particular, a 2018 report by the human rights nonprofit Amnesty International demonstrates extensively, and in deeply disturbing detail, the nature and breadth of abuse directed against women, especially prominent women, on Twitter/X.[31] The same report presents the results of an earlier online poll which demonstrates that across countries, an extraordinarily high percentage of women report abusive and misogynistic tweets directed at them, including 25 percent reporting threats of physical and sexual violence.[32] And unsurprisingly, the report excoriates Twitter/X for failing to adequately address what even Twitter/X executives concede is a huge problem.

The final, striking and unexpected feature of critiques against platforms for permitting doxing, threats, and harassment is that it has a distinct political valence. The people and institutions generally associated with such critiques, such as Professor Citron, Professor Mary Anne Franks (Citron's co-author[33] and the president of the Cyber Civil Rights Initiative, a nonprofit which serves victims of online abuse[34]), and Amnesty International, are generally associated with the political left. On what was then the political far-right, on the other hand, one finds mainly defenses of online misogyny. For example, the conservative activist Milo Yiannopoulos published a blurb at Breitbart about Gamergate titled (without irony) "Feminist Bullies Tearing the Video Game Industry Apart."[35] Breitbart, it should be remembered, is the far-right online news outlet previously led by Steve Bannon, who later ran Donald Trump's 2016 presidential campaign and then served as "senior counselor" in the first Trump White House. More broadly, there is evidence that online attacks such as the Gamergate ones were organized on online forums like 4Chan that are

---

[31] Amnesty International, *Toxic Twitter – A Toxic Place for Women* (March 21, 2018), www.amnesty.org/en/latest/research/2018/03/online-violence-against-women-chapter-1-1/.

[32] Amnesty International, *Toxic Twitter – Women's Experiences of Violence and Abuse on Twitter* (March 20, 2018), www.amnesty.org/en/latest/news/2018/03/online-violence-against-women-chapter-3-2/.

[33] Danielle Keats Citron and Mary Anne Franks, *Criminalizing Revenge Porn*, 49 WAKE FOREST L. REV. 345, 346 (2014); Danielle Keats Citron and Mary Anne Franks, *The Internet as a Speech Machine and Other Myths Confounding Section 230 Reform*, 2020 U. CHI. LEGAL F. 45, 69–74.

[34] *Cyber Civil Rights Initiative: CCRI Board of Directors*, https://cybercivilrights.org/about/board-of-directors/.

[35] Milo, *Feminist Bullies Tearing the Video Game Industry Apart*, BREITBART (Sept. 1, 2014), www.breitbart.com/europe/2014/09/01/lying-greedy-promiscuous-feminist-bullies-are-tearing-the-video-game-industry-apart/.

often associated with the political alt-right because of their lack of content moderation rules.³⁶

None of this is to say, of course, that most conservatives support or condone the sorts of threatening and harassing behavior described in this section. Indeed, prior to 2016 few would have considered Breitbart to be a part of the mainstream right. But in an age in which Steve Bannon has served in the White House, and few on the political right speak out to condemn online harassment, a political gap has certainly emerged on this question.

2.4 HATE SPEECH

Another area in which social media platforms have faced long-standing, sharp, and consistent criticism is in their (alleged) failure to control "hate speech" on their platforms. That hate speech – which we can loosely define as attacks on individuals or groups based on characteristics such as race, sex, religion, disability, sexual orientation, and gender identity – occurs on social media platforms is of course true; and this is true despite the fact that the major platforms (including Facebook, Instagram, Twitter/X, YouTube, and TikTok) all ban hate speech. Content moderation is inevitably imperfect, and at least some critics claim (whether fairly or not) that platforms' commitment to combating hate speech is not particularly strong.³⁷ Indeed, in an audit commissioned by Facebook itself and published in July 2020, the company was sharply criticized for its failures in these areas.³⁸

The inability or failure of platforms to fully curb hate speech, despite their written commitments to do so in their own policies, has inevitably drawn sharp attacks from the progressive left. For example, in January of 2020, a Democratic New York state senator introduced legislation that would fine platforms that failed to create adequate procedures for removing hate speech in a timely fashion.³⁹ In a similar vein, in August of 2020 a group of twenty state attorneys general, all Democrats, sent a joint letter to Facebook

---

[36] Casey Johnston, *Chat Logs Show How 4Chan Users Created #GamerGate Controversy*, ARS TECHNICA (Sept. 9, 2014), https://arstechnica.com/gaming/2014/09/new-chat-logs-show-how-4chan-users-pushed-gamergate-into-the-national-spotlight/.

[37] Charlie Warzel, *When a Critic Met Facebook: "What They're Doing Is Gaslighting,"* N.Y. TIMES (July 9, 2020), www.nytimes.com/2020/07/09/opinion/facebook-civil-rights-robinson.html.

[38] FACEBOOK'S CIVIL RIGHTS AUDIT – FINAL REPORT 42–58 (July 8, 2020), https://about.fb.com/wp-content/uploads/2020/07/Civil-Rights-Audit-Final-Report.pdf.

[39] Stacy Livingston, *New York State Senator Introduces "Social Media Hate Speech Accountability Act,"* JOLT DIGEST (Feb. 12, 2020), https://jolt.law.harvard.edu/digest/new-york-state-senator-introduces-social-media-hate-speech-accountability-act.

demanding that Facebook do a better job of policing hate speech and other forms of harmful speech on its platforms.[40] And while the letter itself does not go beyond calling on Facebook to take voluntary action, in an interview with the *New York Times*, Attorney General Gurbir S. Grewal of New Jersey (one of the signatories) threatened that, if Facebook did not act, "we always have a variety of legal tools at our disposal."[41] In other words, Grewal appeared to be suggesting that if Facebook failed to do a better job of blocking hate speech and other harmful content, state prosecutors would seek legal remedies against it, thus opening the door to direct regulation of Facebook's content moderation policies.

As a preliminary matter, it should be noted that these threats to regulate online hate speech are essentially hot air because any such regulatory efforts would be blatantly unconstitutional under the First Amendment, as interpreted by the US Supreme Court in modern times. In particular, the Court has made it clear that hate speech is fully protected under the First Amendment, absent narrow and unusual circumstances.[42] Indeed, because such speech is considered political speech on matters of public concern, it receives the very highest level of First Amendment protection.[43] And to cap things off, the Court has consistently in recent years treated efforts to suppress hate speech as almost *per se* unconstitutional viewpoint-based regulations.[44] Thus at least within the United States, any efforts to restrict online hate speech necessarily depend on the voluntary actions of platform owners rather than on the law.

Moreover, even if regulations of hate speech were constitutional, it is far from clear that they would be a good idea. Unlike in the United States, most other countries do not constitutionally protect hate speech, and many have moved to regulate it online. Perhaps the most prominent example of this is

---

[40] Letter from Karl A. Racine, Attorney General, District of Columbia, Kwame Raoul, Attorney General, State of Illinois, Gurbir S. Grewal, Attorney General, State of New Jersey, et. al., to Mark Zuckerberg, Chairman and Chief Executive Officer, Sheryl Sandberg, Chief Operating Officer (Aug. 5, 2020), https://int.nyt.com/data/documenttools/facebook-attorneys-general-letter/50738870562dec84/full.pdf.

[41] *See* Davey Alba, *Facebook Must Better Police Online Hate, State Attorneys General Say*, N.Y. TIMES (Aug. 5, 2020), www.nytimes.com/2020/08/05/technology/facebook-online-hate.html.

[42] *See* Matal v. Tam, 137 S. Ct. 1744, 1764 (2017) (plurality opinion); *ibid.* at 1766–67 (Kennedy, J., concurring in part and concurring in the judgment); R.A.V. v. City of St. Paul, 505 U.S. 377, 395–96 (1992). The narrow circumstances in which hate speech can be banned is when it constitutes a "true threat," Virginia v. Black, 538 U.S. 343, 359 (2003), or when it is directed at an individual, in person, in a way that makes the speech "fighting words," Chaplinsky v. New Hampshire, 315 U.S. 568, 571–72 (1942). Since the fighting words doctrine is limited to in-person speech, it is of course irrelevant on the internet.

[43] *See* Snyder v. Phelps, 562 U.S. 443, 458 (2011).

[44] *See, e.g.*, *Matal*, 137 S. Ct. at 1766–67 (Kennedy, J., concurring in part and concurring in the judgment); R.A.V., 505 U.S. 377, 391–92 (1992).

Germany's NetzDG law, which became effective on January 1, 2018. NetzDG provides that websites that do not, within twenty-four hours, remove hate speech that is "obviously illegal" under German law are subject to fines of up to fifty million euros.[45] In an attempt to comply with this law (and enforce its own Terms of Service), Facebook established a deletion center outside of Berlin staffed by over 1,200 content moderators.[46] The results, however, have been less than ideal. In particular, there have also been complaints that Facebook is, out of caution triggered by the risk of large fines, deleting legitimate posts, and that the law is chilling political speech.[47] And worse, nations with less liberal agendas than Germany's have adopted copycat laws with the predictable result of significantly chilling or silencing legitimate speech the government disapproves of.[48] The merits of a strict approach to online hate speech, therefore, remains highly disputed.

Additionally, it is far from clear that the advent of social media has increased the incidence of hate speech, in any empirically measurable way. Of course, social media has no doubt increased the *salience* of such speech, by exposing it more publicly. But it is entirely possible that the same individuals would have expressed precisely the same views in the past in private, as they do today online. Nor is it clear that the greater online salience of hate speech has any impact on general societal attitudes; to the contrary, as discussed later in more detail with respect to political polarization, what research there is suggests that polarized individuals (including hateful ones) seek out polarized content; but exposure to that content does not change preexisting beliefs.

Finally, another notable thing about critiques of online hate speech is that they too are almost entirely located in the political left. Far from encouraging greater moderation of hate speech, as noted in Chapter 1, Republican politicians regularly accuse platforms of using anti-hate speech rules to suppress conservative content. Indeed, under HB 20, the Texas legislation discussed in Chapter 1, suppression of hate speech by platforms would constitute illegal "viewpoint-based" content moderation (since, as noted earlier, under

---

[45] *Germany Starts Enforcing Hate Speech Law*, BBC (Jan. 1, 2018), www.bbc.com/news/technology-42510868.
[46] Katrin Bennhold, *Germany Acts to Tame Facebook, Learning from Its Own History of Hate*, N.Y. TIMES (May 19, 2018, 10:45 AM), www.nytimes.com/2018/05/19/technology/facebook-deletion-center-germany.html.
[47] Rebecca Zipursky, Note, *Nuts about NETZ: The Network Enforcement Act and Freedom of Expression*, 42 FORDHAM INT'L L.J. 1325, 1359–60 (2019); *see* Linda Kinstler, *Germany's Attempt to Fix Facebook Is Backfiring*, THE ATLANTIC (May 18, 2018), www.theatlantic.com/international/archive/2018/05/germany-facebook-afd/560435/.
[48] *See* Rebecca Zipursky, Note, *Nuts about NETZ: The Network Enforcement Act and Freedom of Expression*, 42 FORDHAM INT'L L.J. 1325, 1360–62 (2019).

established Supreme Court precedent hate speech constitutes a viewpoint). In short, hate speech is yet another area where the political left urges more content moderation, and the political right urges less.

2.5 FILTER BUBBLES, IDEOLOGICAL SILOS, AND POLARIZATION

A final, important critique of social media platforms, and indeed of the internet more generally, is that online speech has contributed to ever-increasing political polarization, both in the United States and around the world. As early as 2001, law professor Cass Sunstein, then at the University of Chicago (where I studied with him) and now at Harvard, published a seminal book titled *Republic.com* which expressed concerns of this nature.[49] Sunstein's basic argument, or perhaps more accurately his worry, was that as speech moves onto the internet (this was well before social media became important), individuals would begin filtering the news and speech they were exposed to, limiting it in ways that would confirm their own preexisting beliefs and biases. The consequence would be a society fragmented into groups of like-minded citizens, with little or no communication across those groups. In other words, his concern was that the internet would increase political tribalism and polarization, perhaps to an unsustainable level.

When Sunstein made this argument in 2001, many people (including myself) were skeptical. After all, the impact of the internet was to make speech cheap, and so to enable ever more speech by ever more people. Wouldn't this lead to people being exposed to more perspectives than before, when the institutional media dominated public discourse? Whatever the truth of the matter in 2001, the advent and growth of social media platforms, and their eventual dominance of online discourse, made many of those on the political left (where Sunstein himself firmly belongs – he served as the so-called Regulatory Czar in the Obama Administration) come to see Sunstein's arguments as prophetic. And indeed, in 2017 Sunstein published another book, *#Republic*, which updated his argument for the social media era.[50]

There seems little doubt that there is a large degree of ideological conformity in the content to which social media users are exposed. In other words, social media use really does tend to confirm existing biases and beliefs, just as Sunstein predicted. The reasons for this phenomenon are complex. Many social media critics argue that the problem lies in the algorithms that

---

[49] CASS R. SUNSTEIN, REPUBLIC.COM (2001).
[50] CASS R. SUNSTEIN, *#Republic* (2017).

platforms use to decide what content to display to individual users. Because platforms care first and foremost about maximizing engagement (to maximize profits), these algorithms choose content that matches users' own previously expressed interests and views. The result is confirmation of those beliefs over time, leading to increasingly firmly held views. And, of course, because different individuals have different beliefs confirmed and strengthened, the broader social result is polarization.

Of course, no serious person would claim that the internet, or social media, are the only or even primary causes of increasing political polarization in the United States, which after all long predates these technologies. But important voices on the left, including in a report published by the Brookings Institute (perhaps the epicenter of progressive thinking), endorse the position that platform algorithms play an important role in fueling the phenomenon.[51] Jonathan Haidt, a highly influential scholar at New York University has also advocated this position,[52] as of course have others.[53] Haidt's argument in particular focuses not just on how platform algorithms select content, but more on ways in which platforms are designed to encourage extremist content because such content is much more likely to be retweeted, shared, or liked than more nuanced views. But ultimately, the result is the same, which is that the nature of the operation of the platforms creates exposure to content that confirms, and exaggerates, preexisting beliefs. And the common theme of all of these arguments is to link the desire of platforms to maximize engagement to the phenomenon of polarization.

There is, however, a somewhat peculiar aspect to this criticism of social media. Critics claim that social media recommends divisive content to users because such content is seen to maximize user engagement – and user engagement is, after all, the ultimate goal of platforms who make money by selling targeted advertising. But it is important to notice something. When critics complain that social media firms maximize engagement through their prioritization algorithms, in plain English what they are saying is that social media is at fault for emphasizing content that users *like*, that they want to see. But one might ask,

---

[51] Paul Barrett, Justin Hendrix and Grant Sims, *How Tech Platforms Fuel U.S. Political Polarization and What Government Can Do about It*, BROOKINGS (Sept. 27, 2021), www.brookings.edu/blog/techtank/2021/09/27/how-tech-platforms-fuel-u-s-political-polarization-and-what-government-can-do-about-it/.

[52] Jonathan Haidt, *Why the Past 10 Years of American Life Have Been Uniquely Stupid: It's Not Just a Phase*, THE ATLANTIC (April 11, 2022), www.theatlantic.com/magazine/archive/2022/05/social-media-democracy-trust-babel/629360/. For a collection of Haidt's arguments on this topic, *see* https://jonathanhaidt.com/social-media/.

[53] Bill Whitaker, *Social Media's Role in America's Polarized Political Climate*, CBS NEWS (Nov. 6, 2022), www.cbsnews.com/news/social-media-political-polarization-60-minutes-2022-11-06/.

is that not the job of any entity that provides entertainment? And one might also ask where the real responsibility for bad social outcomes lies here – in social media companies that feed their users' desires or in the users themselves?

It should be noted, moreover, that not everyone (on the political left or otherwise) agrees that platform algorithms are the main reason why social media increases polarization. An important counterpoint to those who point to algorithms is that the "blame" for platforms increasing polarization falls not on the platforms but rather on us, the users. In particular, law professor Jane Bambauer and colleagues at the University of Arizona argue that the real culprit is the internet's enabling of "cheap friendship," which permits people to socialize online almost exclusively with like-minded people – something that is much harder to do in the physical world.[54] And it is this tendency of users to cluster with those like them that produces the confirmation of beliefs and biases, including on seemingly factual matters, which fuels polarization. It should be noted, however, that whether the driving force is algorithms or friend selection, these arguments all support the view that using social media significantly increases polarization.

Of course, not everyone agrees that social media *does* meaningfully influence polarization. Unsurprisingly, senior figures at Meta, the owner of Facebook and Instagram, continue to dispute this point.[55] And importantly, recent research tends to support this view. In particular, a carefully designed recent study published in the leading scientific journal *Nature* suggests that while social media platforms do indeed have a tendency to present users with content consistent with their preexisting beliefs, that exposure does *not* tend to increase political polarization.[56] Of course, there is a correlation between political polarization and politically oriented social media use; but all that shows is that highly polarized individuals (unsurprisingly) tend to seek out the highly politicized corners of social media and the internet. But as with Professor Bambauer's analysis, this is consistent with the thesis that the problem is not platforms and their algorithms; the problem is on the demand side, situated squarely in individual users.

---

[54] Jane R. Bambauer, Saura Masconale, and Simone M. Sepe, *Cheap Friendship*, 54 U.C. Davis L. Rev. 2341 (2021).

[55] *Mark Zuckerberg Opening Statement Transcript: House Hearing on Misinformation* (March 25, 2021), www.rev.com/blog/transcripts/mark-zuckerberg-opening-statement-transcript-house-hearing-on-misinformation; Nick Clegg, *You and the Algorithm: It Takes Two to Tango* (March 31, 2021), https://nickclegg.medium.com/you-and-the-algorithm-it-takes-two-to-tango-7722b19aa1c2.

[56] Brendan Nyhan, Jaime Settle, Emily Thorson, et al., *Like-Minded Sources on Facebook Are Prevalent but Not Polarizing*, Nature (July 27, 2023), www.nature.com/articles/s41586-023-06297-w.

Indeed, another study conducted by many of the same authors and published in *Science*, the other leading scientific journal, strongly suggests that, contrary to what many critics claim, features such as resharing buttons on social media also do not alter beliefs or accelerate polarization. To the contrary, and perversely, the study suggests (though its findings in this regard are less definitive) that disabling such features decreases users' knowledge about current news, without any accompanying benefits.[57] In other words empirical science, that darling of the political left, suggests that progressive palpitations about the polarizing effects of social media might well be baseless.

In truth, it is almost impossible to separate out the impact of the spread of social media from other societal trends contributing to political polarization in the United States, such as increasing racial diversity and the economic impact of globalization on working class Americans. And it is of course possible that social media has played some role in increasing political polarization – though again, the data supporting this view is largely absent. But the left and center's tendency to attribute political polarization mainly to social media, or even the internet, while largely neglecting other causes, such as public policies and public rhetoric associated with the left, is either perplexing or breathtakingly cynical.

Finally, it should be noted that these concerns about polarization *are* of the center and left, and do not appear to be shared by more conservative leaders and thinkers. To the contrary, prominent conservative politicians, such as Marjorie Taylor Greene, President Trump, and Governor Ron DeSantis of Florida, seem to have adopted a strategy of stoking political polarization for personal gain. Nor is this a new, or online, phenomenon, as illustrated by then Speaker of the House Newt Gingrich's conduct during the 1990s. And of course there are plenty of political figures on the far left that behave similarly. But it remains the case that concerns about the role of social media in stoking political polarization and extremism have for the past decade been, and remain, a mainstay of the center-left in the United States.

2.6 CHILDREN, ADDICTION, AND BODY IMAGE

Finally, we should consider one of the most potent recent attacks on social media – this time one shared by the political left and right. It is the argument that social media is causing intense harm to the mental health of children,

---

[57] Andrew M. Guess, Neil Malhotra, Jennifer Pan, et al., *Reshares on Social Media Amplify Political News but Do Not Detectably Affect Beliefs or Opinions*, SCIENCE (July 27, 2023), www.science.org/doi/full/10.1126/science.add8424.

including by promoting addictive behavior, by contributing to elevated levels of depression and anxiety, and by promoting body image issues among teenagers (especially teenage girls). These concerns have generated a bestselling book by Jonathan Haidt,[58] a proposal by Republican Senator Josh Hawley of Missouri to prohibit social media platforms from offering accounts to children under the age of 16,[59] and, that infallible indicator of the concerns of the intelligentsia, an article in The Economist.[60] Given children's perceived heightened vulnerability to undue influences, these concerns unsurprisingly have received a great deal of attention and have led both the European Union and California to adopt legislation designed to protect children.[61]

Before jumping to extreme solutions (such as Senator Hawley's proposal to ban social media for most children), however, it is important to separate, examine, and dissect these concerns more carefully. Take, for example, the most sweeping (and vague) concern, that the combination of the internet, social media, and smart phones has created an addiction crisis among children, interfering with their socialization. The truth is, though, that while everyone is familiar with the phenomenon of "doom scrolling" (something hardly limited to children), there is no good, accepted definition of what internet or social media "addiction" even is.[62] And insofar as casual commentators are associating "addiction" with screen time on smart phones, the difficulty is that some of the most common uses of smart phones by minors, such as texting, are social activities which have merely displaced things such as phone calls. In my long-distant childhood, in an age before even cell phones, parents regularly chastised teenagers for spending too much time on the telephone, but no one in that era pulled out the term "addiction."

Turning from amorphous concepts of addiction, however, to more measurable mental health concerns such as depression and suicide, some serious

---

[58] JONATHAN HAIDT, THE ANXIOUS GENERATION: HOW THE GREAT REWIRING OF CHILDHOOD IS CAUSING AN EPIDEMIC OF MENTAL ILLNESS (2024).

[59] *New: Hawley Introduces Two Bills to Protect Kids Online, Fight Back against Big Tech*, JOSH HAWLEY: U.S. SENATOR FOR MISSOURI (Feb. 14, 2023), www.hawley.senate.gov/new-hawley-introduces-two-bills-protect-kids-online-fight-back-against-big-tech/.

[60] *Time for a Digital Detox?: Demands Grow to Restrict Young People's Access to Phones and Social Media*, THE ECONOMIST, April 20, 2024, at 87.

[61] Regulation (EU) 2022/2065 of the European Parliament and of the Council of 19 October 2022 (Digital Services Act) Art. 28(2), https://eur-lex.europa.eu/eli/reg/2022/2065/oj; European Commission, Directorate-General for Communications Networks, Content and Technology, *The Digital Services Act (DSA) Explained – Measures to Protect Children and Young People Online*, Publications Office of the European Union, 2023, https://data.europa.eu/doi/10.2759/576008; California Age-Appropriate Design Code Act, CAL. CIV. CODE §§ 1798.99.28–1798.99.40.

[62] Caroline Miller, *Is Internet Addiction Real?*, CHILD MIND INSTITUTE (Dec. 8, 2023), https://childmind.org/article/is-internet-addiction-real/.

questions undoubtedly exist. There is no doubt that during the period when social media use has become prevalent (starting around 2010), rates of depression among adolescents have increased sharply, especially among teenage girls.[63] During that same period of time, suicide rates among young people aged 12–17 in the United States increased by almost 50 percent (suicide rates increased across almost all age groups, but the most among the young).[64] And international data suggests that from around 2013 to 2021, suicide rates among adolescent girls (aged 10–19) increased by 50 percent in developed countries (though it should be noted that that group also has by far the lowest suicide rate of any demographic – boys/men have substantially higher suicide rates than girls/women at every age, and suicide rates increase consistently with age).[65] Given the obvious correlation in time between these objective indicia of an adolescent mental health crisis and the rise of social media, it is very tempting to conclude (as many have) that there is a direct causal connection. And perhaps such a causal connection does indeed exist.

The difficulty, however, is that the proof of the pudding is in the eating, and on this issue there simply is no proof. There have been an enormous number of studies conducted in recent years examining the link between social media use and mental health, and politicians such as Senator Hawley, as well as some journalists, have seized upon some of them as a call to arms to regulate social media use by adolescents. In 2024, however, a blue ribbon committee of experts convened by the National Academies of Sciences, Engineering, and Medicine issued a report on the topic, *Social Media and Adolescent Health*, which painstakingly reviewed the extant literature. Its strikingly straightforward conclusion, stated in the summary, was that "[t]he committee's review of the literature did not support the conclusion that social media causes changes in adolescent health at the population level."[66] And on the specific topic of adolescent depression, the report notes that "[s]tudies looking at the association between social media use and feelings of sadness over time have largely found small to no effects."[67] Of course, this conclusion does not rule out the possibility that social media use can negatively affect the mental health of some

---

[63] Sylvia Wilson and Nathalie M. Dumornay, *Rising Rates or Adolescent Depression in the United States: Challenges and Opportunities in the 2020s*, 70 J. ADOLESC. HEALTH 354, 354–55 (2022), www.jahonline.org/article/S1054-139X(21)00646-7/fulltext.

[64] Heather Saunders and Nirmita Panchal, *A Look at the Latest Suicide Data and Change Over the Last Decade*, KFF (Aug. 4, 2023), www.kff.org/mental-health/issue-brief/a-look-at-the-latest-suicide-data-and-change-over-the-last-decade/.

[65] *Time for a Digital Detox?*, supra n. 60.

[66] NAT'L ACADEMIES OF SCIENCES, ENG'G, AND MED., SOCIAL MEDIA AND ADOLESCENT HEALTH 5 (2024) (henceforth *"Academies' Report"*).

[67] *Ibid.* at 104.

individuals, adolescent or otherwise (or for that matter, improve individuals' mental health). But it does strongly suggest that the proposition that social media use is the cause of a societal mental health crisis among adolescents remains unproven.

Digging down deeper into the Academies' report, the reasons for this failure of proof become clearer. The most fundamental problem is the difficulty in teasing out causation. Even if the data shows a correlation between social media use and mental health issues (and the data suggests that a small such association may exist), it is impossible to say whether the reason for this is that social media use harms mental health or, equally plausibly, that adolescents with mental health challenges are more likely to turn to social media.[68] Another problem is that the period when the relevant research was conducted overlaps with the extreme political divisiveness of the 2016 election and Trump presidency, culminating of course with the COVID-19 pandemic and accompanying lockdowns. Especially during the latter period, both social media use and mental health challenges very predictably increased among adolescents (and adults), but teasing out causation here is essentially impossible. Finally, the sheer variety of platforms encompassed by the term "social media," from Instagram to Twitter/X to chats between online gamers, means that studies focused on social media use generally are of limited value.

But wait, I imagine many of you are thinking, didn't the Surgeon General of the United States issue an Advisory regarding social media use by children and adolescents? Indeed he (Surgeon General Vivek Murthy) did, in 2023.[69] And based on that Advisory, the Surgeon General recommended to Congress that warning labels for adolescents be placed on social media platforms (as well as writing an op-ed in the *New York Times* about warning labels).[70] So doesn't that establish that there is solid scientific evidence that social media causes harm, just as the Surgeon General's mandatory labels for tobacco products were based on solid scientific evidence that smoking causes lung cancer? Not exactly.

If one reads the Surgeon General's Advisory through, one sees many studies of the sort discussed in the Academies' report that find some correlation between social media use and depression.[71] But for the reasons just discussed,

---

[68] Ibid. at 93–94.
[69] *Social Media and Youth Mental Health: The U.S. Surgeon General's Advisory*, U.S. PUBLIC HEALTH SERVICE (2023), www.hhs.gov/surgeongeneral/priorities/youth-mental-health/social-media/index.html.
[70] Vivek H. Murthy, *Surgeon General: Why I'm Calling for a Warning Label on Social Media Platforms*, N.Y. TIMES (June 17, 2024), www.nytimes.com/2024/06/17/opinion/social-media-health-warning.html.
[71] *Social Media and Youth Mental Health*, supra n. 69, at 7–8.

those studies do *not* demonstrate a causal connection between social media use and mental health challenges. Indeed, the Surgeon General's Advisory is phrased very carefully, to reflect this; the key sentence reads as follows: "At this time, we do not yet have enough evidence to determine if social media is sufficiently safe for children and adolescents."[72] In other words, we don't know. And toward the end, the Advisory analogizes social media to approval of new medications by the FDA, where approval is contingent on *proof* that the medication is safe and effective.[73]

But this is a category error. It is indeed true that with prescription medications, the United States does not permit their sale unless the relevant pharmaceutical company can prove their safety. And, as the Advisory notes, that is the same approach we take to children's toys (the regulating agency there is the Consumer Product Safety Commission).[74] But that is *not* the approach we in this country take to free speech – which, after all, is what social media is. To the contrary, such an approach to speech, approval before use, is in the speech context called a "prior restraint," and it is almost automatically unconstitutional under the First Amendment to the US Constitution.[75] Under our constitutional regime, if the government wants to restrict speech, the burden is on the *government* to prove that the speech at issue causes significant harm. Moreover, the Supreme Court has made it clear that the government bears the same burden in restricting speech directed at children as it does more generally.[76] And it is quite clear that absent further, more definitive research, that burden has not been met.

Finally, let us close with one of the most often-expressed, specific concerns about social media use by adolescents, which is that it greatly increases body image issues and related eating disorders among adolescent girls (similar concerns regarding boys have not been much studied). There are indeed some studies suggesting a connection between (some forms of) social media use and body image issues. Indeed, the release to Congress and the media in 2021, by former Facebook employee Francine Haugen, of an internal study by Facebook arguably demonstrating such an effect with respect to Instagram use was at the center of the ensuing "Facebook Files" scandal (recall that Meta, then Facebook, owns Instagram).[77] And it is certainly plausible that constant

---

[72] Ibid. at 4.
[73] Ibid. at 14.
[74] Ibid.
[75] New York Times Co. v. U.S., 403 U.S. 713, 714 (1971) (per curiam).
[76] Brown v. Entertainment Merchants Ass'n, 564 U.S. 786, 799 (2011).
[77] Georgia Wells, Jeff Horwitz, and Deepa Seetharam, *The Facebook Files: Facebook Knows Instagram Is Toxic for Teen Girls, Company Documents Show*, WALL STREET JOURNAL (Sept. 14, 2021), www.wsj.com/articles/facebook-knows-instagram-is-toxic-for-teen-girls-company-documents-show-11631620739?mod=hp_lead_pos7&mod=article_inline.

exposure to a platform such as Instagram, which focuses on photographs of peers, often filtered or altered ones, *could* contribute to body image issues and eating disorders.

But once again, the full truth is more complicated. As the Academies' report notes, even in this area the usual causation problems remain. As the report states, concerns about media depictions of female beauty driving body image issues long predates social media.[78] Furthermore, the report notes, while social media use certainly *might* contribute to body image issues and eating disorders, "the psychological factors that influence the development of eating disorders ... can also manifest in disordered behaviors such as overuse of social media."[79] In other words, the causation might well run in the opposite direction, with disorders leading to social media use rather than vice versa. But all that said, there concededly is a realistic risk that certain forms of social media use contribute to the existing, exceedingly concerning problem of poor self-images among adolescent girls.

But even if that point *is* conceded, two complications must be addressed. The first is that while critics often attribute this problem to "social media," in fact the problem appears to be almost entirely associated with specific, photograph-focused platforms, most of all Instagram and Snapchat (though oddly, only the former gets media attention – presumably because of the media's joy in bashing "Big Tech"). After all, while exposure to political trolling on Twitter/X may well be bad for mental health in a colloquial sense, it is hardly likely to contribute to body image issues. As such, using this argument to justify limiting adolescent access to *all* social media is misguided and vastly overbroad.

Furthermore, as law professor Eric Goldman has pointed out, there is a more fundamental complication here that the critics ignore. Goldman focuses on the October 2019 internal Facebook study regarding Instagram, the release of which in 2021 by Francine Haugen triggered a firestorm. The headline chart in this study has been cited, fairly, for the proposition that Instagram use makes almost 20 percent of US teens, and over 20 percent of US teen girls, feel worse about themselves (the number goes up to 25 percent for teen girls in the UK).[80] But what the critics fail to mention is that 41 percent of US respondents reported that Instagram had no effect on their self-worth, and that another 41 percent (including 37 percent of US

---

[78] Academies' Report, supra n. 66, at 97.
[79] Ibid.
[80] Eric Goldman, *The "Segregate-and-Suppress" Approach to Regulating Child Online Safety*, at 21, Working Paper on File with Author (July 30, 2024); *see also* Wells, Horwitz, and Seetharam, *supra* n. 77.

girls) reported that exposure to Instagram made them feel *better* about themselves. Even among teen girls in the UK, the demographic whose study data was most troubling, 30 percent of respondents reported that Instagram made them feel better about themselves.[81] In other words, even among adolescent girls, Instagram apparently makes substantially more of them feel better about themselves than worse (the numbers are much more positively skewed for boys). So, if we take *all* of this data seriously, rather than cherry-picking, blocking adolescent access to Instagram will presumably make more teenagers feel worse about themselves than better. What is an honest, objective observer to make of that?

None of this is to say that concerns about links between children's use of social media and mental health issues are unreasonable or fanciful. They are not; indeed, they are perfectly reasonable and widely shared. But they are not proven, and the underlying dynamic is far more complex than critics acknowledge. In that world, it would certainly be perfectly reasonable for concerned parents to monitor or limit their children's use of social media. Furthermore, there are obvious and largely unrelated reasons that might justify school policies restricting smart phone use in classrooms (the obvious one being distraction). But when we come to regulatory interventions, skepticism seems in order.

2.7 IMPLICATIONS AND CONTRADICTIONS

There are several points to notice about progressive critiques of social media. The first, and perhaps most important, is that other than amorphous concerns about adolescent mental health, the criticisms ultimately come down to a claim that social media should suppress more content than it does because the content is socially harmful. This point is obviously true about the various attacks on the spread of disinformation, hate speech, or harassing speech; but it also is true of the polarization claim, which ultimately comes down to a demand to suppress or hide inflammatory content on platforms. In other words, progressives want platforms to act as gatekeepers of information, shielding the public from content deemed (by whom is not exactly clear) to be harmful. In Chapter 5, I will explain why I think this is a very bad idea, but for now it is the nature of the claim that matters.

Secondly, many or most progressive critiques, like conservatives claims of platform bias, stand on shaky empirical grounds. Why that is so with respect to hate speech and political polarization has already been discussed. But as

---

[81] Goldman, *supra* n. 80, at 21–22.

it turns out, the same is true with respect to mis- and disinformation. In an extremely thoughtful article in the *New Yorker*, Professor Manvir Singh of the University of California at Davis (my own institution) summarizes a great deal of empirical research that raises serious doubts about whether exposure to false information actually changes people's actions.[82] Professor Singh summarizes a swath of social science research which supports the view that people have two distinct kinds of beliefs: "factual" beliefs, rooted in data about the real world, and "symbolic" beliefs that are more akin to faith about the abstract nature of the world. Factual beliefs, the evidence shows, are susceptible to being changed by exposure to evidence; but symbolic beliefs by and large are not, because they are driven more by social ends such as group solidarity and the reinforcement of political identity.

Crucially, however, what the studies Singh summarizes tend to show is that individuals are far more likely to *act* based on their factual beliefs than their symbolic ones, if those actions have consequences for themselves. In other words, when individuals have "skin in the game," they actually do care about empirical facts. It should be emphasized that this does not mean that people's symbolic beliefs are not authentic – to the contrary, they generally seem to be. But individuals clearly recognize, at some level, that symbolic beliefs are different in kind from factual ones, leading both to a greater willingness to reassess factual beliefs than symbolic ones, and a greater willingness to act upon them. All of which does not suggest that mis- and disinformation is not abundant on social media – of course it is. But it does suggest that the real-world impacts of such content are quite limited. And that in turn suggests that the apocalyptic fears that Singh also gathers, suggesting that the spread of online mis- and disinformation spells the end of democracy and of social cohesion, are greatly overstated if not a form of mass hysteria.

Furthermore, it is also deeply unclear, as progressive critics tend to assume, that it is the architecture and algorithms deployed by social media platforms that are causing the spread of false information. To the contrary, a compelling recent paper argues that the online spread of what it calls "bullshit" is not a product of platform design but rather of consumer demand. In other words, the fault lies not in platforms but in ourselves. To this point, the paper argues that rather than platforms favoring low quality content, it is individuals that seek it out (which admittedly incentivizes platforms to serve up such content to those individuals). But comfortingly, the paper also argues (citing empirical

---

[82] Manvir Singh, *Don't Believe What They're Telling You about Misinformation*, NEW YORKER (April 15, 2024), www.newyorker.com/magazine/2024/04/22/dont-believe-what-theyre-telling-you-about-misinformation.

evidence) that the actual market for bullshit is quite limited, focused on a small percentage of users who start out with highly polarized beliefs.[83] All of which again suggests that the progressive attack on platforms as the source of false information is misguided (and that any solutions targeted at platforms, such as requiring changes to their algorithms, will be largely ineffective).

A third point about progressive critiques is that the social ills which they attribute to social media, in fact, are hardly limited to the social media ecosystem and long predate the spread of online platforms. Bigotry, hate speech, misogyny and threats of gender-based violence, conspiracy theories, and irrational attitudes toward science, including fear of vaccines, have all, unfortunately, been pervasive elements of the national culture of the United States for many decades, if not throughout our history. On conspiracy theories in particular, the historian Richard J. Hofstadter noted the influence of such thinking on the American political right in *The Paranoid Style in American Politics*, an essay published in 1964 (in *Harper's Magazine*, and later republished as a book)[84] that in turn was based on a 1959 lecture. And the historical pervasiveness of racism and racist speech in the United States is hardly in need of proof – though the *New York Times*'s 1619 Project does admirable work on that issue.[85]

Of course, this is not to say that the internet in general, and social media platforms in particular, have not increased the breadth and impact of such thinking. Perhaps QAnon has had a greater impact on the conservative movement today than the John Birch Society did in the 1960s, thanks to social media. Perhaps because of social media, vaccine skepticism during the COVID-19 pandemic was more pervasive than in earlier times and had greater health impacts. But then again, perhaps not. There are many trends in American society and politics, other than or in addition to new communications technology, that might explain the disappointingly low quality of public discourse in the modern era. Fox News, after all, predates social media by a decade and has almost certainly contributed more to polarization than the internet.[86]

---

[83] Lia Greenberg, Katherine Marin, Jessica Sparks, and Jane Bambauer, *The Demand for Bullshit, in* THE ELGAR COMPANION TO FREEDOM OF SPEECH AND EXPRESSION (Ashutosh Bhagwat and Alan Chen eds., in press).
[84] RICHARD J. HOFSTADTER, THE PARANOID STYLE IN AMERICAN POLITICS AND OTHER ESSAYS (1964).
[85] *The 1619 Project*, N.Y. TIMES, www.nytimes.com/interactive/2019/08/14/magazine/1619-america-slavery.html.
[86] Gregory J. Martin and Ali Yurukoglu, *Bias in Cable News: Persuasion and Polarization*, 107 AM. ECON. REV. 2565 (2017); David E. Brockman and Joshua L. Kalla, *Selective Exposure and Partisan Echo Chambers in Television News Consumption: Evidence from Linked Viewership, Administrative, and Survey Data*, Working Paper (April 17, 2023), https://osf.io/b54sx/.

Finally, it is noteworthy how stridently progressive critics of social media believe, and insist, that social media firms should have moral, ethical, and (eventually) legal obligations to alleviate or cure the social ills associated with allegedly harmful content. Yet no one appears inclined to impose such obligations on other forms of media, communications technologies, or industries. As an example, consider the fact that Instagram is regularly attacked for exacerbating body image issues among teenage girls and is held responsible for these impacts in public discourse.[87] Yet obviously body imagine issues among teenage girls did not suddenly arise in 2009 (when Instagram was launched); Mark Zuckerberg, in short, has not destroyed an idyllic past.[88] To the contrary, our popular culture has pushed negative body images, especially onto teenage girls, for many, many decades. And yet, there is a remarkable lack of pressure to impose similar ethical or legal obligations as those urged for social media onto Hollywood, fashion magazines, or for that matter the fashion industry. Similarly, while as noted earlier Fox News's role in exacerbating political polarization is well accepted, no one suggests regulating Fox News to limit divisive content. The inconsistency is striking.

---

[87] *See, e.g.*, Billy Perrigo, *Instagram Makes Teen Girls Hate Themselves. Is That a Bug or a Feature?*, TIME (Sept. 16, 2021), https://time.com/6098771/instagram-body-image-teen-girls/; Catherine Pearson, *Alarming New Report Shows Just How Toxic Instagram Is for Body Image*, HUFFPOST (Oct. 4, 2021), www.huffpost.com/entry/new-report-instagram-body-image_l_615b 1419e4b008640eb738e5.

[88] For an unusual perspective making this point *see* Jessica Grose, *The Messy Truth about Teen Girls and Instagram: You Can't Blame Social Media for Everything*, N.Y. TIMES (Oct. 13, 2021), www.nytimes.com/2021/10/13/parenting/instagram-teen-girls-body-image.html.

3

The Data War

Social Media Kills Privacy

Amidst the partisan rancor that has enveloped the United States since the election of President Donald Trump in November of 2016, exacerbated by the COVID-19 pandemic shutdowns which began in March of 2020, Americans have forgotten that they once agreed on the primary ill of social media: its use of Big Data to invade privacy and manipulate users. Concerns about Big Data, privacy, and the power of digital firms in the knowledge economy lie at the center of Shoshana Zuboff's seminal 2019 book *The Age of Surveillance Capitalism*.[1] Privacy and data protection (or the lack thereof) were also the core concerns driving the Facebook/Cambridge Analytica scandal of 2018, in which a political firm associated with prominent Republicans including Steve Bannon – one of President Trump's most prominent advisers – used data obtained by deceit from Facebook to build profiles of voters.[2] And outside of the United States, it is privacy concerns that motivated the most important early regulatory effort in the world directed at Big Tech, the European Union's General Data Protection Regulation (GDPR), which came into effect in May of 2018.[3] Furthermore, in 2018 the State of California adopted a similar, albeit more limited, data privacy law, the California Consumer Privacy Act (CCPA), which voters amended in 2020 to expand its protections (the new provisions came into effect in 2023).[4] Both the GDPR and CCPA are described in more detail in Chapter 7.

---

[1] SHOSHANA ZUBOFF, THE AGE OF SURVEILLANCE CAPITALISM: THE FIGHT FOR A HUMAN FUTURE AT THE NEW FRONTIER OF POWER (2019) [henceforth *Surveillance Capitalism*].

[2] *See* Kevin Granville, *Facebook and Cambridge Analytica: What You Need to Know as Fallout Widens*, N.Y. TIMES (Mar. 19, 2018), www.nytimes.com/2018/03/19/technology/facebook-cambridge-analytica-explained.html.

[3] General Data Protection Regulation 2016/679, 2016 O.J. (L 119), https://gdpr-info.eu/.

[4] CAL. CIV. CODE §§ 1798.100–178.99-100. For a good, short summary of the CCPA, *see California Consumer Privacy Act (CCPA)*, Office of the Attorney General, State of California Department of Justice, https://oag.ca.gov/privacy/ccpa#.

One notable fact about privacy and related concerns raised by Big Data is that they come from across the political spectrum. When the Cambridge Analytica scandal broke, it triggered calls for investigations from both Republican and Democratic leaders in the United States Congress, and generated an investigation by the Democratic attorney general of the State of Massachusetts, Maura Healey (who was later elected governor of that state). Similarly, the GDPR appears to enjoy broad support within the European Union, as does the CCPA in California (except, of course, among tech firms). Moreover, the bipartisan nature of privacy concerns makes sense. The desire to keep one's personal life to oneself surely has no political valence, nor does the desire not to be manipulated (though perhaps there are generational differences regarding both desires). And yet, despite all of the criticisms and scandals, the sound and the fury, the United States Congress has failed to pass any meaningful privacy legislation, and the laws that have passed (notably the GDPR and CCPA) are widely criticized as toothless. Why is this so?

3.1 THE PROBLEM OF BIG DATA

To get at the answer to that question, one must start by acknowledging that Big Data is a real phenomenon, without doubt. Internet firms collect a lot of data about their users.[5] Every time we buy something on Amazon, the firm keeps a record of that purchase. Every time we engage in a Google search, Google tracks the subject matter. Every time we use Gmail to send an email, Google scans and records the content. And every time we post on Facebook, Facebook records the content. Especially for ubiquitous companies such as Google, the information recorded about individuals can be so extensive as to permit the firm to create a robust picture of the lives of particular people. Furthermore, if firms share data with each other, as they sometimes do,[6] they can develop even more extensive pictures of individual lives.

Of course, the problem of information collection and use, or more broadly what Zuboff terms "surveillance capitalism," is not limited to social media platforms, or even internet firms. Home devices such as Nest thermostats, home hubs, and security systems (Nest is owned by Alphabet, Google's parent

---

[5] Jack M. Balkin, *Information Fiduciaries and the First Amendment*, 49 U.C. DAVIS L. REV. 1183, 1187–94 (2016); *see also* Lina M. Khan and David E. Pozen, *A Skeptical View of Information Fiduciaries*, 133 HARV. L. REV. 497, 498–502 (2019) (agreeing with Balkin about the reality of data practices and privacy concerns, but raising doubts about Balkin's proposed solution to the problem).

[6] *Your Data Is Shared and Sold … What's Being Done about It?*, KNOWLEDGE@WHARTON (Oct. 28, 2019), https://knowledge.wharton.upenn.edu/article/data-shared-sold-whats-done/.

company[7]), as well as Amazon's "Echo" line of home hubs (and the smart assistant, Alexa, built into them), engage in what is in practice ubiquitous surveillance. And in this data age, even most brick-and-mortar stores, including such ubiquitous institutions as Safeway (an American grocery chain) and CVS (an American pharmacy chain), incentivize customers to open and use accounts which track all of their purchases. Furthermore, there exists a robust data brokerage industry in the United States and around the world, involving firms who collect vast amounts of data on individuals and sell it to any willing buyer (in 2024 that market is estimated to be worth $400 billion worldwide).[8] But there can be no doubt that internet platforms – notably Alphabet/Google and the social media giants – have perfected the ability to track clicks and likes to develop user profiles like nobody else, which is why their targeted advertising is so strikingly, and creepily, on target.

The reason why platforms have perfected data gathering and use is of course that, unlike brick-and-mortar stores or even home devices, Big Data is not peripheral to their business model; it is utterly central. The key point to understand is that especially for advertising-driven firms, such as Google and social media platforms, users are not the customers – we are the product. And for them to maximize their profits, they must serve their actual customers – the purchasers of online advertising – the precise (or as precise as possible) product that they want. So, if I perform a Google search for best mattresses, lo and behold, my online feeds become filled with mattress ads. Or (more optimistically) after I upload a social media post about planned travel to Italy, hotel and airfare ads show up everywhere.

The basic ways in which online advertising works are, of course, well known. But the significance of this for platform business models is well illustrated by a relatively recent sequence of events. In April of 2021, Apple announced a new privacy feature in the latest version of its operating system for iPhones, which would permit users to block apps from tracking users' behavior on websites and other apps (or more accurately, it required apps to gain consent, which was rarely forthcoming, from users before engaging in tracking).[9] In the past, firms such as Facebook had used tracking information to improve their targeted advertising. This new feature did not, of course,

---

7 Eric Rosenbaum and Aashna Shah, *Nest Labs: How iPod Creator's Smart Thermostat Became a Top Google Brand*, CNBC (July 21, 2022), www.cnbc.com/2022/07/21/nest-labs-how-ipod-creators-thermostat-became-a-top-google-brand.html.

8 www.knowledge-sourcing.com/report/global-data-broker-market.

9 Alison DeNisco Rayome, *Protect Your Privacy By Disabling This App-Tracking iPhone Setting*, CNET (May 31, 2024), www.cnet.com/tech/services-and-software/protect-your-privacy-by-disabling-this-app-tracking-apple-iphone-setting/.

block targeted advertising; it merely reduced the amount of data available to personalize it. Nor did the privacy feature directly impact users' experiences on social media platforms. And finally, because this was an Apple feature, it also had no impact on tracking on Android phones. Nonetheless, in early 2022 Facebook announced that it expected Apple's new privacy policy to reduce its 2022 revenues by $10 *billion*. This announcement in turn contributed to a 26 percent drop in the share price of Meta, Facebook's (and Instagram's) parent company.[10] Other social media platforms faced similar drops in stock price, though in the long term Facebook, the platform most dependent on targeted advertising, seems to have been the biggest loser.

3.2 THE THREAT TO PRIVACY

Why does all of this matter? It matters because the harms associated with data collection and tracking are significant but, given the economic model of most social media platforms, there is little or no chance that the platforms will voluntarily cease or reduce their data collection practices. This is why the European Union and California have adopted privacy regulations, and why there have been continuous (albeit to date unsuccessful) proposals in the United States Congress to adopt a sweeping privacy-protection law. The wisdom, efficacy, and implications of such regulation are the topic of Chapter 7, so for now we will focus on the personal and social harms associated with Big Data.[11]

The most obvious risk associated with the widespread collection and storage of data is, of course, public leaks of personal information. Such leaks might be of embarrassing information about past conduct, which can take a wide variety of forms from infidelity to dishonesty to past crimes. A particularly extreme, intrusive, and troubling example of such leaks is sexually explicit photographs or videos, such as the 2014 release of nude photos of actress Jennifer Lawrence (which had been hacked from her iCloud account).[12] Such invasions of privacy can not only cause reputational harm but can also impose significant psychological trauma and interfere with future economic prospects (even if in utterly irrational and unjustifiable ways, as with the leak of intimate images).

---

[10] Meghan Bobrowsky, *Facebook Feels $10 Billion Sting from Apple's Privacy Push*, WALL STREET JOURNAL (Feb. 3, 2022), www.wsj.com/articles/facebook-feels-10-billion-sting-from-apples-privacy-push-11643898139.

[11] For a broad discussion of the value of privacy, *see* NEIL RICHARDS, WHY PRIVACY MATTERS (2021).

[12] Laura M. Holson, *Hacker of Nude Photos of Jennifer Lawrence Gets 8 Months in Prison*, N.Y. TIMES (Aug. 30, 2018), www.nytimes.com/2018/08/30/arts/hack-jennifer-lawrence-guilty.html.

Other sorts of information leaks can cause more direct, financial, or even physical harm to affected individuals. Leaked social security numbers can lead to identity theft. Leaked credit card or bank information can produce financial theft. Leaked home addresses can enable stalking or other physically threatening behavior. Indeed, leaks can be harmful even if they reveal no truly sensitive information, because public awareness of information such as an individual's political preferences or even reading habits can have significant social repercussions in our highly polarized and geographically politicized society. Woe betide a Republican in Berkeley, California, or a Democrat in Lafayette, Louisiana.

Of course, it is true that internet firms, including especially social media platforms, are quite unlikely to deliberately leak private user data or information to the general public. After all, any public release is likely to harm their relationships with users, with no offsetting benefits. Nor are the major, advertising-driven platforms likely to even sell user data to others. This data, after all, is not just financially valuable to them but the driving force of their profit model. As such, they are hardly likely to share it with potential competitors – and, in fact, both Facebook and Twitter/X explicitly state that they do not sell user data.[13]

Nevertheless, the very *existence* of large amounts of data stored on company servers makes leaks more likely, even if a leak requires bad actors to take advantage of the vulnerability of the stored data. But in the modern world, such bad actors are readily at hand, given the potential financial rewards from mining stolen data. In addition, hacking operations associated with state actors such as Russia[14] and China[15] also pose a constant threat to personal data, albeit the motivations there are less financial in nature (but no less potentially harmful).

Furthermore, even though internet firms are unlikely to engage in broad-based public disclosures of personal data, there are sound reasons to be concerned that they might leak intimate or embarrassing information about critics in order to discredit them, or threaten such leaks to silence critics or perceived enemies. Consider, for example, reports that in 2014 a senior Uber executive tracked the rides of a journalist, and a second senior executive floated a bizarre plan to use such tracking to dig dirt on journalists

---

[13] *Does Facebook Sell My Information?*, FACEBOOK HELP CENTER, www.facebook.com/help/152637448140583; *X Privacy Policy* ¶ 6.1 (Sept. 29, 2023), https://x.com/en/privacy#.

[14] Eileen Sullivan, *U.S. Disrupts Hacking Operation Led by Russian Intelligence*, N.Y. TIMES (Feb. 15, 2024), www.nytimes.com/2024/02/15/us/politics/hacking-russian-intelligence-routers.html.

[15] J. Edward Moreno, *China's Hacker Network: What to Know*, N.Y. TIMES (Feb. 22, 2024), www.nytimes.com/2024/02/22/business/china-hack-leak-isoon.html#.

who criticize the company (in 2014, there were a lot of such journalists).[16] Uber immediately disclaimed these actions and instituted an internal privacy policy; but there can be no confidence that leaders of a firm facing strong public criticism will not be tempted to act similarly in the future. Consider also the fact that in December of 2022 TikTok confirmed that employees of TikTok's Chinese parent company, ByteDance, accessed the user data of two journalists in the course of investigating leaks.[17] The TikTok disclosure was particularly troubling because of concerns that the government of China, which has broad powers over even private Chinese firms such as ByteDance, might access user data for geopolitical reasons. Indeed, the disclosure as well as other long-standing concerns have resulted in numerous restrictions being placed on TikTok. Many countries have prohibited downloading TikTok onto government-issued phones, and India (as well, bizarrely, as the State of Montana) has flatly banned TikTok based on such concerns.[18] All of this culminated in federal legislation in the US that will ban TikTok if ByteDance does not divest its ownership interest in it (as of this writing, it remains unclear whether ByteDance will divest its ownership of TikTok, or whether TikTok will shut down in the US).[19]

Leaving aside leaks, threats of leaks, or misuse of information, even the seemingly legitimate use of personal data such as targeted advertising raises troubling possibilities. At first, targeted advertising of goods and services seems at most annoying, and sometimes useful. But personal information can be

[16] Alex Hern, *Uber Investigates Top Executive after Journalist's Privacy Was Breached*, THE GUARDIAN (Nov. 19, 2014), www.theguardian.com/technology/2014/nov/19/uber-investigates-top-executive-after-journalists-privacy-was-breached; Neil Irwin, *Uber Scandal Highlights Silicon Valley's Grown-Up Problem*, N.Y. TIMES (Nov. 19, 2014), www.nytimes.com/2014/11/20/upshot/ubers-latest-scandal-and-silicon-valleys-grown-up-problem.html.
[17] Clare Duffy, *TikTok Confirms that Journalists' Data Was Accessed by Employees of Its Parent Company*, CNN (Dec. 22, 2022), www.cnn.com/2022/12/22/tech/tiktok-bytedance-journalist-data/index.html.
[18] Kelvin Chan, *Here Are the Countries That Have Bans on TikTok*, AP NEWS (April 4, 2023), https://apnews.com/article/tiktok-ban-privacy-cybersecurity-bytedance-china-2dce297f0aed056efe53309bbcd44a04; https://news.mt.gov/Governors-Office/Governor_Gianforte_Bans_TikTok_in_Montana.
[19] Sapna Maheshwari and Amanda Holpuch, *Why the U.S. Is Forcing TikTok to Be Sold or Banned*, N.Y. TIMES (June 20, 2024), www.nytimes.com/article/tiktok-ban.html. In January of 2025 the US Supreme Court rejected constitutional challenges to the TikTok law. TikTok Inc. v. Garland, 145 S. Ct. 57 (2025) (per curiam) (full disclosure – I participated in an amicus brief in the litigation over the TikTok law, supporting TikTok's position that the law violates the First Amendment). Subsequently, however, President Trump issued an Executive Order suspending enforcement of the law against TikTok. *Application of Protecting Americans from Foreign Adversary Controlled Applications Act to TikTok* (Jan. 20, 2025), www.whitehouse.gov/presidential-actions/2025/01/application-of-protecting-americans-from-foreign-adversary-controlled-applications-act-to-tiktok/.

used to influence and manipulate choices beyond the commercial sphere. As Professors Jack Balkin of the Yale Law School and Jonathan Zittrain of the Harvard Law School recount, during the 2010 midterm election Facebook conducted an experiment in which it added graphics to some users' news feeds that were designed to encourage them to vote.[20] The impact of this post was small (targeted users were 0.39 percent more likely to vote), but given Facebook's enormous user base, that can translate into a lot of votes, potentially enough to swing a close election. The risk, of course, is that because Facebook can pretty reliably predict users' political inclinations based on their personal data, it could manipulate election results by encouraging turnout only of voters of a particular political persuasion.[21] Which is not to say that Facebook, or any other platform, has actually engaged in such behavior, but this possibility poses a rather more serious problem than a consumer being convinced to buy a pair of shoes they do not need. And given Elon Musk's almost-simultaneous takeover of Twitter/X, and embracing his role as a rabid Republican supporter of Donald Trump,[22] the risks of such (mis)conduct are not farfetched.

As Shoshana Zuboff nicely describes it, the basic problem, the social risk, posed by "surveillance capitalism," which is to say the collecting and processing of massive amounts of personal data, implicates the very nature of our society. In the modern digital economy, information about human experience (i.e., personal data) is the key input into a huge amount of economic activity. The result is that those who possess and control that data, primarily the major technology companies such as Alphabet (owner of Google and YouTube), Meta (owner of Facebook, Instagram, and WhatsApp), and Amazon have the power to predict and manipulate a huge range of human choices. Their primary motivations in doing so are, of course, commercial; surveillance capitalism is, after all, *capitalism*. But as noted earlier, the power to extend such manipulation and control into social and political spheres certainly exists. Furthermore, because the tech sector is highly concentrated and (unlike the manufacturing firms that dominated earlier versions of capitalism) tends to employ relatively small numbers of highly educated people, the concentration of power entailed by this system is far more dramatic than in earlier eras.[23] Indeed, as of 2024

---

[20] Balkin, *supra* n. 5, at 1188–89 (internal citation omitted); *see* Jonathan Zittrain, *Facebook Could Decide an Election without Anyone Ever Finding Out*, NEW REPUBLIC (June 1, 2014), www.newrepublic.com/article/117878/information-fiduciary-solution-facebook-digital-gerrymandering.

[21] Jonathan Zittrain, Response, *Engineering an Election*, 127 HARV. L. REV. F. 335, 336 (2014).

[22] Theodore Schleifer, Maggie Haberman, Ryan Mac, and Jonathan Swift, *Musk Is Going All in to Elect Trump*, N.Y. TIMES (Oct. 11, 2024), www.nytimes.com/2024/10/11/us/politics/elon-musk-donald-trump-pennsylvania.html.

[23] *Surveillance Capitalism*, *supra* n. 1, at 500–01.

just a handful of individuals – Elon Musk, Mark Zuckerberg, and Jeff Bezos, notably – exercise complete control over many of the tech giants. As such, it can be argued that the rise of Big Data has fundamentally altered the structure of our societies, making them less democratic and in some sense less free.

3.3 COUNTER CONSIDERATIONS

There is, in short, no serious doubt that we live in a society and economy in which massive amounts of personal data collection and storage occur on a continuous and ongoing basis. There is also no serious doubt that personal data can be easily misused, and that even the possibility of accidental data leaks raises real privacy concerns. If one takes commentators and the media seriously, it is easy to come to the conclusion that the combination of Big Data and the death of privacy imposes constant harms on many people and threatens to change the very nature of our society. But to what extent are these extreme warning cries justified?

The scale of the risks posed by the data practices of modern platforms (and others) is honestly difficult to determine accurately, but there are reasons to believe the risks are somewhat exaggerated. Consider, for example, the concern that personal data will be misused by firms to target enemies and critics. That such a risk exists is certainly true, as demonstrated by the Uber and TikTok revelations. But in both cases the incidents appear to have been isolated ones, which were quickly rectified, and there is certainly no evidence that firms routinely misuse data in this way.

For example, when Montana's Governor Greg Gianforte signed a bill in May of 2023 completely banning TikTok within the state, he cited privacy concerns raised by the fact that TikTok's owner, ByteDance, is a Chinese company. The governor's release stated that the "Chinese Communist Party using TikTok to spy on Americans, violate our privacy, and collect their personal, private, and sensitive information is well-documented."[24] But tellingly, neither the governor nor the legislature could point to any evidence to support this claim, and TikTok insists that it has never shared US user data with the Chinese government or Communist Party.[25] Moreover, cybersecurity experts appear to support TikTok's position, rather than Governor Gianforte's

---

[24] *Governor Gianforte Bans TikTok in Montana*, STATE OF MONT. (May 17, 2023), https://news.mt.gov/Governors-Office/Governor_Gianforte_Bans_TikTok_in_Montana.

[25] David Shepardson, *TikTok CEO: App Has Never Shared US Data with Chinese Government*, REUTERS (March 21, 2023), www.reuters.com/technology/tiktok-ceo-app-has-never-shared-us-data-with-chinese-goverment-2023-03-22/.

unsupported claims.[26] This is not to say, of course, that there is *no* risk that the Chinese government, not known for its concerns about privacy or civil liberties, would coerce TikTok to share data – which is why ongoing pressure on TikTok to store US user data in the US makes sense.[27] But it seems equally clear that public statements by politicians and in the media about TikTok are greatly exaggerated and that TikTok bans, such as the Montana and federal laws, appear to be driven more by anti-China political sentiment than empirically grounded concerns.

Now consider the problem of leaks. Again, there can be little doubt that data leaks happen, as illustrated by the Facebook/Cambridge Analytica fiasco.[28] But how often do these leaks involve truly personal or private, potentially embarrassing, or weaponizable information, as opposed to information which can be harmful if public but otherwise lacking any moral valence, such as social security or credit card numbers? Of course, even the release of information that can be used to steal money or identity is harmful. But for one thing, social media platforms (as opposed to sellers of goods such as Amazon) are relatively unlikely to possess that sort of financial information. Furthermore, leaks of financial information (which, after all, long predate the internet) do not threaten basic societal stability or structures. It is when information can be used to generate social and political power that serious concerns arise.

So, it is worth asking again, how often do data leaks occur which raise such fundamental concerns? As is so often the case, there can be no definitive answer to that question, but all indications are that such events are exceedingly rare. They do of course happen, a prime example being the leak of intimate photos of Jennifer Lawrence and others. But they are not a recurring or common occurrence. None of which is to excuse leaks when they occur, of course, or to reduce the need for those who control data to secure it. But when considering appropriate regulatory initiatives, it is important to ensure that they are proportionate to the underlying problem, because even privacy regulation inevitably has unintended or negative consequences (as discussed further in Chapter 7).

One further point here: The fact that leaks of weaponizable data collected by platforms is rare does *not* mean that third parties/users have not utilized

---

[26] Max Zahn, *No Evidence of TikTok National Security Threat but Reason for Concern, Experts Say*, ABC NEWS (March 28, 2023), https://abcnews.go.com/Technology/evidence-tiktok-national-security-threat-reason-concern-experts/story?id=98149650#.

[27] Echo Wang and David Shepardson, *TikTok Moves U.S. User Data to Oracle Servers*, REUTERS (June 17, 2022), www.reuters.com/technology/tiktok-moves-us-user-data-oracle-servers-2022-06-17/.

[28] Nicholas Confessore, *Cambridge Analytica and Facebook: The Scandal and the Fallout So Far*, N.Y. TIMES (April 4, 2018), www.nytimes.com/2018/04/04/us/politics/cambridge-analytica-scandal-fallout.html.

the internet and platforms to expose and circulate personal information in extremely harmful ways. As discussed in Chapter 2, doxing and the like are troublingly common phenomena. And in the most repulsive such instances, such as sharing nonconsensual intimate images, such propagation can cause extreme, personal harm. The point is, however, that none of these sorts of abuses can be tied to the data collection, storage, and use policies of the big platforms. They instead are a product of bad actors and, on the platforms' part, (arguable) failures of content moderation. In Chapter 8, we will consider possible regulatory responses to this problem; but traditional privacy rules, directed at data practices, are not among them.

Finally, let us consider the risk that platforms (and other owners of large databases) will use the data not to target enemies but to manipulate society as a whole. An example of such behavior was Facebook's experiment during the 2010 election, described earlier, seeking to enhance voter turnout. While Facebook's conduct there was innocuous, as noted earlier similar actions could be used in highly disquieting ways, such as to try and push elections in particular directions. That such manipulation is possible is clear. Further, the extreme concentration of ownership of the major social media platforms – Mark Zuckerberg and Elon Musk, alone, each have dominant positions – makes the possibility greater because it is easier to imagine an individual pursuing such political games than publicly traded companies. Indeed, Musk's increasing politicization is particularly concerning in this regard, as illustrated by claims, admittedly unproven, that in the summer of 2024, Twitter/X interfered with the social media activities of groups supporting Democratic presidential candidate Kamala Harris.[29] But there are also disincentives to such behavior, most obviously that public disclosure of any such attempts would be a public relations disaster. And given that employees of platform companies would have to be aware of, and aid in implementing, such a scheme, ultimate disclosure would be highly likely (if it was not publicly visible, as with Twitter/X's suspension of the pro-Harris account). And lastly, as the Facebook example shows, attempts to use nudges or posts to manipulate conduct appear to have at best marginal effects.

One might ask, however, what the harm is in sharply restricting the data practices of big platforms (as, to some extent, the European Union is doing). After all, the accumulation of small risks can add up to significant ones, so why not act? The short answer is that, while some regulation might be justified,

---

[29] Trisha Thadani, Will Oremus, and Eva Dou, *X Suspends "White Dudes for Harris" Account after Massive Fundraiser*, WASHINGTON POST (July 31, 2024), www.washingtonpost.com/technology/2024/07/30/white-dudes-harris-suspended-x-twitter/.

3.3 Counter Considerations

there are serious downsides to regulation. What those downsides are, and what effective regulation might look like, are the topics of Chapter 7, but for now let us touch upon two.

The first, in brief, is that data collection and use is at the heart of the business models of the major current platforms. That is how they make money. To interfere with that model is to interfere with lucrative economic activity, which itself is problematic in a free market economy (it is no coincidence, in this regard, that the targets of the European Union's regulatory initiatives are almost exclusively US companies, and so have little impact on European companies and profits). But in addition, it is the data/advertising business model that permits platforms to offer their services to users without charge. Eliminate the business model, and the free services will either entirely disappear, or will no longer be free.

Second, it is important to remember that information is speech. To stop the collection and distribution of information is, therefore, definitionally an interference with free speech. This is not to say that restrictions are never permissible – free speech rights are not, after all, absolute. But regulations do raise serious constitutional and political concerns, and so must be considered with care – as we shall do in Chapter 7.

To conclude, the data practices of the major social media platforms undoubtedly threaten serious privacy and other social harms. At the same time, the scale and seriousness of such harms have almost certainly been exaggerated in public debate and criticisms of platforms. Finally, regulation itself threatens serious social and legal harms to users, and to society. Careful consideration and balancing of the harms is therefore essential before sweeping regulatory initiatives are undertaken.

4

Social Media Platforms as Common Carriers

At the heart of the conservative attack on social media sits a basic premise: Because social media is primarily a technology designed to permit individuals in society to communicate with each other, social media platforms should facilitate that communication without preferentialism or interference. In other words, social media platforms should operate like telephone or telegraph companies, or like the postal service, transmitting *all* users' messages to each other without in any way altering them. It was this model that Justice Clarence Thomas was defending when, as discussed in Chapter 1, he advocated regulating social media platforms as "common carriers." And it was also this model that explicitly underpins the Florida and Texas laws, also discussed in Chapter 1, that seek to regulate social media content moderation practices. But is this the correct way to think of social media? Or, in the alternative, are social media platforms more analogous to traditional media entities such as newspapers, who have long been recognized to have First Amendment rights to control the content that they provide? These are the questions this chapter addresses.

As it turns out, a majority of the U.S. Supreme Court has now provided some fairly clear answers to these questions. In the *Moody v. NetChoice* and *NetChoice v. Paxton* cases decided on July 1, 2024 (henceforth called *NetChoice*),[1] six justices of the Supreme Court agreed that social media platforms possess editorial rights under the First Amendment, analogous to the rights that earlier cases granted traditional media such as newspapers and cable television operators (and, weirdly, organizers of parades).[2] And, furthermore, five justices, still a clear majority, went on to specify in detail that with respect to the "feed" feature of social media platforms – focusing in particular

[1] 144 S. Ct. 2383 (2024).
[2] Ibid. at 2399–2403.

on Facebook's News Feed and YouTube's homepage – those editorial rights encompass decisions such as what content to carry, what content to block, and what content to amplify.[3] Finally, that same majority also flatly rejected Texas's argument that the State of Texas had a legitimate interest in regulating social media platforms in order to correct their alleged anti-conservative bias.[4] Justice Samuel Alito, joined by (unsurprisingly) Justice Thomas and Justice Neil Gorsuch, wrote a separate opinion flatly rejecting all aspects of the majority's analysis regarding editorial rights[5] – but of course three votes is substantially short of a majority of the Supreme Court.

Ultimately, the Supreme Court did not finally resolve the legal issues raised in the *NetChoice* cases – whether Florida's S.B. 7072 and Texas's HB 20 violated the First Amendment – because all nine justices agreed that both the lower courts in these cases had failed to properly resolve a complex, preliminary procedural issue.[6] Nor did the justices in the majority directly address the issue of whether social media platforms should be considered common carriers, an argument that Justice Alito (citing Justice Thomas's separate opinion discussed in Chapter 1) did raise.[7] But by squarely recognizing that platforms did enjoy First Amendment editorial rights, the majority quite clearly, if implicitly, rejected that argument, at least as to social media "feeds." In this chapter we will explore the roots of the argument over common carrier status versus editorial rights for social media platforms. We will also look at the implications of the *NetChoice* decision for future efforts to regulate social media, and why it is so important that the Court got the outcome right.

4.1 ARE SOCIAL MEDIA PLATFORMS COMMON CARRIERS?

As noted in Chapter 1, one of the most consistent critiques of social media platforms from the political right is the claim that social media firms are biased against conservative content, and unfairly single out such content for content moderation. According to the critics, such bias has taken the form of disproportionately blocking and/or labeling conservative content, secretly deprioritizing such content, and most famously, deplatforming conservative

---

[3] *Ibid.* at 2403–06.
[4] *Ibid.* at 2407–08.
[5] *Ibid.* at 2430–33 (Alito, J., concurring in the judgment).
[6] The issue concerned the fact that NetChoice and the other plaintiffs in these cases chose to bring a "facial" rather than an "as-applied" challenge to the Florida and Texas laws, and had to do with how to analyze such "facial" challenges, a topic thankfully far outside the scope of this book.
[7] *NetChoice*, 144 S. Ct. at 2438–39 (Alito, J., concurring in the judgment).

users including notably President Donald Trump (though as also noted in Chapter 1, the empirical evidence that such bias exists is weak). It was in response to these concerns that Justice Thomas suggested that social media platforms might qualify as common carriers, which in turn led the States of Florida and Texas to enact the legislation at issue in the *NetChoice* litigation. To understand the theory that drives these actions, we must begin by taking a bit of a deep dive into the concept of common carriage.

Let us begin with the foundational question of what, historically and legally, *is* common carriage – which is to say, what characteristics of particular services have led to them being classified as common carriers subject to extensive legal restrictions. Common carriage, as Justice Thomas pointed out, is an old concept, traceable to the English common law. At its heart, common carriage required certain forms of transportation businesses, as well as related professions such as innkeepers and warehousers, to serve customers on a nondiscriminatory basis (the common law also imposed liability on such businesses for negligence, but that is less relevant to our story).[8] This principle appears to have emerged from much earlier (medieval) law requiring *all* tradesmen who engaged in a "common calling" to serve the public without discrimination.[9] Regardless, however, long before the American Revolution, the common law had evolved to focus squarely on certain specific professions associated with transportation and travel.

That stability was challenged, unsurprisingly, by the technological revolutions of the nineteenth and twentieth centuries. The first challenge was railroads, which were in the transportation business but of course had no precise, common law analogue. Congress resolved that issue by designating railroads as common carriers in the Interstate Commerce Act of 1887.[10] Meanwhile, the telephone was invented (in 1876), and the question emerged whether this new industry should also have common carrier status. Courts originally split on this issue, but Congress resolved it by classifying telephone companies as common carriers in 1910, a designation it confirmed in the Federal Communications Act of 1934 (the foundational statute establishing the framework for federal regulation of the telecommunications and broadcasting industries).[11]

---

[8] Biden v. Knight First Amend. Inst. at Columbia Univ., 141 S. Ct. 1220, 1222–23 (2021) (Thomas, J., concurring) (citing Adam Candeub, *Bargaining for Free Speech: Common Carriage, Network Neutrality, and Section 230*, 22 YALE J.L. & TECH. 391, 398–403 (2020)); James B. Speta, *A Common Carrier Approach to Internet Interconnection*, 54 FED. COMM. L.J. 225, 255 (2002).

[9] Speta, *supra* n. 8, at 253–54 (citing Bruce Wyman, *The Law of Public Callings as a Solution of the Trust Problem*, 17 HARV. L. REV. 156 (1904)).

[10] Angela J. Campbell, *Publish or Carriage: Approaches to Analyzing the First Amendment Rights of Telephone Companies*, 70 N.C. L. REV. 1071, 1120 (1992).

[11] *Ibid.* at 1121–22.

The preceding discussion describes *how* common carrier regulation evolved to cover modern transportation and communications technologies, but it tells us little about what it was, precisely, that led judges and regulators to designate certain industries, but not others, as common carriers – because it is simply not true that all modern communications technologies have been treated as common carriers. The most important counterexamples in this regard are cable television operators[12] and television broadcasters,[13] both of which the courts have explicitly held are not common carriers.

Furthermore, specifically in the telecommunications field (which of course encompasses the internet), the statutory definition of common carrier – "[A]ny person engaged as a common carrier for hire, in interstate or foreign communication by wire or radio"[14] – is notably unhelpful. In an attempt to clarify this muddle, Justice Thomas claims to identify a number of considerations that scholars and courts have associated with common carrier status: market or monopoly power, whether one holds oneself out as serving the public, whether the business is "affected with the public interest," whether the service is in the "transportation or communications industries," and whether the business has received "special government favors."[15] Thomas also argues that modern social media platforms share all of these characteristics.[16]

However, Professor Christopher Yoo of the University of Pennsylvania has argued convincingly that most of the considerations Justice Thomas identifies have little historical basis. Monopoly power, for example, was not historically either sufficient (as demonstrated by Standard Oil) or necessary (as demonstrated by inns in large cities) for common carrier status.[17] As for being "affected with the public interest," the Supreme Court has recognized since 1934 that this phrase does not identify any particular category of businesses.[18] Similarly, a bland statement that "transportation and communications" businesses have tended to be common carriers evades the questions of *why* that is so, and why it is that some, but not all, such services are treated as common carriers – an obviously relevant question when evaluating digital platforms.[19] Finally, regarding "special government favors," while it is true that common

---

[12] FCC v. Midwest Video Corp., 440 U.S. 689 (1979).
[13] Columbia Broad. System, Inc. v. Democratic Nat'l Comm., 412 U.S. 94 (1973).
[14] 47 U.S.C. § 153(h).
[15] Biden v. Knight First Amend. Inst. at Columbia Univ., 141 S. Ct. 1220, 1222–23 (2021) (Thomas, J., concurring).
[16] Ibid. at 1224–25.
[17] Christopher Yoo, *The First Amendment, Common Carriers, and Public Accommodations: Net Neutrality, Digital Platforms, and Privacy*, 1 J. FREE SPEECH L. 463, 466–68 (2021).
[18] Ibid. at 468 (citing Nebbia v. New York, 291 U.S. 502, 536 (1934)).
[19] Ibid. at 469–72.

carrier status has often historically been accompanied by franchises, sometimes granting legal monopolies or limitations on liability, it is simply not true that a franchise or license inevitably results in common carrier status even in communications industries – the obvious counterexamples being cable television operators[20] and television broadcasters.

That leaves "holding out as serving the entire public." Professor Yoo convincingly argues that, as a historical matter, this is probably the most widely accepted definition of a common carrier.[21] This approach to common carriage is also consistent with the approach to this issue taken by the United States Court of Appeals for the District of Columbia Circuit (known as the DC Circuit), the most important regulatory court in the United States. In a case known as *NARUC I*, the court stated that "to be a common carrier one must hold oneself out indiscriminately to the clientele,"[22] or alternatively that "the carrier 'undertakes to carry all people indifferently.'"[23] In a later case with the same name (but different subject matter), *NARUC II*, the court reiterated this definition while clarifying that it was crucial to common carriage that the carrier transmit information of the customer's own choosing, not that of the carrier's.[24]

It should be noted, however, that to identify the "holding out" approach as the dominant historical and regulatory definition of common carriage is to open up a host of very difficult questions. For one thing, this definition appears to leave firms with an easy option to avoid common carriage designation by simply announcing that they do not serve the general public – but surely Congress did not intend telephone companies to avoid regulation through such a simple ploy.[25] In addition, it should be obvious that a simple willingness to serve the general public does not convert a firm into a common *carrier* because if that were so, Walmart would be a common carrier. Something more is clearly required – and that something is "carriage," meaning (as *NARUC II* indicates) a willingness to carry goods or messages chosen by the *customer* to the *customer's* chosen destination without interference.

This discussion of the development and definition of common carrier status goes a long way toward explaining why social media platforms such as Facebook

---

[20] FCC v. Midwest Video Corp., 440 U.S. 689 (1979).
[21] Yoo, *supra* n. 17, at 473–75.
[22] National Ass'n of Regul. Util. Comm'rs v. FCC (*NARUC I*), 525 F.2d 630, 641 (D.C. Cir. 1976).
[23] *Ibid.* (quoting Semon v. Royal Indemnity Co., 279 F.2d 737, 739 (5th Cir. 1960)).
[24] National Ass'n of Regul. Util. Comm'rs v. FCC (*NARUC II*), 533 F.2d 601, 609 (D.C. Cir. 1976).
[25] *See* Yoo, *supra* n. 17, at 475.

and Twitter/X do not conceivably fit within that category, even if Justice Thomas's definition were correct. Indeed, the question is not even a close one.

Starting with the obvious, there is no question that Facebook, with its almost two billion active daily users,[26] possesses some degree of market power, as Justice Thomas argues in his *Knight* concurrence.[27] But its market share, and profits, have been stagnating or declining in recent years because of the rise, as Mark Zuckerberg the CEO of Meta (the owner of Facebook and Instagram) acknowledges, of rival platforms such as TikTok.[28] As such, Facebook hardly constitutes the sort of unavoidable essential facility such as a local landline telephone company (before the rise of cellular telephony) or monopoly railroad facilities[29] that have traditionally been classified as common carriers under the monopoly theory of common carriage (which in any event, as discussed earlier, is a weak one). And Twitter/X, which since Elon Musk bought the platform has seen its daily active users collapse from 229 million daily active users to 174 million daily active users in February of 2024,[30] is even less credibly described as a monopoly of that nature – as demonstrated by the fact that, when deplatformed by Twitter/X, President Trump created his own, competing platform, Truth Social. Yet it was undoubtedly Twitter/X's deplatforming of Donald Trump that triggered Justice Thomas's judicial and Florida and Texas's legislative attacks on social media, given that Twitter/X was Trump's primary medium of communication to his followers (as well as being the subject matter of the litigation which generated Justice Thomas's call for common carriage regulation).[31]

Indeed, the very existence of four or five, if one counts Facebook and Instagram separately despite their common ownership, very large social media platforms (Facebook, Twitter/X, Instagram, YouTube, and TikTok) in the United States alone[32] belies the notion that any one of them is a monopoly

---

[26] Shannon Bond, *Facebook Shrugs Off Fears It's Losing Users*, NPR (Apr. 28, 2022), www.npr.org/2022/04/28/1095147942/facebook-shrugs-off-fears-its-losing-users.

[27] Biden v. Knight First Amend. Inst. at Columbia Univ., 141 S. Ct. 1220, 1224 (2021) (Thomas, J., concurring).

[28] Bond, *supra* n. 26.

[29] *See* United States v. Terminal R.R. Ass'n of St. Louis, 224 U.S. 383 (1912).

[30] *Twitter Daily User Growth Rises as Musk Readies to Take Control*, AL JAZEERA (April 28, 2022), www.aljazeera.com/economy/2022/4/28/twitter-daily-user-growth-rises-as-musk-readies-to-take-control; David Ingram, *Fewer People Are Using Elon Musk's X as the Platform Struggles to Attract and Keep Users, According to Analysts*, NBC NEWS (March 22, 2024), www.nbcnews.com/tech/tech-news/fewer-people-using-elon-musks-x-struggles-keep-users-rcna144115.

[31] *Knight*, 141 S. Ct. at 1221 (Thomas, J., concurring).

[32] If one considers social media at a global scale, one must add to that list platforms such as Telegram, which skirt the line between social media and messaging but enjoy huge user bases (in Telegram's case, larger than Twitter/X's).

essential facility. And finally, the fact that Trump continues to post on his new social media platform, Truth Social, also demonstrates beyond doubt that Twitter/X, or for that matter Facebook, are not the sorts of non-bypassable networks or services that have historically triggered common carrier treatment.

Aside from market power, the factors Justice Thomas identifies as relevant to common carrier status are whether the business "holds itself out as open to the public," is "of public interest," is in the transportation or communications sectors, or has received "special government favors."[33] But Justice Thomas himself concedes that "of public interest" is a meaningless standard.[34] And as for the fact that social media platforms are in the communications sector, no one seriously believes that all communications companies are common carriers. After all, all media companies – including newspapers such as the *New York Times* and cable channels such as Fox News – are involved in "communications" but, everyone appears to agree, cannot be subjected to common carriage regulation. And as also noted earlier, the Supreme Court has specifically rejected common carrier status for television broadcasters and cable television operators, both undoubtedly in the "communications" business. In other words, being in the transportation or communications sectors is neither necessary (see inns) nor sufficient (see cable and broadcasting) to be classified as a common carrier.

That leaves "government favors" and "holding out." Let us begin with the latter because, as discussed earlier, it is the most plausible candidate for the traditional definition of common carriers. But again, obviously not all businesses that serve the public indiscriminately, such as Walmart and Denny's, are common carriers. Even within "communications" companies, being open to the public generally (as the Fox News website is) obviously cannot suffice. This is the insight underlying the DC Circuit's analysis in *NARUC II*, according to which the key to common carrier status is that customers of the communications service at issue communicate content of their own choice and to their own destination of choice. Without that indifference to content on the part of the communications service, common carriage is a nonstarter.

But now consider the absurdity of the argument that social media platforms are common carriers. Justice Thomas and the States of Florida and Texas object to social media platforms because they (allegedly) systematically "discriminate against" (i.e., refuse to carry) certain conservative content and refuse to serve certain conservative customers (in particular, President Trump). Furthermore, conservative voices object that social media firms

---

[33] *Knight*, 141 S. Ct. at 1222–23 (Thomas, J., concurring).
[34] *Ibid.* at 1223 (Thomas, J., concurring).

choose to amplify certain content that platforms favor, while deemphasizing other, disfavored (i.e., conservative) content. In other words, the conservative argument is that social media platforms are or should be common carriers because they do precisely what a common carrier does not, which is having the service itself decide what content to carry, where to send it, and what to emphasize. In short, the Thomas/Florida/Texas argument is that social media platforms are common carriers because they are not common carriers. To quote the famous Supreme Court Justice Robert Jackson from a very different context, himself quoting Mark Twain, "The more you explain it, the more I don't understand it."[35]

Finally, we should briefly consider the argument that platforms are common carriers because they have received "special government favors." It is certainly true that traditional common carriers such as railroads and telephone companies were often granted special franchises or licenses, often with monopoly status, or special governmental powers such as eminent domain (the power to take private property without the owner's consent)[36] – but obviously none of that has any relevance to social media platforms. So in what sense do such platforms receive special "favors"? Justice Thomas does not himself much elaborate on this argument, but an article he cites by Professor Adam Candeub of Michigan State University does. Professor Candeub argues that, historically, what appears to define common carriage "is a bargain that gives special liability breaks in return for the carrier refraining from using some market power to further some public good."[37] And with respect to social media platforms, Candeub argues that the common carrier "bargain" can be found in Section 230 of the Communications Decency Act, a statute which limits platform liability for third-party content.[38]

Section 230, its meaning, and its role in the social media wars is the topic of Chapter 6 of this book. Briefly, however, Section 230, which was enacted by Congress in 1996 (and has been called "the twenty-six words that created the internet"[39]), has two crucial provisions. The first, Section 230(c)(1), provides that internet providers who host third-party content are not legally liable for harms caused by that content. And the second, Section 230(c)(2)(A), similarly provides that that such platforms cannot be held liable for actions "taken in good faith"

---

[35] Securities & Exchange Comm'n v. Chenery Corp., 332 U.S. 194, 214 (1947) (Jackson, J., dissenting).
[36] Adam Candeub, *Bargaining for Free Speech: Common Carriage, Network Neutrality, and Section 230*, 22 YALE J.L. & TECH. 391, 402–03 (2020).
[37] *Ibid.* at 405–06.
[38] *Ibid.* at 418–22.
[39] JEFF KOSSEFF, THE TWENTY-SIX WORDS THAT CREATED THE INTERNET (2019).

to restrict access to harmful content (i.e., for content moderation) even if the moderated content is constitutionally protected. Disputes over the actual meaning of these provisions, their effect, and their wisdom are myriad, and as I said will be taken up in Chapter 6. But for our purposes the question is, assuming that Section 230 grants platforms almost complete immunity for third-party content and for good-faith content moderation, would it then be reasonable for Congress to impose common carriage on platforms as a quid pro quo?

The answer is that it would not, because such a supposed "bargain" creates a fundamental and irreconcilable contradiction. The problem is this: Common carriage is a legal regime whereby platforms would be required to carry any and all legal content. Its very purpose is to eliminate content moderation. But the basic purpose of Section 230(c)(2) was and is to *encourage* content moderation, in order to prevent the internet and platforms from degenerating into sewage (on which more later in this chapter and in Chapter 6). In particular, Section 230 permits, and indeed encourages, platforms to block content that they, in good faith, believe is highly offensive, even if legal. But the whole point of common carriage regulation as proposed by Justice Thomas and Professor Candeub – to prevent platforms from selectively blocking legal content – is the conduct that Congress, by enacting Section 230(c)(2), intended to encourage and protect. In other words, this particular "bargain," Section 230 immunity in exchange for common carriage status, is not just implausible but incoherent.

In short, there is simply no plausible argument that social media platforms are or should be considered analogous to historical common carriers. They bear essentially no similarities to such carriers (other than engaging in "communications"), and certainly do not function as carriers of user-selected content, indifferent to content themselves, the thing that characterizes traditional common carriers such as telephone companies.[40]

4.2 SOCIAL MEDIA, EDITORIAL RIGHTS, AND THE *NETCHOICE* CASES

The alternative model from common carriage for social media platforms would be to analogize social media platforms to traditional media such as newspapers

---

[40] In an article published just as this book was being completed, Professors Ganesh Sitaram and Morgan Ricks of Vanderbilt University argue that internet platforms do qualify as common carriers under the common law. Ganesh Sitaram and Morgan Ricks, *Tech Platforms and the Common Law of Carriers*, 73 DUKE L.J. 1037 (2024). A closer look at their argument (which is not particularly focused on social media) demonstrates, however, that the form of common carriage they support would permit many of the platform behaviors that Justice Thomas, Florida, and Texas seek to prevent. *Ibid.* at 1088–98.

4.2 Social Media, Editorial Rights, and the NetChoice Cases

and cable television operators, and so protect their First Amendment editorial rights to control what content they carry, who to present it to, and what parts of it to emphasize. The Supreme Court, to a substantial extent, endorsed this model in the *NetChoice* cases; but it also left open important questions. I will begin by summarizing what the Supreme Court actually said in *NetChoice*, and then take a step back to explore broader issues regarding the nature of editorial rights and their application to social media platforms. I will also suggest answers to some specific questions regarding how laws can restrict the editorial choices of platforms, which the *NetChoice* Court did not address.

The *NetChoice* litigation arose when two trade associations for tech firms (we can call them NetChoice collectively), whose members include Facebook and YouTube, challenged the constitutionality of the Florida and Texas statutes (S.B. 7072 and HB 20) regulating social media content moderation practices, which are described in Chapter 1. As briefly noted earlier, the Supreme Court did not fully resolve the constitutionality of either law, because all nine justices agreed that both lower courts had misapplied the procedural rules regarding so-called facial challenges to statutes, and so remanded the case to those courts. Along the way, however, a five to six member majority of the justices provided important guidance on how, on remand, the lower courts should apply the First Amendment to platform content moderation practices. And it is this part of the opinion that is our focus.

The crucial and fundamental legal issue underlying the *NetChoice* cases was whether the First Amendment granted *any* constitutional protection to content moderation decisions made by social media platforms. And on that basic question, the lower courts in this litigation took polar opposite positions. One, the United States Court of Appeals for the Eleventh Circuit, held that the First Amendment did protect platforms' "editorial discretion," and so invalidated the key provisions of the Florida statute it was reviewing.[41] The other, the United States Court of Appeals for the Fifth Circuit, concluded that platform content moderation practices had no expressive component at all, and so fell completely outside the First Amendment. As a result, the Fifth Circuit upheld the Texas statute in full.[42] When confronted with this disagreement, the Supreme Court sided firmly with the Eleventh Circuit, describing the Fifth Circuit's reasoning as "rest[ing] on a serious misunderstanding of First Amendment precedent and principle," and as being simply "wrong."[43]

---

[41] *NetChoice*, 144 S. Ct. at 2396 (*citing* NetChoice v. Moody, 34 F.4th 1196, 1209 (11th Cir. 2022)).
[42] Ibid. (*citing* NetChoice v. Paxton, 49 F.4th 439, 466, 494 (5th Cir. 2022)).
[43] Ibid. at 2399.

The most important part of Justice Elena Kagan's majority opinion addressing this issue was joined by six justices (everyone but Justices Thomas, Alito, and Gorsuch). The Court begins by analyzing the key Supreme Court precedents relevant to the issue of editorial rights: *Miami Herald Publishing Co. v. Tornillo*,[44] which held that the First Amendment protected newspapers' "exercise of editorial control and judgment"; *Pacific Gas & Elec. Co. v. Public Util. Comm'n of Cal.*,[45] which held that regulators could not force a utility company to include materials it disagreed with in its billing envelopes; *Turner Broadcasting System, Inc. v. FCC*,[46] which held that cable television operators' decisions regarding what channels to carry implicated their First Amendment right of "editorial discretion"; and *Hurley v. Irish-American Gay, Lesbian and Bisexual Group of Boston, Inc.*,[47] which held that private organizers of a St. Patrick's Day parade had a First Amendment right to exclude groups whose message they did not agree with. (The Court also distinguished two cases in which the Court had not found First Amendment violations, on the grounds that the regulated parties in those cases were not engaging in any expressive activity.)[48]

Based on its analysis of these cases, the Court derived three critical principles. First, "the First Amendment offers protection when an entity engaging in expressive activity, including compiling and curating others' speech, is directed to accommodate messages it would prefer to exclude ... [a]nd that is as true when the content comes from third parties as when it does not." Second, "none of that changes just because a compiler includes most items and excludes just a few." And third, "the government cannot get its way just by asserting an interest in improving, or better balancing, the marketplace of ideas."[49] Note that the last two principles largely resolve, and reject, the key arguments in favor of the Florida and Texas laws: that they did not meaningfully interfere with platform rights because platforms carry most third-party content without objection or change; and that regulation is necessary to cure platforms' anti-conservative bias.

The rest of Justice Kagan's majority opinion, this time on behalf of five justices (so still a majority), considered how these principles applied to social media platforms (Justice Ketanji Brown Jackson, the Court's newest member at the time, thought it unnecessary to get into those details[50]). In particular,

---

[44] 418 U.S. 241 (1974).
[45] 475 U.S. 1 (1986).
[46] 512 U.S. 622 (1994).
[47] 515 U.S. 557 (1995).
[48] *NetChoice*, 144 S. Ct. at 2400–01.
[49] *Ibid.* at 2401–03.
[50] *Ibid.* at 2411–12 (Jackson, J., concurring in part and concurring in the judgment).

the Court focused on their application to social media "feeds," including Facebook's News Feed and YouTube's homepage, because those are the issues that the lower courts had focused on. The Court begins by describing in some detail how platforms moderate content on their feeds via algorithmic prioritization of chosen content, attaching warnings to some content, and completely blocking content deemed particularly harmful.[51] And the Court then unequivocally concluded that all of these activities are protected by the First Amendment because, like traditional media, social media platforms "create a distinctive expressive offering" via their content moderation practices.[52]

Nor did the Court stop there. It went on to emphasize that it was irrelevant that platforms do not moderate the lion's share of content, and so are not tightly controlling the messages they convey. As with the parade organizers in Hurley, the fact that platforms were not seeking to express a "particularized message" did not mean they gave up "their right to reject the few messages they found harmful or offensive."[53] The Court also recognized that the right at issue in these cases was not vitiated because no one was likely to attribute specific user content to the platforms themselves, because the expressive choices being protected here are deciding what content to include, and how to display and organize it.[54] Finally, the Court (following the third "principle" described earlier) flatly rejected the idea that the government could override platforms' First Amendment rights based on a purported state interest in curing platforms' "silencing" of conservative viewpoints. It held, crucially, that the state had *no* legitimate interest in or power to create "greater balance in the marketplace of ideas" or to "chang[e] the balance of speech on the major platforms' feeds."[55]

As noted earlier, for procedural reasons the Court did not ultimately resolve the constitutionality of either the Florida or Texas statutes. And in fact, it may well be that certain services provided by platforms, such as email and direct messaging, may legitimately be regulated because those functions *do* resemble traditional common carriage. But given the Court's analysis, it is crystal clear that the First Amendment fully protects the core content moderation functions platforms use to shape their user feeds, and Florida's and Texas's attempts to regulate those functions are flatly unconstitutional. As such, when a case arises that does clearly raise this question, quite possibly in the form of as-applied challenges by Facebook and YouTube to the Florida and Texas

[51] Ibid. at 2403–04.
[52] Ibid. at 2405.
[53] Ibid. at 2406 (quoting Hurley, 515 U.S. at 569, 574).
[54] Ibid.
[55] Ibid. at 2407–08.

laws, they will certainly be invalidated. Furthermore, as much as Justices Thomas and Alito sought to avoid this conclusion by labeling the majority's analysis "dictum"[56] or "superfluous,"[57] all sensible people understand that the writing is on the wall for the core applications of the Texas and Florida statutes.

Finally, it should be emphasized that the Supreme Court in *NetChoice* was not only clear in extending editorial rights to social media platforms but absolutely correct to do so for many of the same reasons that those platforms are not common carriers. Most fundamentally, the reason to grant social media platforms editorial rights is that unlike common carriers such as telephone companies and unlike Internet Service Providers (ISPs) such as Comcast, social media platforms are intentionally designed to provide a specific experience to users. While it is true that most of the content available on social media platforms is generated by third parties rather than the platforms themselves, social media is not a transparent conduit for speech such as a telephone system or ISPs. To the contrary, platforms famously moderate content extensively, making constant, value-based choices about what third-party content to permit on their platforms.[58] And they also ubiquitously employ algorithms that determine what content to show users, what content to emphasize, and what content to deemphasize. Furthermore, Facebook and other platform owners are constantly tweaking and making deliberate choices about how their algorithms should operate, both for business reasons and for ideological ones (sometimes in response to public pressure). Indeed, prominent commentary Tarleton Gillespie has convincingly said that content moderation "is, in many ways, *the* commodity that platforms offer."[59] For platforms editorial discretion is thus, as with newspapers, a fundamental feature of their operations.

Not only are platforms factually more like traditional media than common carriers, basic free speech theory also supports granting social media platforms editorial rights. The reason we grant editorial rights to other media, such as newspapers and websites that provide their own content, is because we think public discourse is enhanced when publishers are able to present coherent, consistent products with consistent messages. Fox News is not CNN, and the

---

[56] *Ibid.* at 2412 (Thomas, J., concurring in the judgment).
[57] *Ibid.* at 2438 (Alito, J., concurring in the judgment).
[58] Eric Goldman made this point succinctly in a brief essay. *See* Eric Goldman, *Of Course the First Amendment Protects Google and Facebook (and It's Not a Close Question)*, KNIGHT FIRST AMENDMENT INST. AT COLUMBIA UNIV. (Feb. 26, 2018), https://perma.cc/UU8L-R72T. For a thorough description of the process, *see* Kate Klonick, *The New Governors: The People, Rules, and Processes Governing Online Speech*, 131 HARV. L. REV. 1598 (2018).
[59] TARLETON GILLESPIE, CUSTODIANS OF THE INTERNET 13 (2018).

Wall Street Journal editorial pages are not the same as those of the *New York Times*. Furthermore, we believe that this diversity of perspectives advances public debate despite some risk of ideological sorting (conservatives watching Fox News and reading the *Wall Street Journal*, liberals doing the same with CNN and the *New York Times*). Permitting the creation of such coherent and consistent messaging is the very purpose of First Amendment editorial rights because while debate across perspectives is of course a valuable part of public discourse and democracy, so too is discussion *within* ideological groups which permits them to develop (and sometimes share with the public) their own values and views.[60]

Indeed, it would seem fundamental to the very concept of democratic citizenship that we must permit individuals to choose what information and perspectives to focus on. Or conversely, it is entirely inconsistent with our system of popular sovereignty and democratic self-governance to permit the State to choose what information is "appropriate for" or "beneficial to" citizens, and then force it upon them. We do not, after all, require liberals to watch Fox News, or conservatives to watch CNN, and could never do so consistent with the First Amendment. Yet imposing viewpoint neutrality, nondiscrimination, or common carrier requirements on social media platforms does precisely the same thing. It denies platforms the ability to create ideologically coherent packages of content, and so denies platform users the ability to select among such packages. Such regulation is at heart no different than legally *requiring* Fox News to provide airtime to Rachel Maddow or requiring CNN to provide time to Laura Ingraham – laws which presumably all agree, for good reason, would violate the First Amendment editorial rights of those news channels. To deny social media platforms, unquestionably the new dominant media for political and social discourse, the same freedom makes little sense.

If anything, the fact that modern social media platforms rely on third-party rather than their own content strengthens rather than weakens the argument in favor of editorial autonomy. The starting, but widely shared, assumption here is that democratic self-governance relies on public discourse;[61] and further, that this discourse is enhanced when it is truly *public*, meaning open to participation by the public at large. While historically a partisan press (discussed further in the next chapter) permitted those few who had access to the

---

[60] For a fuller development of this argument, tying it to the implied First Amendment right of association, *see* Ashutosh Bhagwat, Our Democratic First Amendment 56–57 (2020).

[61] *See* Robert C. Post, *The Constitutional Concept of Public Discourse: Outrageous Opinion, Democratic Deliberation, and* Hustler Magazine v. Falwell, 103 Harv. L. Rev. 601, 684 (1990).

press (i.e., political and social leaders) to create and shape groupings of citizens with shared values and perceived interests, social media permits citizens themselves to engage in discourse, both with leaders and among themselves, and so to participate in that creative, shaping process. Thus, the internet has democratized not just speech but also association and assembly.[62] Admittedly, granting platforms editorial rights leaves citizen groups at the mercy of the platform owners' decisions to permit or deplatform such groups, including ideologically driven decisions;[63] but to deny platforms such rights would leave such groups at the mercy of government regulation that would inevitably also favor some groups over others, surely a worse outcome. And in any event platforms, unlike the government, do not monopolize power and so if a group is denied access to one platform (say Facebook), it can always migrate to another (say Parler, Truth Social, or Telegram). A group disfavored by the government would have no such exit option.

Finally, the argument some make, that because the major social media platforms today claim *not* to engage in ideologically based moderation they have no need for editorial rights, is wrong for three different reasons. First, it is irrelevant. Even if platforms such as Facebook have not engaged in ideologically based moderation, they still use their algorithms to control users' experiences on their platform, making those experiences more engaging (and arguably more addictive, which is the source of much criticism of Facebook and Twitter/X). It is worth remembering in this context that the First Amendment protects entertainment as well as political and ideological speech, at least in part because of our inability to distinguish between the two.[64]

Second, it is untrue. Social media platforms' terms of service and other moderation rules are replete with ideological choices. The decisions by Facebook to ban hate speech, glorification of violence, electoral falsehoods, and even nudity are in fact ideological choices. To consider just nudity, the enormous struggles Facebook faced early in its existence over defining nudity and determining how to apply its prohibition to breastfeeding women[65] or the famous Napalm Girl photograph[66] illustrate the charged ideological questions

---

[62] *Cf.* John D. Inazu, *Virtual Assembly*, 98 CORNELL L. REV. 1093, 1141–42 (2013).
[63] Such deplatforming decisions are not uncommon. *See, e.g.*, Joshua Partlow, *Facebook's Decision to Shut Down Militia Pages Prompts Backlash among Some Targets*, WASHINGTON POST (Aug. 21, 2020).
[64] *See* Brown v. Entertainment Merchants Ass'n, 564 U.S. 786, 790 (2011); United States v. Stevens, 559 U.S. 460, 479–80 (2010); Winters v. New York, 333 U.S. 507, 510 (1948).
[65] *Radiolab: Post No Evil*, WNYC STUDIOS (Aug. 17, 2018), https://perma.cc/B8SQ-27VM.
[66] Aarti Shahani, *With "Napalm Girl," Facebook Humans (Not Algorithms) Struggle to Be Editor*, NPR (Sept. 10, 2016, 11: 12 PM), https://perma.cc/HE6Q-N7WB.

that can arise in enforcing even seemingly simple rules. Moreover, social media firms' willingness to engage in arguably ideological content moderation is evolving. Twitter/X started life as an "anything goes" platform,[67] but then rapidly moved to exercise extensive control over content,[68] before again relaxing those controls after Elon Musk's purchase and rebranding (to "X") of the platform.[69]

Finally, it is a logical error to condition constitutional rights on their exercise. By that reasoning, only current gun owners would have Second Amendment rights – but that obviously cannot be the law. Similarly, a printer's Ben Franklin-like commitment to generally publish all perspectives[70] cannot mean that the printer has waived their right to reject content that is particularly objectionable in their (evolving) view. For the same reason, even if social media platforms today do not engage in ideological censorship,[71] that is no reason to believe that they have waived that right, given the extensive *other* moderation that they undoubtedly do engage in.

4.3 NETCHOICE AND LEGISLATIVE IMPOSITION OF COMMON CARRIAGE

As noted earlier, the *NetChoice* majority never explicitly addressed the question of whether social media platforms may be regulated as common carriers. Furthermore, Justices Thomas and Alito both strongly suggested in their separate opinions that the issue remains open.[72] This, however, seems quite wrong.

---

[67] *See* Farhad Manjoo, *Twitter, It's Time to End Your Anything-Goes Paradise*, N.Y. TIMES (Nov. 22, 2017); *see also* Lindy West, *This American Life: Ask Not for Whom the Bell Trolls; It Trolls for Thee*, CHI. PUB. RADIO (Jan. 23, 2015), https://perma.cc/5VUC-8KJW. Lindy West's segment on the harms of trolls led to Twitter/X's then CEO admitting the platform's failures to address harassment, Caitlin Dewey, *Twitter CEO Dick Costolo Finally Admits the Obvious: Site Has Failed Users on Abuse*, WASHINGTON POST (Feb. 5, 2015).

[68] *The Twitter Rules*, TWITTER: RULES AND POLICIES, https://perma.cc/GNC7-7Q3R (last visited June 25, 2021).

[69] David Klepper, *Twitter Ends Enforcement of COVID Misinformation Policy*, AP (Nov. 29, 2022), https://apnews.com/article/twitter-ends-covid-misinformation-policy-cc232c9ceof193c505bbc63bf57ecad6.

[70] *See* Benjamin Franklin, *Apology for Printers*, PENNSYLVANIA GAZETTE (June 10, 1731), https://perma.cc/83V7-X8NP.

[71] Whether or not they do so turns entirely on the definition of "ideological." If by that one means that platforms favor "liberal" over "conservative" content, there appears to be no evidence that they do. But if a ban on hate speech can be considered ideological, then the major platforms clearly engage in such behavior.

[72] *NetChoice*, 144 S. Ct. at 2413 (Thomas, J., concurring in the judgment); *ibid.* at 2438 (Alito, J., concurring in the judgment).

Despite never using the term "common carrier," the majority's analysis also clearly, albeit implicitly, rejects the argument that at least with respect to their "feed" functions, either Congress or state governments may impose common carrier obligations on social media platforms (though perhaps they can do so with respect to other, more common-carrier-like platform functions such as email and direct messaging). The reason for this is simple: The Supreme Court's caselaw clearly establishes that legislatures cannot strip entities of First Amendment rights by fiat, simply by labeling them as "common carriers" or the related concept, "places of public accommodation."

That, in fact, is precisely what the State of Massachusetts attempted to do in the *Hurley* case cited by the *NetChoice* majority. In *Hurley*, a group of gay, lesbian, and bisexual individuals of Irish descent formed an organization named GLIB, which sought to participate in Boston's annual St. Patrick's Day parade in a way that would express their pride in their openly gay, lesbian, and bisexual identities as well as in their Irish heritage. After the organizers of the parade (a private group) denied their application, GLIB filed a lawsuit claiming that the denial violated a state law forbidding discrimination on account of sexual orientation by places of public accommodation.[73] Massachusetts state courts concluded that the parade constituted a place of public accommodation, that GLIB's exclusion violated the antidiscrimination statute, and that application of the statute did not violate the parade organizers' First Amendment rights. But the Supreme Court reversed the state court, holding that regardless of the parade's designation under state law, the First Amendment prohibited the government from interfering with the parade organizers' editorial choices regarding what third-party messages to include in their expressive activity.

Another case supporting the conclusion that applying the label "common carrier" or "place of public accommodation" does not eliminate First Amendment rights is *Boy Scouts of America v. Dale*.[74] The case involved a decision by a New Jersey Boy Scouts troop to revoke the adult membership of an assistant scoutmaster, James Dale, after discovering that Dale was gay. After Dale sued, the New Jersey Supreme Court held that the Boy Scouts were a place of public accommodation under state law, and that therefore the Scouts' actions violated the state's ban on discrimination on the basis of sexual orientation. The US Supreme Court held, however, citing *Hurley*, that this application of state public accommodation law violated the Boy Scouts' First Amendment rights.[75] Like *Hurley*, the *Dale* decision thus clearly stands

---

[73] *Hurley v. Irish-American Gay, Lesbian and Bisexual Group of Boston, Inc.*, 515 U.S. 557, 561 (1995).
[74] *Boy Scouts of Am. v. Dale*, 530 U.S. 640 (2000).
[75] *Ibid.* at 659.

for the proposition that legislatures, and courts, cannot strip entities of First Amendment protections, including the right to exclude content or speakers they do not wish to associate with, simply by designating those entities as places of public accommodation. Furthermore, the *Dale* Court held that such legislative action is particularly suspect when a state extends the "places of public accommodation" designation well beyond entities such as "inns and trains" which were traditionally considered in that category.[76]

The lesson from *Hurley* and *Dale* is clear: States (or Congress) cannot strip expressive entities or platforms of First Amendment rights simply by designating them as "common carriers" or "places of public accommodation." Furthermore, this is especially true when the government attaches those labels to things that do not closely resemble the kinds of entities historically recognized as within those labels. But that is precisely what the states of Florida and Texas sought to do in S.B. 7072 and HB 20. What this discussion demonstrates is that Justices Thomas and Alito notwithstanding, legislative attempts to strip platforms of their core First Amendment editorial rights simply by labeling them as common carriers is clearly unconstitutional.

4.4 A DEEPER DIVE INTO EDITORIAL RIGHTS

The Supreme Court's *NetChoice* decision is, for all these reasons, best read to recognize that social media platforms, at least in their core content moderation and presentation functions, enjoy First Amendment editorial rights, and may not, with respect to those same functions, be regulated as common carriers. What the Court did *not* do, however, was to explicate in any detail the nature of those editorial rights, or their limits. In this section we will explore how courts should resolve those questions when eventually they arise.

To understand the scope of editorial rights, we should first consider the source and nature of those rights. Historically, the core protection provided by the Speech and Press Clauses of the First Amendment was the right to express one's own ideas, and to distribute them as widely as one chooses, free of governmental interference. In addition, since the 1943 flag salute case,[77] there has been a related right against the government compelling you to express an ideological message of the government's choosing. Finally, as the *NetChoice* majority recognized, the Court has also recognized that owners of expressive platforms that communicate their own speech *or* the speech of others have a right to choose what to include and what not to include on their platforms.

---

[76] *ibid.* at 656–57.
[77] W. Va. Bd. of Educ. v. Barnette, 319 U.S. 624 (1943).

These editorial rights are somewhat related to both the speech and compelled speech rights, but they are distinct, especially with respect to third-party content. Editorial rights are not a form of pure speech. When a platform carries third-party content, interference with editorial freedom does not involve suppression of the regulated platform's own speech. Nor are editorial rights simply an aspect of compelled speech, for two separate reasons. First, one type of editorial right – the right to carry third-party speech that the government disapproves of – has nothing to do with compelled speech. Second, even when the claimed editorial right is to refuse to carry government-favored speech, pure compelled speech doctrine is a poor fit because, as *NetChoice* held, editorial rights apply even when it is highly unlikely that the speech at issue would be attributed to the regulated entity/platform owner.

For all of these reasons, editorial rights are best understood as a third, distinct right of free expression protected by either the Free Speech or (more plausibly) Free Press Clauses of the First Amendment. But what exactly are those rights? To begin with, a distinction must be drawn between positive and negative editorial rights – that is, between a right to include on one's platform expression that the government disfavors, and a right to exclude information that the government would mandate. This distinction has obvious parallels to the distinction between the basic free speech right and the right against compelled speech; but, as noted earlier, the parallel is not exact.

Nonetheless, it may well be that positive editorial rights should receive stronger constitutional protections than negative editorial rights, just as the right to speak is more robust than the right not to speak.[78] This is because the expressive injury, and potential distortion of public discourse, caused by state restrictions on what content platforms are permitted to include are obvious and severe. Silencing speech they dislike is the quintessential way in which governments control and manipulate public discourse, to the severe detriment of democracy.

It is less obvious, however, that the distortion caused by forced inclusion of unwanted content is so severe – so long as, and this is crucial, the platform owner is permitted to prominently disassociate itself from the required content, and indicate that the content is government-mandated. Without such a right to disassociate, government mandates can seriously distort public discourse, because listeners/users will mistakenly attribute to platforms and other

---

[78] Admittedly, the Court has at times insisted upon "[t]he constitutional equivalence of compelled speech and compelled silence." Riley v. National Fed'n of the Blind of N.C., Inc., 487 U.S. 781, 797 (1988). Given the ubiquity of disclosure obligations in the commercial and campaign finance contexts, however, these assertions cannot be taken entirely seriously.

users views that are in fact the government's, thereby giving them credibility they do not deserve. But if it is clear that mandated speech *does* originate with the government, then the public can judge it appropriately.

Moving on from simple government censorship and mandates, the *NetChoice* majority also clearly recognized that editorial rights also protect *how* to present content and (relatedly) what elements of that content to emphasize. With respect to the traditional media, this editorial right encompasses the decision to highlight some content on a newspaper front page or magazine cover, while burying other content inside the paper or magazine. With broadcast and cable television channels, this editorial power is most obviously exercised when programming is allocated "primetime" slots, while other programming is relegated to 2 a.m. With cable television operators, the decision on which channels to grant preferred (i.e., low) channel numbers is similarly an editorial one. With social media platforms such as Facebook and YouTube, the decision on what content to highlight in users' feeds, and what content to deemphasize, is similarly an editorial one.

Finally, it is important to recognize that even when editorial rights exist, *how* the government interferes with those rights may well be constitutionally relevant because no rights, including First Amendment rights, are absolute. Regarding disfavored (but legal) content, for example, presumably a prohibition on carrying the content constitutes a greater First Amendment burden than, say, a requirement that the content be accompanied by a warning label. After all, labeling is something that platforms today do voluntarily all the time. Admittedly, government-mandated labeling is different, but so long as the label was clearly attributed to the government, the First Amendment burden (while real) seems less severe, suggesting that mandatory labeling may be permissible *if* (for reasons discussed further later) the government has a strong, objectively reasonable (i.e., non-ideological) reason for requiring it.

Similarly, if the government were to mandate that a platform carry particular content, for reasons already noted the harm of such a mandate would be mitigated (though not eliminated) so long as the platform can clearly state that the content is state-mandated, and disown it. Indeed, absent the ability to do so the violation of editorial rights merges with a compelled speech violation of the most egregious form and (by banning the platform disclaimer) a direct violation of the right to speak. So, even if some requirements to carry content might be constitutionally permissible (on which more later), that would be so only if platforms had the right to identify the content as government-mandated and to make clear that the platform does not endorse it.

4.5 IMPLICATIONS

In light of all of the earlier discussion, let us consider specifically what editorial rights platforms should enjoy, and which should be more (or less) robust than others. It seems clear in this regard that the strongest editorial right a platform must possess is the positive right to include any legal content it desires on its platform. For the state to interfere with this right not only directly interferes with the platform's editorial control but also directly infringes on the free speech rights of the individual who posted the content. Since such regulations necessarily specify what content is forbidden, such regulatory intervention is presumptively unconstitutional (i.e., subject to strict scrutiny) under standard First Amendment doctrine, if challenged by the speaker. Even if the speaker does not assert their right to speak, however, a platform should similarly be able to assert its editorial rights in seeking to invalidate any such regulation. As we shall see, however, this simple fact dooms many regulatory proposals (primarily from the political left) directed at social media platforms.

On the other hand, while regulatory interference with negative editorial rights, by requiring inclusion of specified content, certainly remains constitutionally troubling, it might be defensible in specific circumstances. The problem with such inclusion requirements are twofold. First and foremost, as discussed earlier, such inclusion undermines a platform's ability to create a *coherent* user experience; and concomitantly, it interferes with the ability of groups of users to develop shared beliefs and values, by interposing the state's own preferred beliefs into the conversation. As such, forcing content onto platforms interferes with both editorial and associational values. Second, requiring inclusion of content has the potential to distort public discourse, by overemphasizing the preferred positions of the state at the expense of the views of the *public* as expressed in posts by users, a clear violation of the democratic principles that underlie the First Amendment. As James Madison put it, in a "Republican Government ... the censorial power is in the people over the Government, and not in the Government over the people."[79]

For all of these reasons, there should generally exist a presumption against state-imposed inclusion of content onto platforms – and that indeed is what the *NetChoice* Court held. But that presumption need not be absolute, because as noted earlier, inclusion of content clearly has a less severe impact on both editorial integrity and public discourse than suppression of content. Furthermore, inclusion of government-mandated content on a platform constitutes less of an

---

[79] New York Times v. Sullivan, 376 U.S. 254, 275 (1964) (quoting 4 ANNALS OF CONGRESS 934 (1794)).

interference with First Amendment interests than with, say, newspapers, both because platforms are already primarily dedicated to hosting content generated and selected by third parties while exercising modest control; and because, unlike newspapers, the major online platforms do not have capacity constraints, so including government-mandated content does not require removing other content (though if a smaller platform did have capacity constraints, then government-mandated content might pose a more serious First Amendment burden).

Nonetheless, it seems clear that regulations that require platforms to carry content expressing the government's own ideological preferences, or private ideologies that the government supports (as Florida and Texas sought to do), are out of bounds. Such rules create the greatest distortions of public discourse and seem to have no strong justification. The government, after all, remains free to circulate its preferred message using its own means of communication, rather than high-jacking privately owned ones. For this reason, a law that, for example, would require a social media company to display messages discouraging smoking/drug use/premarital sex or encouraging voting/gun ownership/exercise would be clearly unconstitutional.

On the other hand, requirements to carry non-ideological, factual content, even though it is chosen by the government, seem less problematic. Thus regulations that require platforms to prominently disclose their own content moderation practices, for example, are surely not terribly troubling so long as they do not impose a serious burden on platforms' ability to engage in content moderation (whether they do is a disputed point[80]). And one could imagine a myriad of situations where governments may legitimately require the display of factual content, such as displaying the hours and locations of polling places near in time to an election, or displaying the locations of shelters during a natural disaster. Surely these kinds of mandates advance strong state interests while imposing little or no harm to editorial rights or public discourse, so long as the quantity of mandated content remains modest (modest because if mandates become onerous, they could crowd out platform- and user-favored content[81]). And again, given that platforms are in the business of displaying third-party content with few restrictions, requiring some additional, unobjectionable content seems a minor burden on their editorial rights.

---

[80] *See* Eric Goldman, *The Constitutionality of Mandating Editorial Transparency*, 73 HASTINGS L.J. 1203 (2022) (arguing that transparency requirements regarding platform content moderation policies impose substantial First Amendment burdens, and so are presumptively unconstitutional).

[81] *Cf.* Am. Beverage Ass'n v. City & Cnty. of San Francisco, 916 F.3d 749, 757 (9th Cir. 2019) (en banc) (invalidating a warning requirement on advertisements of sugar-sweetened beverages because the size of the warning drowned out the advertisers' speech).

To this point, we have considered interferences with platform editorial control that either prohibit, or require, specified content. The state, however, has a larger regulatory repertoire than that. Consider a hypothetical legal requirement that platforms label specific content as false, or a requirement that platforms post warning labels or links to trusted sources of factual information (as many already do voluntarily) when specific topics such as COVID-19 vaccines are the subject matter of a post. Notice that such requirements implicate both positive and negative editorial rights. They implicate positive rights because a platform's decision to display specific user content triggers legal consequences. They implicate negative rights because the legal remedy is to force platforms to post content of the government's choosing.

Even given that, however, it seems plain that labeling requirements are less intrusive on editorial discretion than flat bans because platforms remain free to post any material they wish, to control the prominence of those materials, and to disassociate themselves from any government-mandated label by captioning the label as imposed by the government. On the other hand, there is an obvious concern that regulatory authorities will select what content to target for labeling for ideological reasons, which would violate the cardinal rule against ideologically based infringements of negative editorial rights. As a consequence, at a minimum courts should approach labeling or linking requirements with a high degree of skepticism, and uphold them only if the government can prove that it is addressing a serious and urgent social problem, the information triggering the requirement is demonstrably factual and false, and the information contained in the mandated label or link is demonstrably factual and true.

4.6 REGULATORY PROPOSALS

Recognizing that platforms should and do possess robust First Amendment editorial rights, and specifying the nature of those rights, provides valuable tools to evaluate the sorts of regulatory proposals discussed in Chapters 1 and 2. Most fundamentally, for reasons already discussed, editorial rights are clearly inconsistent with some of the strongest regulatory proposals coming from conservative critics of social media, such as regulating platforms as common carriers, as Justice Thomas proposed, or requiring "fairness" or viewpoint neutrality in content regulation, as Texas sought to do.

But just as editorial rights are a formidable barrier to the mainly[82] conservative proposals to require viewpoint neutrality on social media platforms, such

---

[82] I say mainly because UC Berkeley School of Law Dean Chemerinsky, who is famously progressive, once made a similar proposal. Prasad Krishnamurthy and Erwin Chemerinsky, *How*

rights also appear to doom most progressive proposals of the sort discussed in Chapter 2 to regulate social media. Examples of such proposals include pressure by Democratic State Attorneys General (backed by the threat of legal action) to force platforms to block more hate speech,[83] as well as legislative proposals and actions by Senator Amy Klobuchar and the State of California, discussed in Chapter 2, which target medical (especially COVID) mis- and disinformation.

The reason such proposals violate the First Amendment is, quite simply, that both hate speech[84] and falsehoods[85] are fully protected under the First Amendment. And the First Amendment's prohibition on the government suppressing protected speech based on its message applies equally to government requirements that private actors suppress such speech.[86] As such, users posting legally prohibited content would surely be able to successfully attack such laws as violating the First Amendment. But what the holding in *NetChoice* establishes is that even if the users themselves fail to advance such legal claims, platforms claiming editorial rights should be able to attack such legislative efforts as usurping *their* core editorial rights to carry whatever legal and constitutionally protected content they choose to.

However, while a flat-out prohibition on falsehoods or hate speech cannot survive constitutional scrutiny, the First Amendment does permit regulation even of protected speech, thereby restricting both speech and editorial rights, so long as the regulation serves urgent social goals and is written narrowly. Thus, a narrow prohibition on falsehoods regarding, for example, voting rules might survive judicial scrutiny if written carefully to target only clearly false, and clearly harmful assertions. Similarly, for reasons already discussed, narrowly written labeling requirements (or requirements to link to truthful information) might also be permissible in such situations, so long as carefully targeted at content that is provably harmful and false.

Furthermore, when speech is *unprotected* there is no question that legislation can ban such speech, overriding both speech and editorial rights. Thus, there is no First Amendment barrier to laws requiring platforms, upon being given notice, to remove false commercial speech[87] or hate speech that crosses

---

Congress Can Prevent Big Tech from Becoming the Speech Police, THE HILL (Feb. 18, 2021, 8:00 AM), https://perma.cc/G8EJ-3XCM.

[83] *See, e.g.*, Davey Alba, *Facebook Must Better Police Online Hate, State Attorneys General Say*, N.Y. TIMES (Aug. 5, 2020), www.nytimes.com/2020/08/05/technology/facebook-online-hate.html.

[84] Matal v. Tam, 137 S. Ct. 1744, 1764 (2017) (plurality opinion).

[85] United States v. Alvarez, 567 U.S. 709, 727–28 (2012).

[86] United States v. Playboy Ent. Grp., 529 U.S. 803, 826–27 (2000).

[87] *See, e.g.*, Va. State Bd. of Pharm. v. Va. Citizens Consumer Council, Inc., 425 U.S. 748, 770–71 (1976).

the line into incitement of violence under the Supreme Court's precedent in this area.[88] Nor would there be any *constitutional* barrier to amending Section 230 to limit or eliminate platforms' statutory immunity for carrying third-party content that is constitutionally unprotected, as Congress in fact did in 2018 with respect to platforms that knowingly permit their services to be used to facilitate sex trafficking.[89] Questions regarding possible Section 230 reforms, and their (troubling) practical consequences, will be taken up in more detail in Chapter 6 but for now it is sufficient to note that the *First Amendment* is not an absolute bar to such legislative actions, so long as platform liability is limited to content the platform knows is illegal (why that is so will be taken up in Chapter 6).

Finally, consider laws that forbid platforms from deplatforming a specific class of users – as Florida did with politicians and journalists,[90] in obvious response to the deplatforming of President Trump in January of 2021. While at first blush such a law seems less troubling than direct restrictions on content moderation, they are nonetheless very problematic. For one, it is highly predictable that if a legislature imposes such a limit, it will almost always be seeking to protect speakers with specific ideological bents (as was surely true in Florida), which makes the law indistinguishable from one directly favoring specific viewpoints. In addition, such legislation has the direct and obvious effect of denying platforms one powerful remedy – temporary or permanent deplatforming – against users who regularly violate content policies. But this in itself sharply interferes with editorial freedom, by making it difficult for platforms to control and deter users who are scofflaws. As such, courts should approach such law with, at a minimum, high levels of skepticism.

4.7 WHY TREATING PLATFORMS AS COMMON CARRIERS IS A *TERRIBLE* IDEA

We should end our discussion of the choice between treating social media platforms as common carriers, similar to railroads and telephone companies, or as media entities, possessing editorial rights, by taking a step away from the law and considering instead policy and practical consequences. To understand

---

[88] Brandenburg v. Ohio, 395 U.S. 444, 447 (1969).
[89] The relevant law is commonly known as FOSTA-SESTA. For a discussion of the legislation's terms and background, *see* Charles Matula, *Any Safe Harbor in a Storm: SESTA-FOSTA and the Future of § 230 of the Communications Decency Act*, 18 DUKE L. & TECH. REV. 353 (2020). For a critique of the law in action, *see* David McCabe and Kate Conger, *Stamping Out Online Sex Trafficking May Have Pushed It Underground*, N.Y. TIMES (Dec. 17, 2019).
[90] S.B. 7072, 2021 Leg. (Fla. 2021).

4.7 Why Treating Platforms as Common Carriers Is a Terrible Idea

why the common carrier model for platforms is not only unconstitutional but also terrible public policy, it is useful to envision what the world would look like if platforms *were* treated as common carriers. Would that world be a better one than the admittedly imperfect status quo? Proponents of regulation appear to believe so (or so one must assume); but they are clearly wrong.

Let us begin first with Justice Thomas's far-reaching proposal to fully regulate social media platforms as common carriers or places of public accommodation, on par with railroads, landline telephony, and telegraphs. At the core of such regulation is a requirement of nondiscrimination – an obligation to serve all customers without distinction and on identical terms, so long as the provider has capacity to do so (I presume that Justice Thomas did not intend to endorse other elements of common carriage status, such as price regulation).[91] As applied to social media, what this would mean is that platforms would be required to carry any and all (legal?) content posted by any person who is or seeks to be a platform user (capacity constraints not being an issue for the major platforms). What would this look like?

First, let us consider the potential caveat limiting platform hosting obligations to *legal* content. While they rarely address the question directly, proponents of platform regulation appear to implicitly assume that even under common carrier regulation, platforms could and would refuse to host blatantly illegal content such as child pornography or violent threats. But it is not clear why that is so. After all, when terrorists use telephone calls to plan an atrocity, or insurrectionists travel by airplane or railroad to attack the Capitol, no one holds the telephone company, airline, or railroad responsible for the resulting violence, even if they had reason to know that illegal activity was afoot. The reason is that imposing obligations to police their customers on common carriers seems completely inconsistent with their broader obligation to serve.

Why then should platforms be different? If platforms are regulated as common carriers, they will presumably dismantle the elaborate content-moderation machinery that they have created.[92] After all, content moderation is a fraught, extremely expensive, and controversial process, so if platforms' ability to engage in such moderation is severely restricted, they will surely not bother incurring the expense. But once the content moderation machinery is dismantled, how and why would platforms suppress illegal content? Left to their own devices, one strongly suspects that they would not.

---

[91] Biden v. Knight First Amend. Inst. at Columbia Univ., 141 S. Ct. 1220, 1222 (2021) (Thomas, J., concurring).
[92] *See* Klonick, *supra* n. 58, at 1625–30 (2018).

A possible response to this argument is that platforms should simply be subject to a legal obligation to block illegal content, while carrying all legal content. But this is also highly problematic. The difficulty arises because, as Eric Goldman and Jess Miers have pointed out, the line between protected and unprotected content is often very blurry.[93] When a communication crosses the line from hyperbole to a "true threat," for example, is often unclear.[94] And even when the legal line is clear, it is often quite difficult to determine if particular content is illegal – for example, whether it is unprotected child pornography portraying a minor engaged in sexual conduct,[95] or protected "virtual child pornography" depicting a young-looking adult.[96] But under a regulatory approach combining common carriage with an obligation to block illegal content, platforms would be liable *either* if they fail to block illegal content *or* if they mistakenly blocked legal content thinking it is illegal, thereby violating their common carrier obligations. Such a legal regime is both profoundly unfair and entirely unsustainable.

Leaving aside the problem of illegal content, however, even with respect to unquestionably legal and constitutionally protected content, common carriage would have highly problematic consequences. As Goldman and Miers also point out, the world is full of content that is "lawful-but-awful," and experience suggests that the internet is particularly likely to be used to spread such content (perhaps because of the pseudo-anonymity of being online,[97] and also because of the lack of online gatekeepers, the topic of the next chapter). Such lawful-but-awful content includes non-obscene pornography, gruesome depictions of violence (sometimes posted by the perpetrator), hate speech, bullying that does not rise to the level of harassment or threats, and of course lies galore about just about anything, including dangerous lies such as medical misinformation. Such content is legal and constitutionally protected, so a common carriage requirement would entirely eliminate social media platforms' power to block such content. Indeed, platforms could not even de-amplify it, because common carriers are required to provide service to all users on equal and nondiscriminatory terms, on a first-come, first-served basis. In the world

---

[93] Eric Goldman and Jess Miers, *Online Account Terminations/Content Removals and the Benefits of Internet Services Enforcing Their House Rules*, 1 J. FREE SPEECH L. 191, 204–07 (2021).
[94] *See, e.g.*, Elonis v. United States, 575 U.S. 723 (2015); Counterman v. Colorado, 600 U.S. 66 (2023).
[95] New York v. Ferber, 458 U.S. 747 (1982).
[96] Ashcroft v. Free Speech Coal., 535 U.S. 234 (2002).
[97] Goldman and Miers, *supra* n. 93, at 208–09.

of social media, this means hosting and displaying *all* legal content without making distinctions, because for the major platforms capacity constraints are a non-issue. That seems a rather troubling outcome.

Furthermore, if platforms were forced to host and display lawful-but-awful content on equal terms with all other content, it seems highly likely that all but the worst users and advertisers will ultimately flee the platforms. Users will flee because most people will quite reasonably not want to waste their time (and harm their emotional well-being) by wading through pornography, violence, hate, and lies. And advertisers will flee because they do not want their products associated with such things – something in the advertising industry called protecting "brand safety." This dynamic was on full display in the wake of Elon Musk's purchase of Twitter/X, whose advertising revenues fell 59 *percent* in the ensuing six months, at least in part because of the rise of hate speech and pornography on the platform.[98]

In the long term, such a downward spiral must lead to platforms' demise. That seems a very bad result, not only for the platforms themselves but for the billions of users worldwide who enjoy interacting with social media. Moreover, whether or not social media is on balance socially beneficial, the precedent of the government effectively destroying a new form of communicative media through regulation seems to set a truly terrible precedent, putting aside constitutionality.

Perhaps because they recognized these problems, the Florida and Texas legislation at issue in *NetChoice*, while giving a nod to the notion that social media platforms operate as "common carriers," both stopped well short of true common carriage requirements. Nonetheless, both laws will, if ever implemented, have highly troubling consequences. The problem with Florida's law is, frankly, that it is bizarre. The special protections it provides to speech by or about politicians suggests that, in the view of the Florida legislature, elected officials are more important contributors to public discourse than the citizens who vote them into office. How such an approach can be reconciled with the basic premises of popular sovereignty that underlie our system of government is beyond understanding. Florida's law favors elected officials over ordinary citizens in the process of setting public opinion by only protecting politicians' posts about public policy (recall that while the Florida law protects private posts *about* politicians, it does not protect posts addressing public policy unless they are posted *by* politicians), and by only protecting politicians from deplatforming. But if James Madison was correct in asserting that "[p]ublic

---

[98] Ryan Mac and Tiffany Hsu, *Twitter's U.S. Ad Sales Plunge 59% as Woes Continue*, N.Y. TIMES (June 5, 2023), www.nytimes.com/2023/06/05/technology/twitter-ad-sales-musk.html.

opinion sets bounds to every government, and is the real sovereign in every free one,"[99] then this has it upside-down.

Finally, let us consider Texas's requirement of viewpoint neutrality in content moderation. On its face, this seems a narrower and more reasonable restriction than full common carriage or Florida's self-serving pro-politician gerrymander, since it would presumably still permit platforms to block some forms of lawful-but-awful content, such as nudity or personal abuse, on a viewpoint-neutral basis. But viewpoint neutrality nonetheless prohibits a great deal of desirable content moderation. For example, outright pro-Nazi or White Supremacist speech is fully shielded by the Texas law as protected viewpoints. The same is true of speech encouraging gender-based violence or self-harm. And the same is true of speech praising and supporting ISIS, and encouraging emulation of terrorist violence.[100] It is ironic in this regard that Twitter/X, which in its early years sought to avoid content moderation, changed its approach precisely because it had become an important venue for ISIS propaganda and recruitment.[101] In the name of protecting conservative viewpoints, Texas would *force* Twitter/X (and Facebook and YouTube and all other platforms) back to that time.

For similar reasons, platform efforts to block hate speech directed at racial or sexual minorities or at women would also be illegal under the Texas statute. The Supreme Court has clearly held that hate speech is a protected viewpoint.[102] As a result, a hate-speech ban on social media would directly violate HB 20's core requirements of viewpoint neutrality.[103] To give just one example of the consequences of this, under Texas's HB 20, Facebook would be required to reverse its decision from October of 2020 to ban Holocaust denial.[104] Indeed, because HB 20 prohibits censorship based on the viewpoint of the user as well as of content, it would also appear to prohibit platforms from banning white supremacist groups such as the Ku Klux Klan from their platform. Not only are these outcomes highly problematic from a public policy perspective, in the long run they will also, as noted earlier, threaten the

---

[99] James Madison, *Public Opinion*, NAT'L GAZETTE (Dec. 19, 1791), https://perma.cc/T92L-ZXM6.
[100] *NetChoice*, 144 S. Ct. at 2405 (listing awful viewpoints protected by Texas law).
[101] Julia Greenberg, *Why Facebook and Twitter Can't Just Wipe Out ISIS Online*, WIRED (Nov. 21, 2015), https://perma.cc/T263-YKUW.
[102] Matal v. Tam, 137 S. Ct. 1744, 1766–67 (2017) (Kennedy, J., concurring in part and concurring in the judgment); R.A.V. v. City of St. Paul, 505 U.S. 377, 391–92 (1992).
[103] Tex. Civ. Prac. & Rem. Code § 143A.002(a)(1)–(3).
[104] Monika Bickert, *VP of Content Policy, Removing Holocaust Denial Content*, FACEBOOK (Oct. 12, 2020), https://perma.cc/X5QK-T3SC.

very existence of social media platforms as users and advertisers flee such a toxic environment.

In short, there are very good reasons, both ethical and business-related, why almost all successful social media platforms moderate content, often extensively. Eliminating that ability, as Justice Thomas's common carrier proposal would do, would have utterly unacceptable social consequences. Furthermore, even Texas's more modest requirement of viewpoint-neutral content moderation would also end up enabling a great deal of speech, such as terrorist propaganda and white supremacist speech, that most reasonable people do not want to be exposed to. Which is to say that these proposals are not just unconstitutional, they are a terrible idea.

5

Social Media as the New Gatekeepers

As discussed in the previous chapter, the preferred regulatory solution to the supposed ills of social media proposed by conservative critics is to strip social media platforms of almost all editorial power. Their progressive counterparts (such as Senator Elizabeth Warren of Massachusetts and Senator Amy Klobuchar of Minnesota), perhaps unsurprisingly, propose exactly the opposite. They want platforms to engage in *more* content moderation, under the guidance of experts and political leaders (such as, presumably, themselves). In other words, progressives want platform owners to operate as gatekeepers of speech and knowledge,[1] excluding from public discourse the kinds of harmful content, described in Chapter 2, to which they object. As this chapter will demonstrate, however, the progressive proposals make as little sense as the conservative ones.

5.1 THE GOVERNMENT AS GATEKEEPER

At the outset, it is important to draw an important distinction between voluntary actions taken by platforms to moderate content (which, for reasons described in Chapter 4, they have a constitutional right to take) and government mandates requiring platforms to block or deemphasize specific, harmful content. While most progressive calls for content moderation seem to envision voluntary steps by platforms, critics sometimes veer into legislative mandates. For example, in 2021 in the midst of the COVID-19 pandemic, Senator Klobuchar introduced legislation that would have made platforms liable for any health misinformation that they algorithmically promoted – specifically,

---

[1] By gatekeepers, I mean entities and/or institutions who control what information and what sources of information the general public is exposed to without great effort on the audience's part.

the legislation would have stripped platforms of the immunity they normally enjoy under Section 230 of the Communications Decency Act regarding such information.[2]

Similarly, in 2020 a group of twenty state Attorneys General sent a joint letter to Facebook, calling on the firm to make greater efforts to block allegedly harmful content.[3] The letter identified a number of different kinds of such harmful speech, including disinformation, cyberstalking, doxing (publishing private information), and swatting (filing false police reports), but the primary focus of the letter was hate speech – which is to say, speech that vilifies specific groups based on characteristics such as race, national origin, sex, religion, or sexual orientation.[4] And while the letter itself did not go beyond calling on Facebook to take voluntary action, in an interview with the New York Times, then-Attorney General Gurbir S. Grewal of New Jersey (one of the signatories) threatened that, if Facebook did not act, "we always have a variety of legal tools at our disposal."[5] In other words, Grewal appeared to be suggesting that, if Facebook failed to do a better job of blocking hate speech and other harmful content, state prosecutors would seek legal remedies against it, thus opening the door to direct legal requirements to engage in content moderation.

The problem with proposals such as these, however, is that they are quite clearly in violation of the First Amendment. It is textbook law that aside from a very few, narrowly defined categories of speech such as obscenity,[6] child pornography,[7] and threats of violence,[8] the First Amendment protects all speech from government censorship. The Supreme Court has made it clear, moreover, that disinformation – which is to say intentional lies – are *not* an unprotected category, and so enjoy full First Amendment protections.[9] Furthermore, despite common misunderstandings among the public and

---

[2] *Health Misinformation Act of 2021*, S. 2448, 117th Congress (July 22, 2021), www.congress.gov/bill/117th-congress/senate-bill/2448/text.
[3] Davey Alba, *Facebook Must Better Police Online Hate, State Attorneys General Say*, N.Y. TIMES (Aug. 5, 2020), www.nytimes.com/2020/08/05/technology/facebook-online-hate.html.
[4] Letter from Karl A. Racine, Attorney General, District of Columbia, Kwame Raoul, Attorney General, State of Illinois, Gurbir S. Grewal, Attorney General, State of New Jersey, et al., to Mark Zuckerberg, Chairman and Chief Executive Officer, Sheryl Sandberg, Chief Operating Officer (Aug. 5, 2020), https://int.nyt.com/data/documenttools/facebook-attorneys-general-letter/50738870562dec84/full.pdf.
[5] Alba, *supra* n. 3.
[6] Roth v. United States, 354 U.S. 476 (1957).
[7] Ferber v. New York, 458 U.S. 747 (1982).
[8] Counterman v. Colorado, 600 U.S. 66 (2023).
[9] United States v. Alvarez, 567 U.S. 709 (2012).

even elected leaders and some lawyers,[10] the Supreme Court has also made it clear, unanimously no less, that "hate speech" is also fully protected by the First Amendment in the United States (unlike in many other countries).[11] Indeed, it is not entirely clear that even doxing is unprotected speech, though on this point the law is somewhat unclear.

The final piece of the puzzle is that under long-standing First Amendment doctrine, when the government singles out protected speech for regulation based on the content or especially the viewpoint of the speech, the regulatory effort is almost always invalidated by courts.[12] Yet by singling out health disinformation, Senator Klobuchar's legislative proposal clearly singles out specific content. And as for former Attorney General Grewal's threats regarding hate speech, current law treats regulations of hate speech as viewpoint-based, and so essentially automatically unconstitutional.[13]

The implications of all of this are clear: Just as the government could not directly prohibit or restrict "disinformation" or "hate speech," it also cannot require social media platforms to remove or limit the availability of such speech. To conclude otherwise would be to permit the government to involuntarily dragoon private companies to do things that the Constitution forbids the government. But just as the government cannot require private security firms to conduct searches that violate the Fourth Amendment, so it cannot require platforms to engage in censorship that violates the First. Then-Attorney General Grewal's threats in that regard were, then, just so much hot air.

Senator Klobuchar's proposal, which could not have completely banned disinformation but merely removed it from the Section 230 protective umbrella, poses a slightly more difficult question but ultimately meets the same fate (the details of how Section 230 operates, as well as proposals to amend it, are the topics of the next chapter). But to begin with, it is not even clear what the legislation would accomplish. In theory, it would open platforms up to liability for spreading health disinformation; but what kind of liability? We do not typically impose civil liability even on *speakers* based on protected speech, or spreaders

---

[10] Eugene Volokh, *No, Gov. Dean, There Is No "Hate Speech" Exception to the First Amendment*, WASHINGTON POST (April 21, 2017), www.washingtonpost.com/news/volokh-conspiracy/wp/2017/04/21/no-gov-dean-there-is-no-hate-speech-exception-to-the-first-amendment/; Eugene Volokh, *California AG's Brief Claims "Hate Speech" Is Constitutionally Unprotected*, REASON.COM (Nov. 25, 2020), https://reason.com/volokh/2020/11/25/california-ags-brief-claims-hate-speech-is-constitutionally-unprotected/.
[11] Matal v. Tam, 582 U.S. 218 (2017); *see also* R.A.V. v. City of St. Paul, 505 U.S. 377 (1992).
[12] Reed v. Town of Gilbert, 576 U.S. 155 (2015).
[13] *Matal*, 582 U.S. at 243 (plurality opinion); *ibid.* at 248–49 (Kennedy, J., concurring in part and concurring in the judgment).

of vaccine disinformation such as Robert F. Kennedy, Jr.[14] could be constantly in the dock. Given that, it is quite unclear under what theory a mere unwitting distributor of such content, such as a platform, would face liability.

But even if liability was a possibility under tort law, what Senator Klobuchar proposed would likely violate the First Amendment. Congress no doubt has the power to entirely repeal Section 230 and so eliminate platforms' statutory protections from liability for third-party content.[15] Furthermore, Congress also probably has the power to selectively deny Section 230 immunity for speech unprotected by the First Amendment – as Congress in fact did with respect to speech promoting sex trafficking.[16] But to permit Congress to selectively strip immunity for *protected* speech – which would effectively force platforms to block speech it was made aware of that even arguably falls within the disfavored category – would be an extraordinarily potent tool of censorship. Surely the First Amendment could not permit Congress to eliminate Section 230 immunity for, say, posts critical of Democratic elected officials, but not Republican ones. But given the porousness of the definition of "health misinformation" – some platforms labeled posts opposed to mask mandates for children, surely a question on which reasonable people could differ given the limited risks children face from COVID, as misinformation – Senator Klobuchar's proposed law seems to be at least analogous.

In short, government mandates that social media platforms moderate constitutionally protected content are quite clearly unconstitutional. As a consequence, despite much talk among politicians and journalists, such laws have not been enacted in the United States. It is noteworthy in this regard that jurisdictions such as Germany, in which hate speech does *not* receive strong protections, *have* adopted and enforced laws requiring platforms to swiftly

---

[14] Anjali Huynh, *5 Noteworthy Falsehoods Robert F. Kennedy Jr. Has Promoted*, N.Y. TIMES (July 6, 2023), www.nytimes.com/2023/07/06/us/politics/rfk-conspiracy-theories-fact-check.html.

[15] Which is not to say that such a repeal would leave platforms liable for all content they host – it seems likely that the First Amendment itself would provide some shield to platforms, though the exact contours of that shield have not been determined because Section 230's existence has made the issue moot.

[16] Tom Jackman, *Trump Signs "FOSTA" Bill Targeting Online Sex Trafficking, Enables States and Victims to Pursue Websites*, WASHINGTON POST (April 11, 2018), www.washingtonpost.com/news/true-crime/wp/2018/04/11/trump-signs-fosta-bill-targeting-online-sex-trafficking-enables-states-and-victims-to-pursue-websites/. Ironically, the bill appears to have completely failed to achieve its goals and instead had perverse consequences. Melissa Gira Grant, *The Real Story of the Bipartisan Anti-Sex Trafficking Bill that Failed Miserably on Its Own Terms*, NEW REPUBLIC (June 23, 2021), https://newrepublic.com/article/162823/sex-trafficking-sex-work-sesta-fosta.

remove hate speech.[17] But in the United States, those who wish platforms to play the role of gatekeepers of constitutionally protected content must necessarily rely on the voluntary cooperation of the platforms themselves. And that, it would seem, is the primary goal of progressive critics of social media: to convince/induce/pressure platforms into performing that role and removing harmful content from public discourse.

One final point on this: While US law draws a strong distinction between government mandates to moderate protected content and encouraging platforms to voluntarily do to same, on the ground the line between these two things is not always clear. In particular, evidence has emerged that during the height of the COVID-19 pandemic, the Biden Administration imposed heavy pressure on the major platforms to remove mis- and disinformation about COVID-19, and COVID vaccines. This eventually led to a lawsuit brought by some social media users whose posts were blocked, as well as Republican politicians, claiming that the Administration's efforts had crossed the line into violating the First Amendment. Ultimately, the Supreme Court dismissed the case on technical grounds, concluding in essence that the plaintiffs had failed to show that government lobbying caused any specific content moderation decisions.[18] Moreover, in a letter to Congress Mark Zuckerberg (the CEO of Meta, which owns both Facebook and Instagram), while expressing regret over his platforms' cooperation with the Administration, insisted that all content moderation decisions had ultimately been made by the platforms themselves, not by the government.[19] But the fact remains that at some point, government cajoling and pressure can cross the line into unconstitutional coercion.

5.2 THE OLD GATEKEEPERS

To understand why there are so many voices, primarily (but not exclusively) on the political left, who endorse a gatekeeper role for platforms, one must take a step back and consider the nature and origins of the gatekeeper function. Underlying the desire to resurrect the gatekeeper function is a pervasive fear among progressive critics, discussed in Chapter 2, that the spread of harmful content is systematically harming society, including especially

---

[17] *Germany Starts Enforcing Hate Speech Law*, BBC (Jan. 1, 2018), www.bbc.com/news/technology-42510868.
[18] Murthy v. Missouri, 144 S. Ct. 1972 (2024).
[19] Gnaneshwar Rajan and Nandita Bose, *Zuckerberg Says Biden Administration Pressured Meta to Censor COVID-19 Content*, REUTERS (Aug. 27, 2024), www.reuters.com/technology/zuckerberg-says-biden-administration-pressured-meta-censor-covid-19-content-2024-08-27/.

vulnerable elements of society such as racial and sexual minorities. But not all "harmful" speech elicits equal amounts of concern. Due perhaps to the COVID-19 pandemic and its corrosive effect on politics and public discourse, there is no question that from the perspective of progressive critics, the most dangerous and corrosive form of online speech is mis- and disinformation, especially (though not exclusively) on matters pertaining to health (as demonstrated by Senator Klobuchar's proposed legislation). Why are falsehoods of such particular concern to these critics?

Driving the campaign against misinformation is a basic, existential worry that the spread of online falsehoods is systematically eroding the common base of facts, accepted by the broader public, that is essential to a system of democratic self-governance. Absent such a common base or factual consensus, it is feared, democratic politics will tend to collapse into polarized camps that cannot accept the possibility of electoral defeat (as they arguably have in recent years in the United States). The only way to combat these developments, these critics believe, is to divert the flow of mis- and disinformation from the public ecosphere. And for that to happen, gatekeepers who can identify and favor trusted and trustworthy sources of information are essential.

But therein lies the nub of the problem. If one wishes to restore a common, factual consensus in the public sphere, one must confront the unavoidable question of "Who to trust?" But underlying *that* question is yet another, more foundational one: "Who *decides* who to trust?" Ultimately, of course, each person must decide for themselves who to trust. But for a societal consensus on this question to emerge, some common source of authority is seemingly needed. If there is one lesson that can be drawn from the modern era of social media, it is that robust, public discourse alone cannot be expected to generate an automatic consensus on who can be trusted (or on what are trustworthy facts). The quest for trusted communicators, then, is in truth a quest for authoritative sources of trust – which is to say, a quest for authority. In the internet era, centralized control over information flows has fragmented and, consequently, so too has the authority to identify trusted communicators. Before seeking to recreate such authority, however, it is important to understand how and why such authoritative sources of information emerged in the pre-internet era – which is to say, during the first six or seven decades of the twentieth century – when modern expectations about trust and a factual consensus developed.

Who were the creators and designators of trust during this period? In short, it was the institutional media. Moreover, through most of the twentieth century, institutional media acted as the gatekeepers of knowledge and news as well. Just who constituted the institutional media gatekeepers, however, changed over time. During the first part of the century, perhaps the crucial period in the development of gatekeepers and trusted communicators, it was major daily newspapers, especially those associated with William Randolph Hearst and Joseph Pulitzer, as well as Adolph Ochs's *New York Times*. As we shall discuss in more detail, in many ways it was cultural clashes between Hearst and Pulitzer on one side and Ochs on the other that generated the dominant gatekeeper/trusted-communicator model.[20]

After the First World War, while newspapers certainly maintained their importance, commercial radio broadcasters emerged as another crucial – and soon more popularly accessible – media institution. The first commercial radio station began broadcasting in 1920 in Pittsburgh, Pennsylvania. Four years later, 600 commercial radio stations were broadcasting in the United States. In 1926, the first national radio network, National Broadcasting Company (NBC), was formed.[21] As evidenced by President Franklin Delano Roosevelt's fireside chats during the Great Depression, radio quickly emerged as a widely available, popular means for institutional media – and those trusted communicators to whom they provided airtime, such as FDR – to reach mass public audiences.

Finally, around the mid century, at the beginning of what many considered the Golden Age of the institutional media, television broadcasters began to complement and eventually supplant radio (and newspapers) as the key institutional media. The Federal Communications Commission (FCC) first authorized commercial television broadcasts in 1941, but because of World War II, commercial television broadcasts did not begin in earnest until 1947.[22] And then the industry exploded. From 1946 to 1951, the number of television sets in use in the US rose from 6,000 to 12 million. By 1955, half of American households owned television sets.[23] Moreover, during the 1940s, the three iconic national television networks – NBC (evolved from the first radio network), Columbia Broadcasting System (CBS) (evolved from a competing radio network), and American Broadcasting Company (ABC) (spun off from NBC by order of the FCC) – had also emerged.[24] Finally, with the creation in 1956 of NBC's *The Huntley-Brinkley Report* (the first national television news broadcast), television's dominance as the primary source of news

---

[20] *See generally* W. JOSEPH CAMPBELL, THE YEAR THAT DEFINED AMERICAN JOURNALISM: 1897 AND THE CLASH OF PARADIGMS (2006).

[21] *KDKA Begins to Broadcast: 1920*, PBS (1998), https://www.pbs.org/wgbh/aso/databank/entries/dt20ra.html.

[22] Mitchell Stephens, *History of Television*, GROLIER ENCYCLOPEDIA, https://stephens.hosting.nyu.edu/History%20of%20Television%20page.html.

[23] ibid.

[24] ibid.

for most Americans (and the concomitant decline in the influence of newspapers) began.[25]

The rise of broadcasting also led to the emergence of the quintessential trusted communicators of this era, the network reporter and, later, anchorman. Coincidentally, the figures that epitomize both roles were affiliated with CBS. Edward R. Murrow first rose to prominence during the radio era through his revolutionary reporting on Hitler's *Anschluss* of Austria in 1938, and he became a household name by reporting live from London during the London Blitz in the early 1940s. He then moved to television and demonstrated continuing enormous influence through broadcasts, including a pathbreaking one in 1954 criticizing Senator Joseph McCarthy's witch hunt against Communists, which contributed to McCarthy's downfall.[26]

The other, even more important trusted communicator of the broadcast era was of course Walter Cronkite. Cronkite first became prominent (among other things, as the first designated "anchorman") during CBS's coverage of the 1952 presidential nominating conventions. But it was with the launch of *The CBS Evening News with Walter Cronkite* in 1962 that Cronkite's central role as *the* trusted communicator emerged.[27] Cronkite's influence was most famously demonstrated when his critical coverage of the Vietnam War in 1968 led to an important swing in public opinion against the war, and contributed to President Lyndon Johnson's decision not to run for reelection. Cronkite's status is illustrated by the fact that a 1972 poll named him "the most trusted man in America."[28] The institutional media and its key figures, epitomized by Murrow and Cronkite, were thus *the* trusted communicators of this era.

Even though their technology and reach varied, the gatekeepers/trusted communicators described earlier shared some basic characteristics. First, they were relatively scarce. The economics of newspapers meant that during most of this period, metropolitan areas could only support one or a handful of major newspapers.[29] With respect to the broadcast medium, the number of radio and television stations in any particular locality that actually produced original content (as opposed to playing music or broadcasting reruns of sitcoms) was limited by the same economic factors (essentially economies of scale) as newspapers. In addition, the fact that the number of possible

---

[25] ibid.
[26] David Mindich, *For Journalists Covering Trump, a Murrow Moment*, COLUM. JOURNALISM REV. (July 15, 2016), www.cjr.org/analysis/trump_inspires_murrow_moment_for_journalism.php.
[27] Stephens, *supra* n. 22.
[28] *Walter Cronkite: American Journalist*, BRITANNICA (Mar. 7, 2022), www.britannica.com/biography/Walter-Cronkite.
[29] *See* Miami Herald Pub'g Co. v. Tornillo, 418 U.S. 241, 249–50 and n.13 (1974).

broadcast frequencies was physically limited – electromagnetic spectrum, as the Supreme Court has put it, is a "scarce resource"[30] – necessarily limited the number of broadcast outlets in any particular market. Indeed, in practice, the broadcast television market, especially in its role as disseminator of national news and general knowledge, was completely dominated by the three major networks (NBC, CBS, and ABC) until the launch of the Fox network in 1986 – and that only added one additional player. This situation only changed with the spread of cable television in the 1980s (and thus the end of spectrum scarcity because of the large channel capacity of cable systems), resulting in the launch of cable-only CNN in 1980 and then of Fox News in 1996.

The second shared characteristic between different types of gatekeepers and trusted communicators was that these gatekeepers sought to construct an "objective," nonpartisan image. The roots of this development, which has become an essential element of modern journalistic ethics,[31] can be found in the conflict between the sensationalist journalism championed by newspaper tycoons William Randolph Hearst and Joseph Pulitzer, and the "counteractivist," nonpartisan model of Adolph S. Och's *New York Times* (which Och purchased in 1896[32]). While the Hearst/Pulitzer model was dominant in the late nineteenth and early twentieth centuries, Ochs's commitment "to give the news impartially, without fear or favor, regardless of party, sect, or interests involved," a commitment Ochs announced on his first day of ownership of the *Times*,[33] eventually won out.[34] By 1920, this norm of objectivity[35] (which had previously gone by the name of "realism"[36]) was becoming the dominant paradigm of journalism, as reflected by the fact that the Society of Professional Journalists' first Code of Ethics, adopted in 1926, calls for journalistic "impartiality," meaning that "[n]ews reports should be free from opinion or bias of any kind."[37]

---

[30] Red Lion Broad. Co. v. FCC, 395 U.S. 367, 391 (1969).
[31] See SPJ Code of Ethics, SOC'Y PROF. JOURNALISTS, www.spj.org/ethicscode.asp ("Ethical journalism should be accurate and fair").
[32] BILL KOVACH AND TOM ROSENSTIEL, THE ELEMENTS OF JOURNALISM: WHAT NEWSPEOPLE SHOULD KNOW AND THE PUBLIC SHOULD EXPECT 76 (4th ed. 2021).
[33] ibid.
[34] See generally CAMPBELL, supra n. 20; Invisible Men: The Future of Journalism, THE ECONOMIST, July 18, 2020, at 67.
[35] Andrew Porwancher, Objectivity's Prophet: Adolph S. Ochs and the New York Times, 36 JOURNALISM HIST. 186, 187 (2011), www.americanpressinstitute.org/journalism-essentials/bias-objectivity/lost-meaning-objectivity/.
[36] Walter Dean, The Lost Meaning of "Objectivity," AM. PRESS INST., https://perma.cc/6CRR-EWWL.
[37] Sigma Delta Chi's New Code of Ethics, SOC'Y PROF. JOURNALISTS, http://spjnetwork.org/quill2/codedcontroversey/ethics-code-1926.pdf.

5.2 The Old Gatekeepers

It is important to note, however, that this goal of objectivity was a historical anomaly. Prior to the early twentieth century, newspapers and publishers did not pretend to be objective – to the contrary, they were explicitly partisan. Important historical examples include *The Aurora*, the newspaper edited by Benjamin Franklin Bache (Ben Franklin's grandson) in the late 1790s, which was tied to the Democratic-Republic Party of Jefferson and Madison (Bache and other Jeffersonian newspaper editors were prosecuted by the Adams Administration for sedition),[38] and Horace Greeley's *New York Tribune*, which was closely associated with the Republican Party before and during the Civil War.[39] Needless to say, these newspapers were *not* viewed as trustworthy by their political opponents (as demonstrated by Bache's prosecution). After World War I, however, economic pressures led to the consolidation of newspapers and a notable decrease in the number of daily newspapers – as epitomized by the merger in 1924 of the old rivals the *New York Herald* (which, though claiming to be nonpartisan, often supported Democratic Party policies during the Civil War) and Greeley's *New York Tribune*.[40] As a consequence, newspapers began to seek broader (and so bipartisan) audiences, which required them to abandon their partisan affiliations. Not coincidentally, journalistic ethics during this period also embraced objectivity as a desirable norm, as noted earlier.

The trend toward objectivity continued as newspapers were gradually supplanted by broadcast media: first radio, then (even more dominantly) television. For television broadcasting in particular, the push for objectivity was driven by similar economic motivations to maximize audience share because of the effective monopoly on national news held by the three national networks. In addition, the FCC's Fairness Doctrine, in effect from 1949 to 1987, strongly incentivized objectivity on the part of both radio and television broadcasters by requiring them to present opposing views on public issues, and by creating a right of reply on the part of individuals subject to a "personal attack" during broadcast programming.[41] Facially objective news coverage avoided triggering either requirement.[42]

---

[38] For a good discussion of this episode, see GEOFFREY R. STONE, PERILOUS TIMES: FREE SPEECH DURING WARTIME 35 (2004).

[39] JAMES M. MCPHERSON, BATTLE CRY OF FREEDOM: THE CIVIL WAR ERA 251–52 (1988).

[40] *New York Herald: American Newspaper*, BRITANNICA, www.britannica.com/topic/New-York-Herald.

[41] Red Lion Broad. Co. v. FCC, 395 U.S. 367, 375–79 (1969); Matt Stefon, *Fairness Doctrine*, BRITANNICA, www.britannica.com/topic/Fairness-Doctrine.

[42] The FCC itself, when it repealed the Fairness Doctrine in 1987, recognized that "the fairness doctrine provides broadcasters with a powerful incentive not to air controversial issue

This performed objectivity, playing out in a highly concentrated broadcast market, enabled a small set of individuals and institutions to emerge as "trusted communicators" in the eyes of a broad swath of the American public. We might call this the Murrow–Cronkite Effect. Furthermore, this institutional structure permitted trusted media figures to extend public trust to elite, designated "experts" *outside* the media by giving those experts the gatekeepers' imprimatur in the form of interviews and airtime (as an example, consider Edward R. Murrow's famous 1955 interview of Jonas Salk, the inventor of the polio vaccine[43]). As a consequence, during this "golden era," most of American society obtained news and knowledge from a few common and generally trusted sources.

What engendered this broad-based trust,[44] which in today's fractured world seems inconceivable? I would argue that the answer, in short, was a lack of alternative voices. The public trusted media gatekeepers because they had no choice – there were no significant opposing voices to question or undermine that trust because of concentration within the institutional media. It was precisely these factors – concentration and lack of choice – that made the institutional media, especially the three television networks, gatekeepers who exercised effective control over the flow of information into almost every American household. Indeed, it is hard to imagine how a media institution could play gatekeeper without this kind of option scarcity.

Furthermore, for economic reasons discussed earlier, these gatekeepers adopted an "objectivity" that overwhelmingly tended to reflect the views of the political center, in order to maximize their potential audience. As a consequence, there were simply no opportunities for the public to question consensus facts, or to become aware of what the institutional media was not telling them (such as President Kennedy's philandering, or the CIA's secret foreign coups during President Eisenhower's Administration). I am not insinuating that Murrow and Cronkite did not earn the public's trust – I have no doubt that they did, through ethical and insightful journalism. But that trust ultimately depended on a lack of access to alternative, non-mainstream voices.

Eventually, of course, this system of institutional concentration and consensus collapsed. The first developments along these lines are probably traceable

programming." *In re Complaint of Syracuse Peace Council against Television Station WTVH Syracuse, New York*, FCC 87-266, 2 FCC RCD. 5043, 5049-50 (1987).

[43] Michael Hiltzik, *On Jonas Salk's 100th Birthday, a Celebration of His Polio Vaccine*, L.A. TIMES (Oct. 28, 2014), www.latimes.com/business/hiltzik/la-fi-mh-polio-vaccine-20141028-column.html.

[44] To be fair, it is far from clear that the trust I am describing here extended to minority communities, but that is another story ... Thanks to Helen Norton and Erin Carroll for (independently) pointing this out to me.

to the FCC's repeal of the Fairness Doctrine in 1987,[45] which in turn led to the rise of right-wing talk radio, a medium which did not pretend or aspire to objectivity.[46] In addition, the explosion of the cable television medium during the 1980s ended the era of television concentration, because television no longer required scarce electromagnetic spectrum.[47] This in turn permitted the launch of the overtly partisan Fox News in 1996,[48] at the very dawn of the internet era. But while these developments began undermining the era of (supposed) media objectivity and the media's gatekeeper function, there can be little doubt that the internet, and especially the rise of social media, put a final end to the institutional media's control over public discourse. These, however, are relatively recent events. Twitter/X was founded in 2006,[49] the same year that Facebook became available to the general public.[50] But at first, these were relatively obscure platforms. It was not until the availability and widespread adoption of smartphones – the first iPhone was not released until 2007,[51] and smartphones did not come into common use for several years after then – that social media became mobile and easily usable, leading to its exponential growth.[52]

By the 2010s, the importance of social media in displacing traditional media as the primary engine of public discourse was evident – so much so that by 2017, that most hidebound of American institutions, the United States Supreme Court, recognized social media as "the most important places ... for the exchange of views."[53] Every citizen became a potential publisher and people suddenly possessed a plethora of choices regarding what voices

---

[45] Stefon, *supra* n. 41.
[46] It is no coincidence that *The Rush Limbaugh Show* was launched nationally in 1988. *America's Anchorman*, RUSH LIMBAUGH SHOW, www.rushlimbaugh.com/americas-anchorman/.
[47] During the 1980s, the number of cable networks exploded from 28 to 79, and cable penetration in American households enjoyed similar growth. *See* Brad Adgate, *The Rise and Fall of Cable Television*, FORBES (Nov. 2, 2020), www.forbes.com/sites/bradadgate/2020/11/02/the-rise-and-fall-of-cable-television/?sh=4b6145b76b31.
[48] Michael Ray, *Fox News Channel*, BRITANNICA (Mar. 2, 2022), www.britannica.com/topic/Fox-News-Channel.
[49] Jack Meyer, *History of Twitter: Jack Dorsey and the Social Media Giant*, THE STREET (Jan. 2, 2020), www.thestreet.com/technology/history-of-twitter-facts-what-s-happening-in-2019-14995056.
[50] *Who We Are*, META, https://newsroom.fb.com/company-info/.
[51] *Apple Reinvents the Phone with iPhone*, APPLE (Jan. 9, 2007), www.apple.com/newsroom/2007/01/09Apple-Reinvents-the-Phone-with-iPhone/.
[52] As an illustration, from 2008 to 2012, the number of Facebook users grew from 100 million to 1 billion – the latter being greater than the combined populations of the United States and the European Union. Kurt Wagner and Rani Molla, *Facebook's First 15 Years Were Defined by User Growth*, VOX (Feb. 5, 2019), www.vox.com/2019/2/4/18203992/facebook-15-year-anniversary-user-growth.
[53] Packingham v. North Carolina, 137 S. Ct. 1730, 1735 (2017).

to pay attention to, ending once and for all the gatekeeper function of the institutional media. And for the same reason, the range of opinions expressed publicly became massively more diverse, ending the media's role in creating consensus around a common set of facts and beliefs. The Murrow–Cronkite Effect had vanished.

With the collapse of the gatekeeper function also came the collapse of trusted communicators. There are no Edward Murrows or Walter Cronkites in the social media/Fox News era; instead we have Tucker Carlsons and Robert F. Kennedy, Jrs. (Mr. Kennedy, the son of Bobby Kennedy, is an active anti-vaccine propogandist who ran for President in the 2024 election cycle, before ultimately endorsing Donald Trump and then serving as Trump's Secretary for Health and Human Services[54]). This development is frankly unsurprising if one accepts, as I argued earlier, that much of the public's trust during the Murrow-Cronkite era was a product of the institutional media's gatekeeper function. No more gatekeepers, no more trust.

To be fair, the elimination of gatekeepers is not the only development that has contributed to the loss of trusted communicators. Most obviously, political polarization has also played an important role. As many people have drifted into more radicalized political positions, they inevitably cease to trust the traditional trusted communicators of the center (or, more honestly, the center-left) that made up the institutional media. Individuals whose views sit in the far-right or far-left have no reason to trust institutional speakers such as *The New York Times* or CNN. But here, too, the loss of gatekeepers plays an important causal role. During the peak of the gatekeeper era, most people had no access or exposure to radical voices unless they actively sought them out – and such voices were, as a result, quite rare. Today, social media and other internet forums provide easy access to a vast range of viewpoints and alternative "facts," permitting individuals to trust whomever they please – usually voices that reinforce and intensify their existing views. Of course, there have always been radical movements and conspiracy theories, but the rapid spread and sheer scope of the QAnon conspiracy theory, for example, would not have been possible in the pre-internet era; its ideas would never have gotten past the gatekeepers.

---

[54] Adam Nagourney, *A Kennedy's Crusade against Covid Vaccines Anguishes Family and Friends*, N.Y. TIMES (Feb. 26, 2022); Rebecca Davis O'Brien, Simon J. Levien, and Jonathan Swan, *Robert F. Kennedy Jr. Endorses Trump and Suspends His Independent Bid for President*, N.Y. TIMES (Aug. 23, 2024); Sheryl Gay Stolberg, *Senate Confirms Kennedy, a Prominent Vaccine Skeptic, as Health Secretary*, N.Y. TIMES (Feb. 13, 2025), https://www.nytimes.com/2025/02/13/us/rfk-jr-hhs-senate-confirmation.html.

5.3 THE NEW GATEKEEPERS?

The loss of faith in institutional elites, including the institutional media, and the resulting collapse of consensus has had profound consequences. Most fundamentally, the loss of gatekeepers and trusted communicators has either threatened or eliminated the possibility of an ideology-free consensus on even basic facts. For individual media consumers, ideology seems to play a heavy role in shaping factual perceptions, regardless of objective reality. As an example, consider the fact that, in 2016, 72 percent of Republicans expressed doubts about Obama's birthplace, despite his Hawaiian birth certificate being in the public record.[55] And this loss of what one might call "consensus reality" has created an intellectual atmosphere of existential angst in some elements of American society. This is most evident within the mainstream media (perhaps unsurprisingly), but it is also an important part of the dialogue in politics (mainly on the left) and in academia (almost definitionally on the left).

To be clear, there is no question that a lack of factual consensus has had negative social consequences. It has made compromise – or even dialogue – across partisan lines far more difficult. And as the United States' experience with COVID-19 demonstrates, it can lead to deeply irrational policy choices (both on the left and right, to be clear). But the intellectual angst that I describe is often expressed in an existential manner, as fear for the very survival of our society (caused by such factors as the false belief among many Republicans, fostered by President Trump and elements of the conservative media, that the 2020 presidential election was stolen from Trump[56]).

As we saw in Chapter 2, the practical ways in which these elements of society have operationalized their angst has been to place enormous amounts of pressure on social media platforms such as Facebook, Twitter/X, and YouTube to actively block (among other things) online falsehoods in order to recreate a consensus reality. These critics want social media platforms to become the *new* gatekeepers, replicating the role of the twentieth-century institutional media in deciding what information and sources of information the public should be exposed to. Their logic appears to be that because a small number of social media platforms now host such a large portion of public discourse, the owners and controllers of those platforms should therefore ensure that the

---

[55] Josh Clinton and Carrie Roush, *Poll: Persistent Partisan Divide over "Birther" Question*, NBC NEWS (Aug. 10, 2016), www.nbcnews.com/politics/2016-election/poll-persistent-partisan-divide-over-birther-question-n627446.

[56] *See, e.g.*, Zachary Ross, *The Five Biggest Threats Our Democracy Faces*, BRENNAN CTR. FOR JUST. (Dec. 15, 2020), www.brennancenter.org/our-work/analysis-opinion/five-biggest-threats-our-democracy-faces.

flow of information to individuals is accurate and "clean," just as twentieth-century institutional media entities did when they controlled a similar bottleneck position.

And in fact, given their dominant market positions, the "big four" owners of the key social media platforms on which political discourse occurs – essentially Meta (which owns Facebook, Instagram, and Threads), Twitter/X, Alphabet (formerly Google, which owns YouTube), and ByteDance (which owns TikTok) – might well jointly possess the power to shape discourse akin to the three broadcast television networks of the twentieth century. But *should* social media firms be in the business of screening out false information and determining who is and is not a trusted communicator? Leaving aside the question of whether this is even possible (does anyone believe that Mark Zuckerberg can replace Walter Cronkite as "the most trusted man in America"?), I will argue that they should not.

There are several reasons why social media firms are ill-suited to be effective gatekeepers (or, as Mr. Zuckerberg would have it, "arbiters of truth"[57]). First and foremost, they have no economic incentives to do so. The traditional institutional media emphasized their objectivity and sought to develop reputations as trusted gatekeepers because it was in their economic interest. Objectivity and trust increased viewership and market share. The same is not true with social media. Social media platforms do not suffer from scarcity, and so can serve up an almost unlimited variety of content. Consequently, their algorithms emphasize relevance to users, not truth. That is what increases engagement, and so profits. Asking for-profit companies to take on roles that they have no economic incentive to adopt strikes me as both dubious policy and likely futile.

Second, social media firms have absolutely no expertise or training that would enable them to be either effective gatekeepers or effective identifiers of trusted communicators. As a practical matter, while social media algorithms are quite effective at sorting by relevance and interest, I am doubtful that they can be designed to identify "truth" or its opposite, given the tenuous and disputed nature of truth. More fundamentally, the people who work for the large tech firms are unlikely to be effective at the gatekeeper function. They are, after all, software engineers, not journalists or trained experts on subject matters such as science, history, or economics, and it seems unlikely, given the culture of Silicon Valley, that they will become so. Training the Mark

---

[57] Yael Halon, *Zuckerberg Knows Twitter for Fact-Checking Trump, Says Private Companies Shouldn't Be "The Arbiter of Truth,"* FOX NEWS (May 27, 2020), www.foxnews.com/media/facebook-mark-zuckerberg-twitter-fact-checking-trump.

5.3 The New Gatekeepers?

Zuckerbergs of the world to be journalists is likely to be about as successful as it would have been to train Walter Cronkite to code.

Furthermore, social media platforms do not themselves generate content, unlike many traditional experts, which significantly reduces the incentives for these firms to develop serious in-house expertise (or for highly qualified experts to want to work for them – fact-checking is boring compared to content creation). Moreover, recent history suggests that when social media firms do rely on "expert" elites to identify misinformation, the results can be dicey – as illustrated by the fiascos of originally labeling the lab-leak theory of COVID-19's origins as misinformation,[58] or the decision to suppress a negative story about Hunter Biden and his laptop on the eve of the 2020 presidential election.[59] Indeed, social media critics are notably vague about how exactly social media firms are to identify "truth" (or its opposite, misinformation) going forward ... other than, that is, strongly suggesting that misinformation is whatever they themselves – the political and media elites – deem it to be.

Finally, I would question whether *any* gatekeepers of information and/or "trusted communicators" are ultimately beneficial to society or consistent with principles of free expression. First, it is important to acknowledge that "truth," especially ideologically tinged truth, is a slippery thing.[60] While I do not deny the existence of objective facts (e.g., COVID-19 is real, and vaccines do work and do not cause autism), that sort of objectivity falls apart very soon after one gets beyond simple, provable facts. Certainly, COVID-19 is a real and dangerous disease, but where did it originate? Maybe a lab in Wuhan, maybe not – we may never know. Was closing primary schools for lengthy periods of time necessary to combat the spread of COVID-19? Teachers and parents may have different answers. Is it necessary or wise to vaccinate young children against COVID-19, given their low risk of severe illness? The experts-provided answers to these questions are, in truth, guesswork or opinions (albeit informed ones) dressed up as objective fact (or "science"). Should disagreement with these experts really be suppressed or labeled as misinformation? One would think not, even though that is precisely what progressive critics seem to be after.

The more fundamental question, once we get beyond a very narrow range of objective facts, is whether gatekeepers and deference to designated "experts" (i.e., trusted communicators) really offer the best way to identify "truth" and,

---

[58] See Brett Stephens, *Media Groupthink and the Lab-Leak Theory*, N.Y. TIMES (May 31, 2021).
[59] Andrew Prokop, *The Return of Hunter Biden's Laptop*, VOX (Mar. 25, 2022), www.vox.com/22992772/hunter-biden-laptop.
[60] For a thoughtful, extended discussion of this problem, see Jane Bambauer, *Snake Oil Speech*, 93 WASH. L. REV. 73 (2018).

conversely, misinformation. Those who favor gatekeepers, including social media gatekeepers, assume that gatekeepers and experts are necessary to hold back the tide of fake news. But there is a deep tension between this institutional approach and basic theories of free speech, as most famously encapsulated by Justice Oliver Wendell Holmes's foundational metaphor of the "marketplace of ideas": "that the best test of truth is the power of the thought to get itself accepted in the competition of the market."[61] Nor is it consistent with Justice Louis Brandeis's equally fundamental adage that, when faced with false or dangerous speech, "the remedy to be applied is more speech, not enforced silence."[62]

Both Holmes's and Brandeis's theories of free speech, while differing in details, are premised on the assumption that citizens should be permitted to freely engage in political debate, to the point even of advocating lawless behavior. This is because, according to Holmes, only then can truth emerge, and, according to Brandeis only then can citizens fully engage in our democracy. The concept of gatekeepers is simply inconsistent with both these visions. Gatekeepers are anathema to competition, and they are also quintessential silencers rather than enablers of "more speech."

Put differently, the gatekeeper solution advanced by progressive critics of social media, whereby a handful of elite actors control public discourse, is not consistent with either principles of free expression or the role of citizens in our democracy. Instead of trying to recreate a bygone (and, frankly, deeply flawed) era, perhaps we should be thinking about how to reinvigorate a marketplace of ideas and encourage genuine democratic deliberation that both surmount political polarization.

5.4 HARASSMENT AND HATE SPEECH

Aside from mis- and disinformation, the other type of speech regarding which progressives have been most critical of platforms is hate speech, as exemplified by the letter to Facebook from the group of Attorneys General discussed at the start of this chapter. Hate speech, which is to say attacks on groups based on protected characteristics, can take the form of general, political invective, or harassing speech directed at individuals. Either way, such speech, so long as it is online,[63] retains constitutional protections unless it rises to the level of an actual

---

[61] Abrams v. United States, 250 U.S. 616, 630 (1919) (Holmes, J., dissenting).
[62] Whitney v. California, 274 U.S. 357, 377 (1927) (Brandeis, J., concurring).
[63] If a racial or other epithet were hurled at an individual in person, it would almost certainly constitute unprotected "fighting words," but the fighting words category is limited to in-person insults and so does not apply to online speech. Cohen v. California, 403 U.S. 15, 20 (1971).

threat of harm (it should be noted, however, that threats remain unprotected speech, even if the speaker has no intention of carrying out the threat[64]).

Despite the fact that hate speech enjoys constitutional protection, however, all the major social media platforms maintain and enforce bans on hate speech, either in the form of broad political statements or personal attacks.[65] It is noteworthy that Twitter/X retained its ban on hate speech after its purchase and renaming by Elon Musk, despite Musk's claims that he would prioritize free speech (though the actual incidence of hate speech on Twitter/X appears to have increased significantly after Musk's takeover, due to a dramatic reduction in company resources dedicated to content moderation[66]). Of course, progressive critics such as the state Attorneys General regularly criticize platforms for failing to adequately enforce their hate speech policies. For example, one prominent critic and activist described Facebook's response to complaints in this regard as "gaslighting."[67] But there is little doubt that the platforms seek to restrict hate speech (or in the case of Twitter/X under Musk, refuse to amplify it), regardless of how effectual their efforts are.

That all of the major platforms are willing to invest substantial resources – though perhaps Twitter/X less so than the others – to limit hate speech may seem surprising, but it shouldn't be. The reason is simple economics. The goal of social media platforms is to maximize user engagement, because engaged users can be sold as advertising targets. But realistically, the vast majority of users are repulsed by outright hate speech, and so the prevalence of such speech is likely to drive users away. And even more fundamentally, advertisers (who, after all, are the actual and ultimate customers of the platforms) most definitely do not want to be associated with hate speech, or for that matter any content that will drive away their own potential customers. In the jargon, advertisers are committed to "brand safety."[68]

---

[64] Virginia v. Black, 538 U.S. 343, 359–60 (2003).
[65] See *Hate Speech*, META, https://transparency.fb.com/policies/community-standards/hate-speech/ (current as of July 10, 2023) (Facebook); *Hate Speech Policy*, YOUTUBE HELP, https://support.google.com/youtube/answer/2801939?hl=en&ref_topic=9282436 (current as of July 10, 2023) (YouTube); *Hate Speech and Hateful Behaviors*, TIKTOK COMMUNITY GUIDELINES (March 2023), www.tiktok.com/community-guidelines/en/safety-civility/#2 (TikTok); *Hateful Conduct*, TWITTER, https://help.twitter.com/en/rules-and-policies/hateful-conduct-policy (April 2023) (Twitter/X).
[66] Christian Martinez, *One Billionaire Owner, Twice the Hate: Twitter Hate Speech Surged with Musk, Study Says*, L.A. TIMES (April 27, 2023), www.latimes.com/business/technology/story/2023-04-27/hate-speech-twitter-surged-since-elon-musk-takeover.
[67] Charlie Warzel, *When a Critic Met Facebook: "What They're Doing Is Gaslighting,"* N.Y. TIMES (July 9, 2020), www.nytimes.com/2020/07/09/opinion/facebook-civil-rights-robinson.html.
[68] Vikram David Amar and Ashutosh Bhagwat, *Why Elon Musk's (and X's) Lawsuit against Companies Who Have Stopped Advertising on the X Platform Is Weak*, Verdict: Legal Analysis

The reality of this phenomenon is demonstrated by the fact that from April–May of 2022 to April–May of 2023, Twitter/X's advertising revenues declined by 59 *percent*, almost certainly as a result of Twitter/X's purchase by Elon Musk in the fall of 2022 and the subsequent rise in the prevalence of hate speech and pornography on the platform.[69] At least one CEO of a major advertiser who pulled ads from Twitter/X, Mondelez International (the maker of Oreos), publicly acknowledged that the reason was concerns about their ads appearing in proximity to "wrong messages" such as hate speech.[70] Indeed, the phenomenally fast uptake of Threads, the Meta/Facebook/Instagram app which was launched in July of 2023 to compete with Twitter/X (it shattered all previous records on download rates[71]), is almost certainly attributable to similar concerns among users.

Given the obvious incentives that platforms face, and react to, regarding hate speech (aside, perhaps, from the mysteries of Twitter/X under Elon Musk), why does so much hate speech remain available on platforms? Critics claim it is a lack of commitment, but this seems rather implausible given both economic incentives and the sheer scale of content moderation efforts by platforms. For example Facebook, traditionally the most criticized platform, employs both artificial intelligence and an army of 15,000 human content moderators globally to moderate content.[72] Rather, a simpler and more plausible explanation is the sheer scale of social media, combined with the difficulty of clearly defining what constitutes hate speech.

The scale is, of course, familiar. Facebook, Instagram, WhatsApp, YouTube, and TikTok all have over a billion monthly users (over two billion in the case of Facebook), producing an extraordinarily high number of daily posts. The simple,

---

and Commentary from Justia (Aug. 26, 2024), https://verdict.justia.com/2024/08/26/why-elon-musks-and-xs-lawsuit-against-companies-who-have-stopped-advertising-on-the-x-platform-is-legally-weak.

[69] Ryan Mac and Tiffany Hsu, *Twitter's U.S. Ad Sales Plunge 59% As Woes Continue*, N.Y. TIMES (June 5, 2023), www.nytimes.com/2023/06/05/technology/twitter-ad-sales-musk.html.

[70] Sheila Dang, *Analysis: Twitter's Advertising Business Seen Facing Slow Recovery*, REUTERS (April 13, 2023), www.reuters.com/technology/twitters-advertising-business-seen-facing-slow-recovery-2023-04-13/; For an analysis of litigation arising out of advertisers' efforts to impose brand safety standards on a post-Musk Twitter/X, see Amar and Bhagwat, *supra* n. 68.

[71] Jay Peters and Jon Porter, *Instagram's Threads Surpasses 100 Million Users*, THE VERGE (July 10, 2023), www.theverge.com/2023/7/10/23787453/meta-instagram-threads-100-million-users-milestone. The more recent emergence of Bluesky as a potent Twitter/X alternative reflects similar trends. Callie Holtermann, *With Surge in New Users, Bluesky Emerges as X Alternative*, N.Y. TIMES (Nov. 12, 2024), www.nytimes.com/2024/11/12/style/bluesky-users-election.html.

[72] *How Does Facebook Use Artificial Intelligence to Moderate Content?* FACEBOOK HELP CENTER, www.facebook.com/help/1584908458516247; David Pilling and Madhumita Murgia, *"You Can't Unsee It": The Content Moderators Taking on Facebook*, FINANCIAL TIMES (May 17, 2023), www.ft.com/content/afeb56f2-9ba5-4103-890d-91291aea4caa.

practical barriers to reviewing this volume of material is obvious. It is true that algorithms and artificial intelligence can generally identify the most obvious forms of hate speech such as well-known epithets (though it should be noted that even the most odious such epithets, such as the N-word, are not always used as hate speech). But on the margins, what constitutes "direct attacks against people – rather than concepts or institutions – on the basis of ... protected characteristics" (Facebook's definition of hate speech) is not always easy to tell. Does a religiously based condemnation of homosexual conduct qualify as hate speech? Or what about a condemnation of such a religiously based condemnation?

The truth of the matter is that given the inevitable errors generated by scale, and the difficulty of defining hate speech at the margins, platforms will inevitably either under- or over-enforce their prohibitions on hate speech. In the United States, the perception on the political left is that platforms under-enforce. But of course the perception on the political right is exactly the opposite; and in practice, no doubt both are true, in that sometimes hate speech slips through, and sometimes content that is not hate speech is blocked or mislabeled. Whether platforms (other than Twitter/X) are systematically under- or over-enforcing is therefore impossible to tell, and conclusions in that regard are more likely driven by a priori assumptions about what constitutes the "right amount" of content moderation than any real data.

Unlike in the United States, in Germany (and the European Union more generally), hate speech does not enjoy protected status. As a consequence, Germany adopted legislation commonly known as the NetzDG, effective January 1, 2018, imposing severe restrictions on online hate speech. Under that law, websites that do not, within twenty-four hours, remove hate speech that is "obviously illegal" under German law are subject to fines of up to fifty million euros.[73] The impact of this law is telling. While it successfully incentivized the platforms to restrict hate speech, commentators convincingly argue the law has also led to deletions of legitimate posts, and the chilling of political speech.[74] And worse, nations with less liberal agendas than Germany's have adopted copycat laws with the predictable result of significantly chilling or silencing legitimate speech the government disapproves of.[75] There are thus clear downsides to placing too much (whatever that means) legal or political pressure on platforms to increase content moderation of hate speech.

---

[73] *Germany Starts Enforcing Hate Speech Law, supra* n. 17.
[74] Rebecca Zipursky, Note, *Nuts About NETZ: The Network Enforcement Act and Freedom of Expression*, 42 FORDHAM INT'L L.J. 1325, 1359–60 (2019); Linda Kinstler, *Germany's Attempt to Fix Facebook Is Backfiring*, THE ATLANTIC (May 18, 2018), www.theatlantic.com/international/archive/2018/05/germany-facebook-afd/560435/.
[75] Zipursky, *supra* n. 74, at 1360–62.

Finally, what about speech that even in the United States lacks constitutional protection, such as true threats (or for that matter child pornography)? All the major platforms unsurprisingly ban such speech (for reasons discussed at the end of this chapter), but should we hold platforms legally responsible when they fail to block threats? Current law, in the form of Section 230 of the Communications Decency Act, immunizes platforms, but should we change that? The answer, I would argue, is no. The reality is that even assuming that platforms are making good faith efforts to block personal threats, their efforts will inevitably be imperfect.

Consider the phrase "I'm going to kill you." Those words are uttered, written, and posted online thousands of times every day, and in almost every case the phrase at most is intended to convey anger, but usually is more of a joke. Yet precisely those words can, of course, constitute a serious threat of violence. Context is all, and most of us can, from context, easily figure out how the words are meant. But algorithms are terrible at context, and so will guess wrong with some frequency about the true meaning of such phrases. And because context is often cultural, even English-speaking human content moderators, if they were not raised in the United States, could easily misunderstand the intended meaning.

Now also consider the fact that the United States Supreme Court recently (in 2023) held that for speech to constitute an unprotected threat, the speaker must have acted recklessly – that is, "that a speaker is aware 'that others could regard his statements' as threatening violence and 'delivers them anyway.'"[76] How, exactly, is an algorithm (or even a distant human moderator) to determine the mental state of an individual who posts a potentially threatening statement online? Even after full, criminal trials mental states are notoriously difficult to pin down, so to expect content moderation, which happens constantly and necessarily quickly, to make such determinations is absurd.

Given the inevitability of mistakes, it becomes clear that just as NetzDG has led platforms to over-moderate potential hate speech in Germany, legal liability will cause platforms to block any speech that could plausibly be considered threatening. But as the "I'm going to kill you" example demonstrates, that is a huge amount of speech. Furthermore, given the vehemence of modern, online political discourse, a substantial fraction of that speech will be sharp political criticisms rather than actual threats. The line is often very difficult to draw, and if they face liability platforms will not take the risk. The burden on speech this would impose is, I would argue, simply not worth the marginal benefits of amending Section 230.

---

[76] Counterman v. Colorado, 600 U.S. 66, 79 (2023) (quoting Elonis v. U.S., 575 U.S. 723, 746 (2015) (Alito, J., concurring in part and dissenting in part)).

5.5 POLITICAL MANIPULATION AND POLARIZATION

Political manipulation, such as Russian interference in the 2016 and 2020 presidential elections, and its sister phenomenon, political polarization, are unquestionably serious concerns. And it is possible that the rise of social media has enabled and increased both phenomena – though, as discussed in Chapter 2, the degree to which social media contributes to polarization is quite unclear. But to what extent can platforms be cajoled or forced to moderate manipulative or polarizing content?

As to political manipulation, all of the major platforms (except perhaps Twitter/X in the Elon Musk era) appear to be firmly committed to combating such efforts, and what evidence we have does suggest that the platforms were far more effective in combating manipulative content in 2020 and 2024 than in 2016. Nonetheless, the media and public opinion should certainly continue to press platforms to fight political manipulation. But as with so many things, difficulties in distinguishing between legitimate and illegitimate online strategies makes legal intervention essentially impossible, especially when manipulation consists of spreading true but divisive information.

None of which is to say that no action is possible. Platforms do, and undoubtedly will, continue to block bots and other fake accounts, especially those seeking to manipulate elections in the United States but originating from outside the country. Nor does official pressure to block such accounts raise serious constitutional concerns, because foreign actors outside the territory of the United States do not enjoy First Amendment rights.[77] But with respect to content that is domestically produced or distributed by legitimate users, there is in truth little to be done because such content constitutes legitimate, and constitutionally protected, political speech.

Polarization is, however, a very different matter. Polarization is not, primarily, a product of disinformation, or even of manipulation. It is rather an increasingly prevalent element of political culture in the United States (and elsewhere, though seemingly not to the same degree in most other countries). Social media platforms' role in stoking polarization is unclear but probably limited. Even if, as Jonathan Haidt argues,[78] social media algorithms do increase polarization, however, the ultimate cause and source of political

---

[77] Agency for International Development v. Alliance for Open Society International, Inc., 591 U.S. 430 (2020).

[78] Jonathan Haidt, *Why the Past 10 Years of American Life Have Been Uniquely Stupid: It's Not Just a Phase*, THE ATLANTIC (April 11, 2022), www.theatlantic.com/magazine/archive/2022/05/social-media-democracy-trust-babel/629369/. For a collection of Haidt's arguments on this topic, *see* https://jonathanhaidt.com/social-media/.

polarization is not Facebook or Twitter/X. It is rather we, the users. And this fact poses a fundamental problem for those who would regulate social media to combat polarization.

Consider first the possibility that the pathway by which social media enhances political polarization is not via platform algorithms, but rather through users' choice of friends who share their political preferences, as (recall from Chapter 2) Professor Jane Bambauer and her co-authors argue.[79] If that is the case, then to reduce the polarizing impact of social media, either the state or platforms would have to force users to friend or follow individuals they disagree with, and as a result probably do not like. But the very thought of doing so seems incredibly manipulative, and ultimately frankly ridiculous. Coercing users in this way would deeply reduce people's enjoyment of social media and probably drive many users way. Perhaps some of the sharpest critics of social media would think this is a good outcome; but most of society should surely recoil at the thoroughly Luddite "solution" of destroying an important, new technological tool which has many, many legitimate uses (especially in commerce), and which most people enjoy – why, after all, would they spend so much time on social media if they did not.

But perhaps Professor Haidt is correct and the real source of increasing polarization is platform algorithms, which seek to maximize user engagement by serving up extremist or overwrought content. If that were the case, then legally requiring platforms to tweak their algorithms might reduce the tendency toward polarization (I say legally require because platforms, which are after all for-profit enterprises, are unlikely to voluntarily take steps that reduce engagement, and so advertising profits). The difficulty is that polarizing material is almost always fully legal and constitutionally protected. Indeed, because such content is typically political in nature, it sits at the very heart of public discourse and so constitutional protections. As such, legally restricting the spread or amplification of such content would violate the First Amendment rights of both users, and of platforms themselves. After all, a platform's decision to amplify specific content is itself an expressive act, as well as an editorial one as discussed in Chapter 4, both aspects of which receive First Amendment protections.[80]

But if legal requirements are a nonstarter, should the public and the media not seek to cajole, and the government jawbone, platforms into altering their algorithms? Perhaps, but even here it is important to take a pause. When

---

[79] Jane R. Bambauer, Saura Masconale, and Simone M. Sepe, *Cheap Friendship*, 54 U.C. DAVIS L. REV. 2341 (2021).

[80] Daphne Keller, *Amplification and Its Discontents: Why Regulating the Reach of Online Content Is Hard*, 1 J. FREE SPEECH L. 227 (2021).

commentators criticize platforms for seeking to maximize engagement, consider what they are really saying. They seem to be saying that platforms should serve up content that users don't like, or like less, so that they spend less time on the platform. This is the equivalent of trying to convince restaurants to serve food that customers will not enjoy, so as to convince them to spend less time and money at restaurants. But even if the goal was less problematic – say, to have customers eat less fatty food – we still do not typically interfere with private choices in this way, or force businesses to take steps that will make customers unhappy. In other words, criticizing platforms for "maximizing engagement" is essentially criticizing them for providing content that users desire and prefer.

Finally, for all the noise about "addiction" and the like, social media platforms are hardly heroin. In our world of infinite entertainment and communications options from Netflix to texting, no one is forced to use social media even for entertainment. And when social media is used for other functions, such as commercial sales, no one thinks that problematic or socially destructive. In short, social media platforms, like most commercial businesses, provide the products that in their view will maximize sales. And absent evidence that the provided product causes severe harm, as in the case of opioids, in a capitalist society that is generally considered normal and desirable even if, as with fatty foods, alcohol, and (perhaps) social media, the desired product is not necessarily good for the consumer.

5.6 INCENTIVES, MOTIVES, AND THE CASE FOR HUMILITY

Where does all of this leave us? The answer is clearly not no content moderation, because the platforms themselves agree (for reasons touched on in Chapter 4) that some level of moderation is essential, both for societal good and their own business models. This fact, combined with the very different incentives and motives of private internet firms versus the government, leads me to conclude that platforms are best left to their own devices in creating and enforcing content moderation rules, within broad limits.

Let us start with government incentives. The starting point is the perhaps grim but inevitable fact that political leaders of all stripes like to stay in power. In democracies, that means winning elections. In autocracies, it means suppressing dissidents. But the goal remains the same; and this fact alone creates strong motivations for political leaders vis-à-vis free speech and platforms.

Let us first consider the motivations of democratically elected leaders. In democracies, free speech is foundational and essential. Without free speech, citizens cannot meaningfully discuss public policy or the achievements and failings of elected leaders, and so cannot cast their vote intelligently. And more broadly, freedom of expression and related liberties such as assembly and association are the crucial, necessary tools with which citizens engage and communicate with their leaders. But from the point of view of elected officials, free speech is of course a threat, because it can be used to reveal their errors and weaknesses. Over time, this in turn can undermine support for them, and so their ability to prevail in elections. Hence the motivation to censor unfavorable speech. Of course, elected leaders must be careful in how they censor, or the censorship itself becomes a political problem, but so long as leaders target minority or unpopular viewpoints, they can often get away with suppression. After all, democratic leaders do not need universal support, just that of a majority of citizens. That is why constitutional protections for freedom of speech, ideally enforced against elected leaders by an independent judiciary, are an essential element of a successful democracy.

Now consider autocracies. Here, the motivation to suppress speech is even more obvious – speech is the primary and essential means to organize opposition to autocratic leaders. It is no coincidence that the largest and most successful autocracy in the world – China – also has the most elaborate and successful censorship systems. And unlike democratic leaders, autocratic leaders do not face democratic checks on their desire to censor.

Finally, consider the motivations of private social media platforms. Unlike government officials, at heart the goal of such firms is to maximize speech, because that is in some sense the product there are providing. To be more precise, platforms host speech to attract users, and then make money by selling access to those users to advertisers. Platforms cannot adopt aggressive rules restricting content because their financial goal is to maximize users; and to maximize users they need to host a great variety of speech that attracts a broad range of users, with a broad range of tastes. Furthermore, from the point of view of the platform, it is entirely irrelevant if the speech they host is favorable to the government, unfavorable to the government, or has nothing to do with government – the more the merrier.[81] Furthermore, even content which is

---

[81] The one caveat here is that if the government and/or political parties affiliated with the government are themselves a major source of platform profits, say from purchasing political advertising, then there might be occasions when platforms find it profitable to block anti-government speech in order to retain government business, to the detriment of other users. Such situations seem likely to be relatively uncommon, however, because political advertising constitutes a tiny fraction of overall advertising revenues for platforms – Facebook, for example, is the single largest conduit for online political ads, yet political advertising constituted less than 1 percent of company revenues. Katie Canales, *Mark Zuckerberg Said Facebook Makes a "Relatively Small" Amount from Political Advertising. The Company Has Made $2.2 Billion From Political Ads since Mid-2018*), BUSINESS INSIDER (Oct. 28, 2020), www.businessinsider.com/zuckerberg-facebook-political-ad-revenue-2020-10.

unpopular with the majority of users typically is of interest to some elements of the population, and so to maximize users, platforms are incented to permit that speech. It is only when speech is so unpopular with users that it is likely to chase them off the platforms that platforms have will want to suppress it. That, then, is the role of content moderation policies: not to suppress speech broadly or to tilt the political dialogue. Rather, it is to suppress the worst of the worst – like terrorist propaganda, hate speech, threats, and (for some platforms such as Facebook) pornography – that is likely to repel significant numbers of users, while otherwise maximizing speech in order to maximize engagement and profits. This is unlike with governments, which even in democracies have no incentive to permit unpopular speech, since their interests are in pleasing the majority, not niche minorities.

These points may seem obvious, but they have an important implication. Contrary to current orthodoxy, we should be far more trusting of platforms restricting speech than politicians restricting either speech or platforms because platforms have no systematic anti-speech bias, but government officials most certainly do (at least as to speech critical of them). As a result, it is as predictable as the sun rising in the east that *anytime* a government regulates in the expressive sphere, including regulating platforms, one of the core purposes of the regulation will be to maximize speech favorable to the government, and to minimize speech unfavorable to it. This is obviously true in autocratic states like China; but it is also true of democratically enacted legislation such as the laws recently enacted in the US states of Florida and Texas, both of whose governors publicly admitted (indeed, emphasized) that the purpose of the laws was to enhance conservative voices (both governors are leading conservatives, and members of the Republican Party).[82]

In short, government remains a much greater threat to free speech than social media platforms, not only because of the former's monopolies on violence and control but also because of their perverse incentives. The primary motivation of internet companies, on the other hand, is to make money, which in the free speech sphere is actually quite innocuous – after all, that is the motivation that drives all privately owned media. So, just as we leave it to the owners of legacy media to decide what (legal) content they will publish, so too the best solution at hand may be to leave that power in the hands of the platforms.

---

[82] NetChoice, LLC v. Att'y Gen., Fla., 34 F.4th 1196, 1205 (11th Cir. 2022); NetChoice, LLC v. Paxton, 1:21-CV-840-RP, 2021 WL 5755120, at *1 (W.D. Tex. Dec. 1, 2021).

6

Making Social Media Pay for Its Sins

Repealing or Amending Section 230

Section 230 of the Communications Decency Act[1] has been described as "the twenty-six words that created the internet."[2] Though initially widely supported, in recent years Section 230 has become a lightning rod for attacks on social media platforms and concerns about the social impact of the internet. Section 230, as we shall discuss in more detail, provides platforms with immunity from legal liability both for third-party content that they host *and* for the platforms' good faith efforts to moderate harmful content. In essence, critics argue that Section 230 has operated as a "get out of jail free" card for social media platform operators, permitting them to ignore harmful content when it suits them, but at the same time to block content that they do not like, both free of legal restraints.

As a result of this continuing criticism, there have been innumerable calls for Section 230 reform coming from across the political spectrum. Remarkably, during the 2020 presidential campaign *both* President Joe Biden and President Donald Trump called for Section 230 to be "revoked" outright. Biden, for example, said in an interview with the *New York Times* in December 2019 that "Section 230 should be revoked, immediately should be revoked."[3] The reason he gave was Facebook's failure to block harmful speech (with a particular focus on falsehoods), though around the same time House Speaker Nancy Pelosi cited harassment and abuse as another reason to eliminate Section 230 immunity.[4]

---

[1] 47 U.S.C. § 230.
[2] JEFF KOSSEFF, THE TWENTY-SIX WORDS THAT CREATED THE INTERNET (2019).
[3] Editorial Board, *Joe Biden*, N.Y. TIMES (Jan. 17, 2020), www.nytimes.com/interactive/2020/01/17/opinion/joe-biden-nytimes-interview.html.
[4] Bobby Allyn, *As Trump Targets Twitter's Legal Shield, Experts Have a Warning*, NPR (May 30, 2020, 11:36 AM), www.npr.org/2020/05/30/865813960/as-trump-targets-twitters-legal-shield-experts-have-a-warning.

In May 2020 President Trump joined the bandwagon, tweeting "REVOKE 230!" in response to a dispute with Twitter/X,[5] a position he reiterated in December 2020 in the course of vetoing a major defense appropriation bill.[6] Importantly, Trump's calls to revoke Section 230 were triggered not by awful content but rather by social media firms' alleged anti-conservative bias; but the two presidents' agreement on the needed *remedy* for the different problems they identify with social media is noteworthy. Nor are Trump and Biden alone in calling for repeal of Section 230.[7]

6.1 SECTION 230: WHAT IT DOES AND WHY IT DOES IT

Section 230 was enacted by Congress in 1996, in the early days of the internet long before the rise of social media platforms and ubiquitous user-generated content. It was a part of the Communications Decency Act, which in turn was part of the Telecommunications Act of 1996, which is why in popular parlance the provision is often described as Section 230 of the Communications Decency Act, or CDA.[8] Section 230 was a direct congressional response to two early defamation cases brought against internet service providers who hosted bulletin boards and discussion forums containing third-party, user-generated content.[9] Read in combination, the two decisions appeared to establish the principle that internet platforms hosting user- or third party-generated content could be held liable as publishers of defamatory content if, but only if, they made efforts to control and suppress harmful or offensive content on their platforms. If the platform owners did *not* exercise such control, they could be held liable only as distributors, meaning that they were liable only for defamatory content of which they were aware, or should have been aware, but nonetheless took no action to stop distributing.

It was immediately apparent that the legal regime created by these decisions would have been an utter disaster for the development of the internet, and especially for those corners of the internet that specialized in hosting third-party content – including what eventually become social media platforms.

---

[5] *ibid.*
[6] *Presidential Veto Message to the House of Representatives for H.R. 6395*, WHITE HOUSE (Dec. 23, 2020), www.whitehouse.gov/briefings-statements/presidential-veto-message-house-representatives-h-r-6395/.
[7] See, e.g., Steve Randy Waldman, *The 1996 Law That Ruined the Internet: Why I Changed My Mind about Section 230*, THE ATLANTIC (Jan. 3, 2021), www.theatlantic.com/ideas/archive/2021/01/trump-fighting-section-230-wrong-reason/617497/.
[8] www.govinfo.gov/link/uscode/47/230.
[9] The cases were Cubby, Inc. v. CompuServe, Inc., 776 F. Supp. 135 (S.D.N.Y. 1991), and Stratton Oakmont, Inc. v. Prodigy Service Co., 1995 WL 323710 (N.Y. Sup. Ct. 1995).

For one, the cases in combination strongly disincentivized any form of content moderation, for fear of opening the door to publisher liability. But it was apparent to observers – and to Congress – that some forms of content moderation are unquestionably desirable. At the same time, the possibility of distributor liability incentivized providers to pull down information at the first hint that it might be defamatory or otherwise illegal, inevitably resulting in the suppression of large amounts of marginal but legal speech. Furthermore, such platform actions opened the door to publisher liability, putting platforms between a rock and a hard place. The internal contradiction here – and the resulting chaos – should have been and were apparent to all.

Section 230 was Congress's response. The first, key operative provision of that law, Section 230(c)(1), states that "No provider or user of an interactive computer service shall be treated as the publisher or speaker of any information provided by another information content provider."[10] The clear intent and effect of this language is to flatly preclude imposing publisher liability on platforms for user-generated or other third-party content that they host. As such, this provision ensures (contrary to the early *Stratton Oakmont* decision described earlier) that engaging in some content moderation does not open platforms to unlimited liability. This protection was in itself essential to permit providers of hosting services (including, eventually, social media platforms) to provide controlled and curated experiences, as opposed to the anything-goes chaos of the public square – though, of course, if a particular platform *wants* to provide fully open, unmoderated spaces they are welcome to do so, as the Telegram and increasingly Twitter/X platforms do.

Important as this immunity was, courts quickly expanded the immunity provided by Section 230(c)(1) well beyond the obvious scope of its language. The key case in this regard was the very important 1997 decision in *Zeran v. American Online*,[11] issued by the United States Court of Appeals for the Fourth Circuit (the regional federal court of appeals covering the states of Maryland, Virginia, West Virginia, North Carolina, and South Carolina). *Zeran* held that Section 230(c)(1) shielded platforms not only from publisher liability but also from *distributor* liability – meaning that even if a platform *knew* or had reason to know that it was hosting illegal or harmful content, it still could not be held legally liable for it. This holding, which has been widely followed by other courts, eliminated any *legal* obligation or incentive (business incentives, as we have seen, are another thing) for platforms to moderate harmful or illegal third-party content.

[10] 47 U.S.C. § 230(c)(1).
[11] 129 F.3d 327 (4th Cir. 1997).

In recent years, the *Zeran* decision and its progeny have come under sharp attack.[12] In particular, in an important separate opinion US Supreme Court Justice Clarence Thomas expressed serious doubts about *Zeran* and urged the Supreme Court (which has never ruled on the issue) to reconsider the scope of Section 230(c)(1) and whether it should be limited to publisher immunity.[13] The Court has not yet taken up Justice Thomas's invitation, but with the growing unpopularity of social media platforms, especially on the political right, it would be unsurprising if it does so soon. It should be noted, however, that at the time *Zeran* was decided its holding was broadly supported. The judge who authored the decision was then-Chief Judge J. Harvey Wilkinson, one of the most respected judges in the federal judiciary (and, it should be noted, an appointee of President Ronald Reagan). And, as already noted, other courts quickly adopted Chief Judge Wilkinson's reasoning. It is only when the implications of the *Zeran* rule for *social media* platforms (which did not exist in their modern form in 1997) became clear that the decision became controversial.

The impact and importance of Section 230 does not end, however, with providing immunity from publisher or distributor liability. Its second key provision, subsection (c)(2)(A), also grants platforms immunity for their affirmative actions in moderating harmful user-generated and other third-party content. It reads as follows:

> No provider or user of an interactive computer service shall be held liable on account of any action voluntarily taken in good faith to restrict access to or availability of material that the provider or user considers to be obscene, lewd, lascivious, filthy, excessively violent, harassing, or otherwise objectionable, whether or not such material is constitutionally protected.[14]

Several things should jump out from this language. First, unlike the immunity provided by subsection (c)(1), this immunity is not absolute, it is limited to *good faith* content moderation. But given the extreme difficulty of proving lack of good faith, this limitation has not turned out to be terribly important in practice.

Second, as the last phrase of this provision suggests, Section 230(c)(2)(A) immunity is *not* limited to platform actions imposing restrictions on illegal content or content beyond the scope of the First Amendment. It is true that

---

[12] For a careful discussion of the difficulties raised by the *Zeran* decision, *see* Alan Z. Rozenshtein, *Interpreting the Ambiguities of Section 230*, 41 YALE J. REG. BULL. 60, 68–71 (2024).

[13] Malwarebytes, Inc. v. Enigma Software Group USA, LLC, 141 S. Ct. 13, 15–16 (2020) (Statement of Justice Thomas respecting the denial of certiorari).

[14] 47 U.S.C. § 230(c)(2)(A).

legally "obscene" content does fall outside First Amendment protection,[15] as perhaps does "harassing" content; but the other forms of content listed, including notably "excessively violent" content, quite clearly are protected by the First Amendment under well-established Supreme Court precedent.[16]

The final important question about the scope of subsection (c)(2)(A) immunity concerns the meaning of the final category of content listed, that which is "otherwise objectionable." Many courts have interpreted this language in an open-ended way, granting platforms immunity for decisions to block or restrict *any* content that a platform, in good faith, finds "objectionable" for any reason.[17] There is an argument to be made, however (and indeed has been made by Professors Adam Candeub and Eugene Volokh), that the phrase "otherwise objectionable" should be interpreted in light of the words preceding it, and so limited to content that is "objectionable" for similar reasons to the other listed categories – i.e., objectionable because it was highly sexual, vulgar, or violent.[18] If such a reading was adopted by, say, the Supreme Court (the question remains unresolved as of this writing), that would severely curtail the power of social media platforms to moderate content because it is false (for example, mis- or disinformation about, say, vaccines), hateful (e.g., racist, sexist, homophobic, and other hate speech), or ideologically troubling (e.g., pro-ISIS/Islamic State or pro-KKK propaganda that is not itself "excessively violent").

One further point about the relationship between the two subsections of Section 230 discussed earlier. On its face, the language of the two provisions would appear to protect distinct things. Subsection (c)(1) immunizes internet service providers regarding third-party content that remains on their platforms, thereby eliminating (on the *Zeran* reading) any obligation on the part of platforms to remove objectionable material. Subsection (c)(2)(A), on the other hand, immunizes platforms when they *do* choose, in good faith, to remove objectionable content (leaving aside for now the meaning of the word "objectionable"). But in fact, some courts have read the first subsection more broadly, to immunize *any* platform decision made in their role as a "publisher," including "reviewing, editing, and deciding whether to publish *or to withdraw from publication* third-party content."[19]

---

[15] Roth v. United States, 354 U.S. 476 (1957).
[16] *See* Brown v. Entertainment Merchants Association, 564 U.S. 786 (2011) (violent speech); Cohen v. California, 403 U.S. 15 (1971) (curse words); United States v. Playboy Entertainment Group, 529 U.S. 803 (2000) (non-obscene pornography).
[17] Adam Candeub and Eugene Volokh, *Interpreting 47 U.S.C. § 230(c)(2)*, 1 J. FREE SPEECH L. 175, 177 n.4 (2021).
[18] *Ibid.* at 179–83.
[19] Barnes v. Yahoo!, Inc., 570 F.3d 1096, 1102 (9th Cir. 2009) (*citing* Fair Housing Council of San Fernando Valley v. Roommates.Com, LLC, 521 F.3d 1157, 1170–71 (9th Cir. 2008)) (emphasis added).

This reading creates serious overlap between the two separate provisions of Section 230, seemingly making subsection (c)(2)(A) redundant and eliminating that provision's limitation of immunity to content moderation decisions made in "good faith." Courts have justified this by arguing that (2)(A) is not redundant because it also immunizes a decision to moderate non-third-party (i.e., at least in part platform-generated) content.[20] But this expansion of subsection (c)(1) immunity is in deep tension with the statutory language, and indeed in the separate opinion mentioned earlier, Justice Clarence Thomas also raised and criticized the judicial interpretation of subsection (c)(1) to reach decisions to remove content.[21]

The reason why all of this matters is simple. It demonstrates that there are several ongoing disputes about the precise scope of Section 230 immunity for platforms. Because the Supreme Court has never spoken to *any* of these issues to date, it remains possible that moving forward Section 230 immunity will become less expansive than what courts have granted in the past. But regardless of how these various disagreements are ultimately resolved, few people seriously doubt that the existence of *some* statutory immunity has been essential for platforms to develop and expand as they have since the turn of the Twenty-First century.[22] And so, any proposals to repeal or reform Section 230 must be evaluated in light of that broad consensus.

6.2 THE WAR ON SECTION 230

As noted at the beginning of this chapter, Section 230 is currently not a very popular law. To the contrary, it is fair to say that Section 230 is loathed across the political spectrum, with few or any politicians or journalists coming to its defense (academics are another matter[23]). And the basic shape of the attack on Section 230 is also familiar and predictable. It is, as noted earlier, that Section

---

[20] *Ibid.* at 1105.
[21] Malwarebytes, Inc. v. Enigma Software Group USA, LLC, 141 S. Ct. 13, 16–17 (2020) (Statement of Justice Thomas respecting the denial of certiorari).
[22] The primary argument *against* the need for some form of Section 230 immunity, aside from Luddites who wish to simply extinguish platforms for third-party content as a technology, rests on the idea that even absent statutory protection, the First Amendment to the Constitution would give platforms the space they need to operate. Professor Eric Goldman has strongly and articulately refuted that view, however. Eric Goldman, *Why Section 230 Is Better than the First Amendment*, 95 Notre Dame L. Rev. Reflection 33 (2019).
[23] While there are many members of the academy who defend Section 230 in its current form, including this author, probably the most vociferous defender is Professor Eric Goldman of Santa Clara University. One can get a good sense of Professor Goldman's views on his Technology and Marketing Law Blog: https://blog.ericgoldman.org/.

230 operates as a "Get Out of Jail Free" card, permitting social media (and other) platforms to do whatever they want, safe in the knowledge that the two parts of Section 230 permit them to leave harmful speech on their platforms and to "censor" whatever content they oppose, in both cases with confidence that they will be free of liability. As a result, platforms can cause great harm both to individuals and to society as a whole in the pursuit of unprecedented profits, without taking any responsibility for their actions.

Despite this seeming unanimity about the ills of Section 230, there exists a basic conundrum: While critics of Section 230 across the political spectrum agree that it enables misbehavior by platforms, they disagree fundamentally regarding the *kinds* of allegedly bad conduct Section 230 enables – which should come as no surprise given the discussion in Chapters 1 and 2 about the nature of conservative and progressive critiques of social media more generally. As a result, the two sides take polar opposite positions regarding *how* Section 230 should be reformed. This is not true, admittedly, about the most extreme calls, such as those from Presidents Biden and Trump described earlier, for the complete repeal of Section 230 – a call Senator Linsey Graham of South Carolina echoed in early 2024, when grandstanding about online child safety issues.[24] But it is not clear what repeal advocates envision taking the place of Section 230, given the unworkability of the legal regime that preceded it. And one suspects that conservatives and progressives would not agree on that replacement.

In any event, few people take calls to totally repeal Section 230 seriously because such a complete repeal would, realistically, make it impossible for platforms to host any user or other third-party content. This is because given the sheer scale at which social media platforms operate, perfect policing of defamatory and other illegal content is effectively impossible (especially defamation of private persons, which is exceedingly hard to factcheck). Repealing Section 230, in short, would completely eliminate the role of platforms as *social* media, and instead put them in the business of traditional media, which is to say serving up content created or carefully selected and vetted by the platform owners.

The destruction of social media may well be the unstated goal of some politicians and journalists, for whom social media has been deeply disempowering – most significantly, as discussed in Chapter 5, by eliminating the gatekeeper power that traditional media enjoyed and that politicians sometimes exploited. Furthermore, in the case of journalists the growth of social media

---

[24] Editorial Board, *Congress's Social-Media Spectacle*, WALL STREET JOURNAL (Feb. 1, 2024), www.wsj.com/articles/big-tech-hearing-congress-meta-social-media-mark-zuckerberg-1aeb2044.

platforms has been financially ruinous. But there are billions of people worldwide who use social media, presumably because they find engaging with their friends and acquaintances as well as the broader public on platforms a net positive experience. For them, the elimination of social media would hardly be a positive outcome or one they would support.

Indeed, moving beyond purely individual desires, eliminating social media as a technology would be a net negative for society and – yes – democracy. Such a move would reverse the profoundly democratizing impact of the internet, which has for first the first time in human history permitted millions of ordinary individuals to reach and engage with large audiences and communities. Perhaps from the point of view of some elites (notably media elites) such a reversal would not be such a bad thing; but from the perspective of most people and of society as a whole, eliminating platforms for user-generated content because they cause some social harm would truly be throwing out the baby with the bathwater.

That then leaves more modest reform proposals. But here, we again face the conundrum of fundamental inconsistency between conservatives and progressives. Conservative critics are focused mainly on weakening the provisions of Section 230 that shield platform moderation of third-party content from liability, on the grounds that they enable platform owners to effectuate their alleged anti-conservative bias. Conservative reform proposals thus consistently seek to restrict the scope of platform authority to moderate content. This would certainly be the result of Justice Thomas's argument, described earlier, that subsection (c)(1) of Section 230 should *not* have been read to immunize platform decisions regarding content moderation. If such an interpretation prevailed, this would mean that platforms could only evoke subsection (c)(2)(A) when defending decisions to remove or deemphasize content, which in turn would permit an attack based on claims of bad faith on the part of platforms – which, arguably, political discrimination would qualify as.

Similarly, the proposal – advanced among others by Professors Candeub and Volokh – to read the "otherwise objectionable" language of subsection (c)(2)(A) narrowly would also severely limit platform immunity for content moderation decisions (especially in combination with Justice Thomas's narrow reading). In fact, as noted earlier, such as reading would probably completely eliminate platform power to suppress speech, including hate speech and some terrorist propaganda, based on the viewpoint expressed in such content (note the parallel to Texas's HB 20, discussed in Chapters 1 and 4).

But conservative attempts to limit Section 230 immunity for content moderation decisions go beyond interpretive arguments, to legislative proposals. Most notably, in September 2020 the Trump Administration Justice

Department sent legislation to Congress proposing substantial revisions to Section 230.[25] Among other things (some discussed later), this proposal would have completely eliminated platforms immunity under subsection (c)(2)(A) for decisions to remove content that it believes to be "otherwise objectionable," thereby mooting the interpretive debate. Under such a regime, in practice platform owners' discretion to remove harmful content would be limited to sexual, violent, or unlawful materials.

Other examples of conservative efforts to amend Section 230 in response to allegations of political bias include proposals by Republican Senators Josh Hawley of Missouri and Marco Rubio of Florida that would condition Section 230 immunity for social media platforms on their making politically neutral and/or viewpoint-neutral content moderation decisions.[26] Another, narrower example of such an legislative initiative, also proposed by Senator Hawley, would condition Section 230 immunity on tech platforms passing an independent audit which confirmed that the platforms were not politically biased.[27] All these initiatives, like the Texas HB 20 and Florida S.B. 7072 laws discussed in Chapter 1, are at bottom efforts to attack platform content moderation power head-on (the only difference being that as states, Texas and Florida have no power to amend a federal statute such as Section 230).

In contrast to conservative proposals, unsurprisingly, progressive reform efforts take exactly the opposite tack, seeking to incentivize *more* rather than less content moderation by platforms by limiting immunity under subsection (c)(1) of Section 230. For example, Senator Amy Klobuchar, a Democrat from Minnesota (and former presidential candidate) proposed legislation in July of 2021 that would have created an exception to Section 230 for platforms whose algorithms promoted health misinformation (July of 2021 was of course in the middle of the COVID-19 pandemic).[28] Senator Elizabeth Warren of Massachusetts, another prominent Democrat (and former presidential

---

[25] *The Justice Department Unveils Proposed Section 230 Legislation*, U.S. DEP'T OF JUST. (Sept. 23, 2020), www.justice.gov/opa/pr/justice-department-unveils-proposed-section-230-legislation.

[26] *See Senator Hawley Introduces Legislation to Amend Section 230 Immunity for Big Tech Companies*, JOSH HAWLEY, U.S. SENATOR FOR MISSOURI (June 19, 2019), https://perma.cc/HFM2-93VA; *see also* Jane Coaston, *A Republican Senator Wants the Government to Police Twitter for Political Bias*, VOX (June 26, 2019, 3:30 PM), www.vox.com/2019/6/26/18691528/section-230-josh-hawley-conservatism-twitter-facebook.; *Rubio Introduces Sec 230 Legislation to Crack Down on Big Tech Algorithms and Protect Free Speech*, MARCO RUBIO, U.S. SENATOR FOR FLORIDA (June 24, 2021), https://perma.cc/43R6-HRWV.

[27] Allyn, *supra* n. 4.

[28] S.2448 – Health Misinformation Act of 2021, www.congress.gov/bill/117th-congress/senate-bill/2448/text; Shannon Bond, *Democrats Want to Hold Social Media Companies Responsible for Health Misinformation*, NPR (July 22, 2021), www.npr.org/2021/07/22/1019346177/democrats-want-to-hold-social-media-companies-responsible-for-health-misinformat.

candidate) has similarly criticized social media platforms, including especially Facebook, sharply for failing to block misinformation in political advertising – in one famous instance by taking out an ad on Facebook containing false information about Facebook and its CEO Mark Zuckerberg.[29]

Nor, of course, is left-wing criticism limited to politicians. Left-leaning journalistic outlets, including well-respected ones such as the New York Times and the Washington Post, have repeatedly published stories and editorials criticizing social media platforms' failure to block mis- and disinformation, as well as their spreading of polarizing content. And several of those editorials have strongly suggested that Section 230 reform was the only way to incentivize better behavior[30] – though as with politicians, the journalists are typically notably short on details on what should take Section 230's place.

Needless to say, not all Section 230 reform proposals are as relentlessly aggressive (or politically motivated) as this. Law professors Danielle Keats Citron and Mary Anne Franks have proposed a set of more thoughtful, and more limited, reforms of Section 230. One would limit Section 230 immunity to *speech*, thereby clarifying that online commercial transactions and the like would not fall within the provision.[31] They would also deny immunity to truly bad actors, meaning websites that knowingly keep up illegal content, encourage illegality, principally host illegal content, or solicit illegal content.[32] Such a revision would presumably have little impact on major platforms such as Facebook and YouTube, but would permit action against the seediest parts of the internet.

Finally, Citron and Franks propose language that would condition Section 230 immunity on platforms taking "reasonable steps to address unlawful uses of its service that create serious harm to others."[33] Such a provision would, of course, require courts to determine what constitutes "reasonable steps" in a world in which, all acknowledge, content moderation will necessarily be imperfect. Citron and Franks argue, however, that courts have proven capable

---

[29] Cecelia Kang and Thomas Kaplan, *Warren Dares Facebook with Intentionally False Political Ad*, WASHINGTON POST (Oct. 12, 2019), www.nytimes.com/2019/10/12/technology/elizabeth-warren-facebook-ad.html.

[30] *See, e.g.*, Jennifer Rubin, *It's Time to Stand Up to Facebook*, WASHINGTON POST (Oct. 4, 2021), www.washingtonpost.com/opinions/2021/10/04/its-time-stand-up-facebook/; Joe Scarborough, *Zuckerberg Says He's "Disgusted" by Trump's Rhetoric. It's Just Crocodile Tears*, WASHINGTON POST (June 18, 2020), www.washingtonpost.com/opinions/why-are-facebook-and-its-founder-not-held-responsible-for-the-damage-they-deal/2020/06/18/85c4017e-b0cb-11ea-856d-5054296735e5_story.html.

[31] Danielle Keats Citron and Mary Anne Franks, *The Internet as a Speech Machine and Other Myths Confounding Section 230 Reform*, 45 U. CHI. LEGAL F. 45, 69–74 (2020).

[32] *Ibid.* at 70–71.

[33] *Ibid.* at 71.

of making such judgments in the past, and that over time best practices will emerge.[34]

Interestingly, the Trump Administration's 2020 proposal to reform Section 230, discussed earlier, picked up on some of Citron and Frank's proposals. In particular, the Trump Administration would have amended Section 230 to deny immunity to "Bad Samaritans," meaning platforms that knowingly facilitate criminal behavior, or knowingly failed to remove material that violated criminal law.[35] The proposed amendments would also have eliminated Section 230 immunity for actions brought under a wide swath of laws, including laws regulating terrorism, child sex abuse, cyber-stalking, as well as antitrust laws. Some of these proposals, notably the Bad Samaritan exception, respond to widely shared concerns. However, it seems fairly clear, given President Trump's disputes with social media firms, that a major objective of some of these proposals, especially the removal of the "otherwise objectionable" language discussed earlier, was to restrict social media platforms' ability to block politically charged posts by conservative politicians.

6.3 THE LIMITS OF SECTION 230

Finally, the idea that Section 230 completely shields platforms from liability for their actions – i.e., Section 230 is an unlimited "Get Out of Jail Free" card – is an exaggeration. Certainly Section 230 has been read by courts (perhaps mistakenly, as noted earlier) to immunize platforms against essentially all claims arising from third-party content, or their efforts to moderate such content; but it does *not* immunize the platforms' own actions aside from content moderation, including the platforms' own speech. Thus if I post content defaming someone else on Facebook, Meta is immune. But if Meta itself posts defamatory content, Section 230 provides no defense. Furthermore, courts have consistently held that decisions platforms make about how to design their platforms, and what features to offer on platforms, are not protected by Section 230. Two examples can help illustrate what this means.

In May of 2017, three Wisconsin teenagers were speeding in a car at well over 100 MPH when they swerved off the road and hit a tree, killing all three of them. In 2019, the parents of two of the boys sued Snap, Inc., the owner of the Snapchat platform, in a federal district court in California (Snap's headquarters are in Santa Monica) claiming that the crash was a result of a Snapchat design feature. In particular, the parents' complaint claimed that at the time

---

[34] Ibid. at 71–73.
[35] *The Justice Department Unveils Proposed Section 230 Legislation*, supra n. 25.

6.3 The Limits of Section 230

of the crash, Snapchat had a feature called a "Speed Filter" which permitted users to record their actual current speed, and overlay that information on content they were uploading to Snapchat. The parents claimed a belief had emerged among Snapchat users that the app rewarded uploads taken at 100 MPH or higher, and that shortly before the accident, one of the boys (not the driver) opened Snapchat and used the Speed Filter.[36] The basis of their claim was that Snapchat was negligent in designing the Speed Filter feature, knowing as they did or should have that it incentivized dangerous conduct among their (mainly young) user base.

After the parents filed their lawsuit against Snap, Snap sought to have the case dismissed on the grounds of Section 230 immunity. Snap succeeded at the trial court level, but on appeal the United States Court of Appeals for The Ninth Circuit (covering the western states) reversed. In doing so the court drew a crucial distinction between claims which seek to treat a defendant platform as a "publisher or speaker" of third-party content, and claims based on negligent design of the platform itself. In this case, the court said, the parents were not seeking to impose liability on Snap based on the content uploaded just before the accident, but rather on the design of the Speed Filter feature itself. Of course, the accident was ultimately related to the fact that the boys were uploading content; but that was not the basis of the claim against Snap. As a result, the court permitted to lawsuit to proceed.[37]

The importance of the Ninth Circuit's *Lemmon* decision (the title of the case was *Lemmon v. Snap*) should be obvious. It clarifies that Section 230 does not generally shield social media platforms from responsibility for all misconduct, but only for their actions with respect to third-party content. The decision has, unsurprisingly, been highly influential, and has opened an (admittedly narrow) door to holding platforms accountable for harm for which they, themselves, are directly responsible. And it is widely accepted and supported, so much so that even the Electronic Frontier Foundation, one of the preeminent cyber-libertarian organizations in the world and a prominent defender of Section 230, expressed support for it.[38]

Important though it is, however, it should be acknowledged that the exact scope of the distinction drawn in *Lemmon* is unclear. Perhaps the greatest unresolved issue in this regard is whether Section 230 permits holding platforms liable for the results of computer algorithms they use to recommend

---

[36] Lemmon v. Snap, Inc., 995 F.3d 1085, 1088–89 (9th Cir. 2021).
[37] Ibid. at 1091–94.
[38] Sophia Cope, *Lawsuit against Snapchat Rightfully Goes Forward Based on a "Speech Filter," Not User Speech*, ELECTRONIC FRONTIER FOUNDATION (May 18, 2021), www.eff.org/deeplinks/2021/05/lawsuit-against-snapchat-rightfully-goes-forward-based-speed-filter-not-user.

specific content to specific users. The Supreme Court was faced with this issue in its 2022–2023 Term in a pair of cases alleging that the major social media platforms (Facebook, Twitter/X, and YouTube) had facilitated terrorist attacks abroad by permitting the Foreign Terrorist Organization ISIS (also known as Islamic State) to use their platforms as recruiting tools. The lower court (as it happens, the Ninth Circuit again) had dismissed the plaintiffs' claims under the authority of Section 230, and crucially, had reaffirmed its conclusion in an earlier case that Section 230(c)(1) immunity barred legal claims based on platform recommendation algorithms, so long as the algorithms were not designed to favor illegal content.[39] On appeal, however, the Supreme Court ducked the Section 230 issue and instead held that the relevant federal anti-terrorism statutes did not reach the platforms' conduct.[40]

Of course, the Court's decision to avoid determining the scope of Section 230 did not either resolve the issue or make it go away, and the question of whether Section 230 *should* be read to immunize algorithmic recommendations has important implications for ongoing and future litigation.[41] Most notably, in the wake of the *Lemmon* decision (and others) literally hundreds of lawsuits were filed by local school districts, as well as a bipartisan group of state attorneys general, against the major platforms based on the allegedly "addictive" nature of platforms, which the claimants say has contributed to a mental health crisis among adolescents[42] (as noted in Chapter 2, the empirical basis for such claims remain highly disputed, but that is a separate question from the scope of Section 230 immunity). Though they vary slightly, the essential element of all of these lawsuits are claims that the platforms have intentionally created a series of features, including recommendation algorithms and endless loops, designed to addict children in ways that cause child users significant mental harm.

These lawsuits have all been consolidated before a single federal judge, Judge Yvonne Gonzales Rogers, who sits in Oakland, California. In the most recent significant development in this litigation as of this writing, on November 14, 2023, Judge Rogers issued a long and careful opinion resolving a motion by the platforms to dismiss the litigation. She concluded that based on Ninth Circuit precedent which she was bound to follow (including *Lemmon* and the terrorism cases discussed earlier), claims against the platforms based

---

[39] Gonzales v. Google LLC, 2 F.4th 871, 894–97 (9th Cir. 2021).
[40] Twitter, Inc. v. Taamneh, 598 U.S. 471 (2023); Gonzales v. Google LLC, 598 U.S. 617 (2023) (per curiam).
[41] The arguments are summarized in Rozenshtein, *supra* n. 12, at 71–73.
[42] Isaiah Poritz, *Social Media Addiction Suits Take Aim at Big Tech's Legal Shield*, BLOOMBERG LAW (Oct. 25, 2023), https://news.bloomberglaw.com/tech-and-telecom-law/hundreds-of-social-media-addiction-suits-face-first-legal-hurdle.

on the features built into the platforms, rather than on decisions directly tied to specific third-party content, fell outside Section 230 as interpreted in the *Lemmon* decision.[43] However, Judge Rogers also confirmed that some of the claims against platforms, based on such things as failing to limit the length of time users could spend on platforms, creating endless streams of content, and using algorithms "to promote addictive engagement," *were* barred by Section 230 because in practice, such claims, if accepted, could be cured only by publishing less third-party content.[44] And notably, in reaching these conclusions Judge Rogers fully embraced the view that Section 230 immunity extends to recommendation algorithms.[45]

In short, despite the seemingly broad consensus among social media critics that Section 230 is fatally flawed, those critics cannot come close to agreeing *why* it is flawed. And furthermore, there remain important, open questions about the actual scope of Section 230 immunity vis-à-vis various kinds of legal claims, including (outside the Ninth Circuit) claims based on the results of platform recommendation algorithms.

6.4 IN DEFENSE OF SECTION 230: IMMUNITY FOR THIRD-PARTY CONTENT

One reason why the basic protections that Section 230 provides to social media platforms are socially beneficial is that to some significant degree, Section 230 protections overlap with First Amendment protections already available to social media (though this does *not* mean that the First Amendment makes Section 230 unnecessary[46]). Significant parts of modern First Amendment law are driven by an insight about "chilling effects": the idea that imposing broad or ill-defined liability on speakers and other First Amendment actors will cause those actors to "voluntarily" silence themselves or others out of fear of inadvertently crossing a legal line. This idea was the driving force behind one of the most influential and significant First Amendment decisions of all time, *New York Times v. Sullivan.*[47] In that case, which arose during the Civil Rights era, an Alabama city official sued the New York Times as well as four individuals active in the civil rights movement for libel, based on factual errors in a fundraising advertisement that the individuals had placed in the Times. The US

---

[43] In re Social Media Adolescent Addition/Personal Injury Products Liability Litigation, 2023 W.L. 7524912 at *11–13 (N.D. Cal. 2023).
[44] *Ibid.* at *13–16.
[45] *Ibid.* at *14.
[46] The reasons why are ably explained by Professor Eric Goldman. Goldman, *supra* n. 22.
[47] 376 U.S. 254 (1964).

Supreme Court held that when public officials sought to recover damages for defamatory speech about their official conduct, they were required to prove that the falsehood was made with "actual malice," meaning that speaker acted with "knowledge that it was false or with reckless disregard for the truth." Later cases in this line extend First Amendment immunity to defamation claims by all public figures, and to liability claims other than defamation.[48]

The crucial aspect of the decision, however, was that the Court did not base its new rule, which protected even negligent falsehoods from liability, on the supposed value of false speech. Rather, all these decisions were driven by the insight that imposing liability on the media even for seemingly low value or unprotected speech can lead to the "voluntary" suppression of valuable, protected speech. It was this "self-censorship" that, in the Court's view, would seriously interfere with the public discourse at the center of our democracy.

There is an obvious analogy between the chilling effects the *Sullivan* Court identified and the position of social media platforms today – and indeed, it was concerns about such chilling effects that drove Congress to adopt Section 230 in the first place. To understand why that is so, one must first absorb the sheer scale of content moderation that social media platforms engage in. Consider the largest of the platforms, Facebook. Facebook is available in almost every country in the world, in over 100 languages (Reuters reported in 2019 that Facebook was available in 111 languages supported by Facebook, and another thirty-one without support[49]). That translates to over 2 *billion* daily active users on Facebook, a substantial percentage of the human race. And with that scale comes an enormous amount of content moderation. The Supreme Court's recent *NetChoice* decision (discussed in detail in Chapter 4) reports that in one quarter of 2021, Facebook blocked 25 million pieces of content just under its rule against hate speech, and another 9 million under its bullying and harassment policy (YouTube similarly reported blocking 6 million videos in one quarter alone).[50] Indeed, it is fair to say that for massive platforms such as Facebook, Instagram, YouTube, and TikTok, content moderation practices are not only a major part of their businesses; they are industrial in scale.[51]

---

[48] Curtis Publ'g Co. v. Butts, 388 U.S. 130, 155 (1967) (extending *Sullivan* holding to public figures); Hustler Magazine v. Falwell, 485 U.S. 46, 56 (1988) (extending *Sullivan* holding to claims by public figures for intentional infliction of emotional distress).

[49] Maggie Fick and Paresh Dave, *Facebook's Flood of Languages Leave It Struggling to Monitor Content*, REUTERS (Apr. 23, 2019), www.reuters.com/article/us-facebook-languages-insight/facebooks-flood-of-languages-leave-it-struggling-to-monitor-content-idUSKCN1RZ0DW.

[50] Moody v. NetChoice, LLC, 144 S. Ct. 2383, 2406 (2024).

[51] The classic, albeit at this point slightly dated, account of how platform content moderation operates is Kate Klonick, *The New Governors: The People, Rules, and Processes Governing Online Speech*, 131 HARV. L. REV. 1598 (2018).

6.4 In Defense of Section 230: Immunity for Third-Party Content 133

But with that scale comes an inevitable byproduct: mistakes. A 2020 report issued by the NYU Stern School of Business suggests that content moderation mistakes are ubiquitous. Indeed, Mark Zuckerberg, the CEO of Meta (which owns Facebook and Instagram), himself conceded that one out of ten content moderation decisions are mistaken – which translates to 300,000 mistakes *a day* for Facebook alone.[52] And while recent advances in Artificial Intelligence (AI) *might* help mitigate this problem in the future, it could also make the problem more intractable given the scale at which generative AI can produce and post content, including problematic content. And note that the inevitability of content moderation mistakes has implications for both sides of the Section 230 puzzle: It means that platforms will inevitably sometimes block content that does not violate their rules (or the law), and sometimes fail to block content that does.

These well-known facts lead to a simple conclusion: Without some basic form of Section 230 immunity, social media as we know it could not exist. Indeed, without Section 230, defamation liability alone would shut down social media as we know it. But this principle itself has implications for Section 230 "reform." In particular, for the same reasons that, as discussed in Chapter 4, the Supreme Court extended First Amendment editorial rights to social media platforms in the *NetChoice* cases, it seems very likely that the principles underlying *Sullivan* and later cases will also apply to social media. Thus, it may well be that the First Amendment requires any reductions in Section 230 immunity to be tempered with some sort of scienter requirement for platforms, such as the *Sullivan* "actual malice" standard. Or to put it differently, it may well be that the Constitution itself forbids imposing *publisher*, meaning strict or negligence, liability on platforms regarding the types of speech that fall within the protection of the *Sullivan* line of cases, even if distributor liability, based on actual knowledge, was permissible.

I will discuss later why reading (or amending) Section 230 to permit distributor, but not publisher, liability creates its own set of serious problems. For now, however, we should note that the *Sullivan* case and its progeny do not in any way shield media from liability to entirely private individuals when the speech at issue does not involve matters of public concern.[53] As such, at least under current law private defamation, whether published in traditional media or posted to platforms, does not trigger First Amendment protections. For newspapers, this is not a major problem because most content in such

---

[52] John Koetsier, *Report: Facebook Makes 300,000 Content Moderation Mistakes Every Day*, FORBES (June 9, 2020), www.forbes.com/sites/johnkoetsier/2020/06/09/300000-facebook-content-moderation-mistakes-daily-report-says/.

[53] Dun & Bradstreet, Inc. v. Greenmoss Builders, Inc., 472 U.S. 749 (1985).

publications is presumed to be of public concern. Unlike with *news* media, however, with *social* media there can be no such assumption; to the contrary, much content on social media is purely private and often personal (I for one tend to use Facebook to report on nice hikes).

This legal regime, which favors political and social commentary over private speech about private persons, certainly reflects the current state of First Amendment law; and it might well have made sense with respect to traditional media whose focus was public affairs. But its consequences for social media are quite troubling – and in this regard the Constitution is almost beside the point. The reality is that online defamatory statements about private figures are actually much harder to police than potential defamation of public figures, because information about private individuals is not readily accessible from available and trustworthy records. Nor, as just noted, would such statements receive First Amendment protections. So, without Section 230 immunity from at least publisher liability, platforms would have to simply ban potentially defamatory content, which is to say any critical statements about private persons. That, in practice, is the end of the "social" aspect of social media (aside from happy thoughts and cat videos, since cats can't sue for defamation).

Nor is the problem limited to defamatory statements. Consider threatening speech. It is well-established law that "true threats" are a form of unprotected speech under the First Amendment to the US Constitution.[54] However, in a recent case involving systematic, online harassment of a women by a stranger, the Supreme Court held that threats and harassment may be punished under the First Amendment only if the speaker was "reckless," meaning that he or she was consciously aware that others could see the speech at issue as threatening but decided to proceed anyway.[55] This is obviously an extraordinarily difficult line for courts and victims to draw, but for platforms it is an impossible one given their lack of access to the state of minds of individual users. Thus if platforms did face publisher liability for what are called "true threats" posted by users, their only recourse would be to block *all* sharp criticisms that could possibly be read to implicate violence, including sharp criticisms of public figures. Such chilling effects raise serious First Amendment concerns and have very troubling implications for democratic discourse.

The way to think about the consequences of eliminating or significantly limiting publisher liability is that doing so would leave platforms with effectively two choices: either to stop carrying unvetted third-party content (and so effectively end the social element of social media) or to massively ramp up

---

[54] Virginia v. Black, 538 U.S. 343, 359 (2012) (plurality opinion).
[55] Counterman v. Colorado, 600 U.S. 66, 79–80 (2023).

content moderation to catch all (or almost all) content that creates the risk of liability. The former "solution" would destroy a multi-billion-dollar industry that provides services that billions of people around the world evidently value, an outcome only a Luddite could support. And as for the second potential solution, massively tightening content moderation, that poses its own problems. First of all, for all of the reasons described earlier such almost-perfect content moderation is impossible, even (or especially) in the age of AI. Furthermore, even if a behemoth such as Facebook could afford to undertake the enormous amounts of content moderation that repeal of Section 230 would require, several of its smaller competitors have already expressed concerns about their ability to do so,[56] which means that such Section 230 "reform" would further concentrate an already overly concentrated industry.

Finally, however, excessive content moderation is objectively troubling for policy reasons. For one thing, some commentators have pointed out that eliminating or severely restricting Section 230 immunity will inevitably lead social media firms to over-filter borderline speech on topics such as sexuality, which could work to the detriment of marginal groups such as LGBTQ youth.[57] In addition, such a change would turbocharge conservative complaints (discussed on Chapter 1) about platform "bias" against conservative voices. And more generally, tightening up content moderation will inevitably result in the silencing of huge amounts of legitimate and protected speech, especially political speech, throughout the world. There is evidence that this is precisely what happened at Facebook when Germany adopted its so-called NetzDG law that imposed massive fines on platforms that, after being notified, permitted hate speech to remain available.[58] Eliminating Section 230 immunity would simply spread that political chill to the United States, on a much more massive scale.

Moreover, essentially all of the bad results I have argued will result from amending Section 230 to permit *publisher* liability would also follow from amending (or as Justice Thomas proposes interpreting) Section 230 to permit imposing *distributor* liability on platforms. Recall that while publisher liability

---

[56] Todd Shields and Ben Brody, *Facebook Worries Smaller Rivals with Openness on Liability*, YAHOO! FIN. (Dec. 23, 2020), https://finance.yahoo.com/news/facebook-support-liability-reform-little-070000635.html.

[57] See Bill Easley, *Revising the Law that Lets Platforms Moderate Content Will Silence Marginalized Voices*, SLATE (Oct. 29, 2020), https://slate.com/technology/2020/10/section-230-marignalized-groups-speech.html.

[58] Rebecca Zipursky, Note, *Nuts about NETZ: The Network Enforcement Act and Freedom of Expression*, 42 FORDHAM INT'L L.J. 1325, 1359–60 (2019); Linda Kinstler, *Germany's Attempt to Fix Facebook Is Backfiring*, THE ATLANTIC (May 18, 2018), www.theatlantic.com/international/archive/2018/05/germany-facebook-afd/560435/.

would hold platforms liable, either strictly or upon a showing of negligence, for harmful third-party content, distributor liability kicks in only if a platform *knew* or had reason to know that it was hosting illegal or harmful content. Justice Thomas and others would (contrary to the *Zeran* case) read Section 230 to permit distributor liability, and others have proposed amending Section 230 to do so. The problem is that distributor liability effectively forces platforms to implement a take-down regime, under which once *anyone* tells a platform that some specific content it is hosting is illegal, that platform must immediately make a judgment about whether to risk keeping the flagged content up or take it down. But of course, the incentives faced by platforms in this situation are asymmetric. Ideally, a platform would like to make the right call every time and only take down actually illegal, flagged content. But, given blurry lines between protected and illegal content, that is impossible. So, in case of doubt a platform has two choices – take down the content and irritate a single user, or leave up the content and potentially face massive fines. That is precisely the choice that the German NetzDG law gave to platforms, and their reaction was utterly predictable: in case of *any* doubt, take it down. The result is a significant burden on the speech of countless users who have posted sharply worded but legal content.

Even worse, a take-down regime not only creates perverse incentives for platforms; it also creates an opening for bad actors among the public. Platforms host lots of content that, while perfectly legal and even legitimate, angers others. That includes honest but negative online reviews, sharp criticisms of individuals, political opinions outside the mainstream (in either direction), and so forth. Take-down regimes effectively encourage those who dislike specific posts to flag them to the platform. Doing so is almost effortless (since take-down regimes inevitably require platforms to create easy means to flag content) and has little downside from the point of view of the flagger, with the potential "upside" of (at least temporarily) getting rid of the content. As a consequence, it is utterly predictable that take-down regimes will encourage huge numbers of dubious or even clearly false notices, with the consequent negative effects on free speech. Indeed, the take-down regime created by the US Digital Millennium Copyright Act regarding intellectual property has been so thoroughly abused that it has led the Electronic Frontier Foundation to create a "Takedown Hall of Shame."[59] Laws like NetzDG, or interpreting Section 230 to permit distributor (even if not publisher) liability, would spread this burden beyond speech implicating intellectual property to *all* speech, including especially political speech, on platforms.

---

[59] Electronic Frontier Foundation, *Takedown Hall of Shame*, www.eff.org/takedowns.

In fact, the kind of take-down regime I describe is precisely what the European Union (EU) put into place in late 2022 when it adopted its "Digital Services Act" (DSA).[60] Article 6 of the DSA states that platforms shall not be liable for third-party content that they host so long as the platform "does not have actual knowledge of illegal activity or illegal content" *and* "upon obtaining such knowledge or awareness, acts expeditiously to remove or to disable access to the illegal content"[61] – in other words, the DSA imposes distributor liability. And Article 16 implements this approach by mandating that platforms create "notice and action" (i.e., notice and take-down) mechanisms that permit individuals to flag content that an individual "considers to be illegal content."[62] Finally, another part of the DSA requires platforms to give priority to notices submitted by "trusted flaggers," which are entities that a member EU government has designated as trusted.[63]

While it is early days, the full impact of these provisions of the DSA is potentially appalling. For one thing, the DSA applies to any content that is illegal under the law of any member state. As Professor Dawn Nunziato points out, that extends to hate speech, Holocaust denial, and glorification of Nazi ideology in Germany; but also to criticism and parody of the President of France under French law, to pro-LGBTQ+ content accessible to minors under Hungarian law, and to *blasphemy* under Austrian and Finnish law.[64] Furthermore, the creation of the "trusted flagger" program is a clear invitation to illiberal governments (yes, they exist in the EU) to drown platforms in complaints – to which platforms are required to give priority – by designating "trusted flaggers" who will repeatedly objecting to content the government dislikes. This would surely put pressure on platforms to voluntarily block speech to which the authorities object, even if that speech is probably legal, simply to avoid the burden of processing complaints (and as a useful side effect, to get into the relevant government's good graces).

But even assuming official good faith, the DSA regime clearly creates a system ripe for abuse by individual flaggers, for reasons already explained. But the only response to this problem is Article 23(2) of the DSA, which states that platforms must stop accepting, "for a reasonable period of time," notices from individuals or entities "that frequently submit notices or complaints that are manifestly unfounded."[65] Presumably in the EU's view false flagging resulting

---

[60] https://eur-lex.europa.eu/eli/reg/2022/2065/oj ("DSA").
[61] *Ibid.*, Art. 6.
[62] *Ibid.*, Art. 16.
[63] *Ibid.*, Art. 22.
[64] Dawn Carla Nunziato, *The Digital Services Act and the Brussels Effect on Platform Content Moderation*, 24 CHI. J. INT'L LAW 115, 119–20 (2023).
[65] DSA, Art. 23(2).

in wrongful take-downs is fine so long as it is not "frequent" and "manifestly unfounded." It is too early to know (as of this writing) what the long term consequences of the DSA for free speech in Europe will be; but the prognosis is not good.

Finally, while I have focused on the EU's DSA, the problem I describe is not unique to Europe. In particular India, the largest democracy in the world and (not coincidentally) home to the largest number of Facebook users,[66] has a similar problem. In 2021, India released what are commonly known as the Information Technology Rules (or "2021 IT Rules"),[67] which implemented provisions of the Information Technology Act of 2000.[68] Sections 14 and 15 of the Rules, acting on the authority of Section 69A of the 2000 Act, create a mechanism permitting executive branch officials to order the blocking of online content deemed to be illegal or otherwise unprotected. In addition, like the DSA, Rules 3(2) and 4(c) of India's 2021 IT Rules also provide the public with a mechanism to file complaints with platforms, to which platforms must respond. But given gaps in enforcement, the primary impact of the Indian IT Rules has been to greatly enhance the power of the central government, led by Prime Minister Narendra Modi and his Bharatiya Janata Party, to pressure platforms to block content – especially because Indian law permits criminal prosecution of tech executives for violations of these rules. Press reports strongly suggest that the consequence has been a dramatic increase in government control over, and censorship of, online content the government considers objectionable.[69]

6.5 IN DEFENSE OF SECTION 230: IMMUNITY FOR CONTENT MODERATION

The discussion to this point demonstrates why any serious curtailment of platform immunity for third-party content that they carry would have (and in some countries has had) very bad consequences for the liberty of social media

---

[66] Tom Fish, *These Countries Have the Most People on Facebook*, NEWSWEEK (Sept. 2, 2021), www.newsweek.com/counties-most-people-facebook-1624911. China has more total users, but famously blocks the major US platforms.

[67] Information Technology (Intermediary Guidelines and Digital Media Ethics Code) Rules, 2021.

[68] Information Technology Act, 2000.

[69] Karishma Mehrotra and Joseph Menn, *How India Tames Twitter and Set a Global Standard for Online Censorship*, WASHINGTON POST (Nov. 8, 2023), www.washingtonpost.com/world/2023/11/08/india-twitter-online-censorship/; Varsha Bansal, *India's Government Wants Total Control of the Internet*, WIRED (Feb. 13, 2023), www.wired.com/story/indias-government-wants-total-control-of-the-internet/

6.5 In Defense of Section 230: Immunity for Content Moderation

users, and more broadly for free public discourse. But in fact, significantly altering the *other* aspect of Section 230 immunity – freedom to moderate content in good faith without fear of liability – would be even worse.

To understand why, it is important to recall that the internet is full of content that is "lawful but awful," meaning content that most people do not want to have to confront but that constitutes fully protected speech under the First Amendment to the US Constitution (though not, in many cases, in other countries). Examples of lawful-but-awful content under US law include almost all hate speech,[70] non-obscene pornography,[71] calls for political violence that do not fall within the extremely narrow definition of "incitement" adopted by the US Supreme Court[72] (including expressing praise and support for terrorist organizations such as ISIS/Islamic State and Hamas), and even deliberate lies that do not cause tangible and provable harm.[73] At first cut, eliminating platform immunity for good faith content moderation would open platforms up to lawsuits for blocking any of this content. Indeed, presumably the whole purpose of Section 230 reform is to prevent platforms from blocking political content they do not like. But hate speech and ISIS propaganda are no less "political viewpoints" than speech supporting Democrats or Republicans. As such, proposals such as those advanced by Senators Rubio and Hawley that condition Section 230 immunity on viewpoint-neutral content moderation[74] would, strikingly, give terrorists and hate groups a free pass on social media.

Another possibility is to amend Section 230 to distinguish between legal and illegal (i.e., constitutionally unprotected) content and to limit Section 230(c)(2)(A) immunity to content moderation of illegal content – the effect of which would be to make it financially risky for platforms to moderate legal content. But this will not work because, as Chapter 4 discusses in more detail, it is extraordinarily difficult for platforms to easily distinguish between legal and illegal, for two separate reasons. The first is that the law is often far from clear in defining unprotected content. And second, even when the law is clear (as with child pornography), it can be very difficult to determine which side of the line any particular piece of content falls on. This, indeed, is precisely why the drafters of Section 230 did not attempt to draw such lines, instead saying

---

[70] Matal v. Tam, 582 U.S. 218, 243–44 (2017) (plurality opinion); *ibid.* at 248–50 (Kennedy, J., concurring in part and concurring in the judgment); R.A.V. v. City of St. Paul, Minn., 505 U.S. 377, 391–92 (1992).

[71] United States v. Playboy Entertainment Group, Inc., 529 U.S. 803, 811 (2000).

[72] Under that definition, speech calling for violence falls outside the First Amendment only if it is "directed to inciting of producing imminent lawless action and is likely to produce such action." Brandenburg v. Ohio, 395 U.S. 444, 447 (1969).

[73] United States v. Alvarez, 567 U.S. 709 (2012).

[74] See *supra* n. 26–27.

explicitly that Section 230(c)(2)(A) immunity extended to content moderation of constitutionally protected content.

Moreover, an approach distinguishing legal and illegal content would do nothing to solve the "lawful but awful" problem. To do *that*, Section 230 would have to somehow draw a legally enforceable distinction between "good" and "bad" *legal* content, immunizing only content moderation of "bad" content. But again, it turns out that this is also a nonstarter.

For one thing, such a move may well violate the First Amendment. As explained in Chapter 4, the Supreme Court clearly held in the *NetChoice* cases that the First Amendment protects platforms' editorial rights to choose what content to carry and what content not to carry. This means that a direct government command to favor certain content – as Texas and Florida sought to impose – violates the First Amendment. But surely what the government cannot do directly, it also cannot do indirectly. And so, while there is no Supreme Court case that directly addresses this question, it seems likely that the Court would strike down a law, such as a gerrymandered version of Section 230(c)(2)(A), that legally incentivizes privately owned platforms to carry some government-favored viewpoints ("ISIS is terrible") while blocking government-disfavored viewpoints ("ISIS is great").

In addition, such a distinction is often impossible to make. Consider the problem of pornography. Presumably Section 230 reformers would want to permit platforms to block non-obscene pornography without fear of liability. But at the same time, surely not all nudity falls within this category, as illustrated by an episode in which Facebook first blocked, then unblocked, the iconic "Napalm Girl" photograph from the Vietnam War.[75] Drawing the line between pornography and valuable but explicit materials in a meaningful way has confounded courts for decades; which is why they do not try to draw such lines, and why Section 230 reformers will be unable to do so as well.

Or consider praise for political violence. Presumably reformers, especially conservative ones, would want to continue to permit platforms to block ISIS propaganda or praise for ISIS attacks, foreign and domestic. At the same time, presumably many conservatives would *not* want to immunize efforts to block praise for the January 6, 2021, incursion on the US Capitol, or calls for similar actions in the future. But imagine trying to draw *that* line in any coherent way. The reality is that distinguishing between content based on its social value in an objective, enforceable, and constitutional manner is well nigh impossible.

---

[75] Aarti Shahani, *With "Napalm Girl," Facebook Humans (Not Algorithms) Struggle to Be Editor*, NPR (Sept. 10, 2016, 11:12 PM), www.npr.org/sections/alltechconsidered/2016/09/10/493454256/with-napalm-girl-facebook-humans-not-algorithms-struggle-to-be-editor.

6.6 IN DEFENSE OF SECTION 230

Finally, it should be evident that as bad as repealing either specific provision of Section 230 would be, it would be worse if, as Presidents Trump and Biden proposed, we repealed Section 230 altogether. Under such a regime, platforms would be extremely reluctant to moderate any content because drawing lines between legal and illegal content is so difficult, and making the wrong decision (as they inevitably would do) creates serious financial risks. But on the other hand, failing to block content also creates risks. In a publisher-liability regime, the risks are so severe that platforms would need to block any content that could conceivably cross the line into illegality (meaning a potential source of liability). And even in a distributor-liability regime, the moment a platform was informed that particular content *might* be illegal, the same incentives apply.

So, without Section 230 in place, platforms both *cannot* block any content that might be legal and *must* block all content that could conceivably be illegal, to be safe. Obviously, doing both things at once is not possible, placing all platforms carrying third-party content between a rock and a hard place. Perhaps the very largest and wealthiest platforms (meaning Meta and Google/YouTube) could find a way to navigate these opposing risks, but for smaller platforms this would spell doom. And in truth, it is not clear that even the larger platforms could find a way through. Which would leave them with two ways forward: either block *all* third-party content and eliminate the "social" aspect of social media; or permit utterly anodyne third-party content that raises no risk of liability either way (lots of cat videos) but nothing else.

Either way, social media as the home of vibrant social and political dialogue would come to an end. And that is an outcome we should all be very, very wary of, involving as it does an inconceivable reversal in the democratization of public discourse that the internet has enabled. For that reason Section 230, mainly in its current form, must stay despite all of its weaknesses; the alternatives are much worse.

6.7 CODA: A FEW THOUGHTS ON ALGORITHMS

Moving forward, some of the most contentious and legally troubling issues surrounding social media will focus on the use of computer algorithms to recommend or amplify certain content (which means by implication not amplifying other content). As noted in Chapter 4, in the *NetChoice* litigation the Supreme Court strongly suggested that the use of algorithms to recommend and amplify favored content, as well as to deamplify or block other content, is itself an exercise of editorial rights protected by the First Amendment.[76] But the exact scope of that First Amendment protection remains quite unclear – in her concurring opinion, Justice Barrett (who provided the crucial fifth vote for the relevant parts of the majority opinion) suggested that such protection *might* not apply "if a platform's algorithm just presents automatically to each user whatever the algorithm thinks the user will like" (i.e., if the algorithm is not enforcing substantive community standards chosen by the platform).[77] She also suggested that protection might be denied if platforms turn over enforcement of their content standards (whatever they are) to AI.[78] Finally, she also raised questions about protection for content moderation decisions made under the influence of foreign owners of platforms – an obvious allusion to ongoing controversies over TikTok's Chinese ownership.[79] So it remains important whether Section 230, which unlike the First Amendment does not limit the scope of the immunity it grants, applies to algorithmic (and eventually AI-driven) recommendations and amplification.

To date, as noted earlier, this issue has not been addressed by the US Supreme Court, but the lower courts have tended to treat algorithmic recommendations as an aspect of the "publication" process protected by Section 230(c)(1).[80] However, in the important Ninth Circuit *Gonzalez* decision regarding platform liability for terrorist acts (which later made its way to the Supreme Court), two of the three judges on the panel that decided the case raised doubts about applying Section 230 to recommendation algorithms (albeit one of the two voted for immunity on the grounds that she was bound by precedent);[81] and in a similar case in the Second Circuit, one of the three judges disagreed with the majority on the immunity point.[82] The issue thus remains very much a point of contention among judges, and also among commentators.

---

[76] Moody v. NetChoice, LLC, 144 S. Ct. 2383, 2403–06 (2024).; *see also ibid.* at 2410 (Barrett, J., concurring).
[77] *Ibid.* at 2410 (Barrett, J., concurring).
[78] *Ibid.*
[79] *Ibid.*
[80] Dryoff v. Ultimate Software Grp., Inc. 934 F.3d 1063, 1098 (9th Cir. 2019); Force v. Facebook, Inc., 934 F.3d 53, 64–72 (2nd Cir. 2019); Gonzalez v. Google LLC, 2 F.4th 871, 894–97 (9th Cir. 2021).
[81] *Gonzalez*, 2 F.4th at 912–18 (Berzon, J., concurring); *ibid.* at 920–21 (Gould, J., concurring in part and dissenting in part).
[82] *Force*, 934 F.3d at 80–84 (Katzmann, C.J., concurring in part and dissenting in part). In a recent decision, the Third Circuit held that in light of the Supreme Court's reasoning in the *NetChoice* cases the output of recommendation algorithms should be considered a platform's own speech, and so outside of Section 230 immunity. Anderson v. TikTok, Inc., 116 F.4th 180, 183-84 (3rd Cir. 2024).

The truth is that the strictly correct "legal" answer is to this question is almost impossible to resolve because when Section 230 was adopted by Congress in 1996 nothing like modern social media platforms, much less recommendation algorithms, existed. And while a fairly straightforward analogy can be drawn (based on plain language) between modern platforms and the message boards and discussion forums of 1996, the same is simply not true of algorithms. So, to ask what Congress "intended" in 1996 regarding recommendation algorithms is nonsensical. Furthermore, a purely linguistic analysis of Section 230 is also indeterminate. On the one hand, deciding what content should be emphasized on a platform (like what story goes on the front page of a newspaper) is an intrinsic part of the process of hosting third-party content protected by Section 230(c)(1); but on the other hand, arguably making recommendations goes beyond merely hosting "any information provided by another information content provider," the thing that Section 230 was designed to protect. As such, the idea that this disagreement can be clearly resolved using narrow legal tools of statutory interpretation is wishful thinking.

So, I would turn the issue around and ask, *should* Section 230 be read to protect algorithmic recommendations – and concomitantly, if courts conclude it does not provide such protection, should Congress amend Section 230 to add such protections? I think that the answer is clear – it should, and Congress should (what Congress actually *would* do, in its current state of dysfunction, is of course a separate question).

The reason for this is simple: In today's world, given the sheer scale of social media platforms, recommendations are an absolutely essential element of running platforms for third-party content, if they are to function at all. The alternative, after all, is to serve up content in either random or chronological order, which would make most feeds useless, especially on open-ended platforms like YouTube and Twitter/X, but also on platforms like Facebook that serve up a combination of posts by friends and other, more generalized content. Indeed, it is precisely because of this that recommendation and amplification choices are central to "publishing" third-party content on a social media platform, just as choosing what stories to run on the front page is an essential element of publishing a newspaper. Or as Tarleton Gillespie put it, content moderation "is, in many ways, *the* commodity that platforms offer."[83]

Now consider what Congress intended to accomplish in creating Section 230 immunity. It intended to permit platforms to serve up third-party content without fear of liability *and* to make sure that platforms did not lose that immunity by making choices about what content to carry (i.e., to engage in content

---

[83] TARLETON GILLESPIE, CUSTODIANS OF THE INTERNET 13 (2018).

moderation). Remember in this regard that Section 230 was a response to judicial decisions imposing publisher liability on platforms who engaged in content moderation. In those early days of the internet, the relevant content moderation consisted only of blocking harmful content, since, given low volumes of users and content (remember, we are talking about message boards and discussion forums), that was all that was required. Today, however, recommendation and amplification decisions are as essential an element of running a platform for third-party content as is blocking harmful content, given exponentially higher volumes of users and content. Without incorporating such a function, platforms would serve up mainly useless and random garbage, from the point of view of users. Publication of third-party content, in other words, *requires* making choices about what content to amplify and to which users to amplify it.

Furthermore, precisely because of the volume of content and users, algorithms are the only feasible way to implement those decisions. It is simply impossible to imagine human beings making the millions of decisions that social media algorithms constantly make, twenty-four hours a day, across the world, regarding what content to recommend to each individual user. So again, if we wish to accomplish Congress's goal of permitting effective platforms for third-party content to thrive, we must protect not only their right to make recommendations but also their ability to use algorithms to make and implement those recommendation and amplification decisions.

Finally, for practical purposes Section 230 immunity is essential if platforms are going to be able to make and implement those algorithmic choices. Just as it is practically impossible for platforms to ensure that all third-party content they carry is legal and does not cause harm, so too there is no way to ensure that their algorithms will never end up directing users to harmful content (whether harmful to themselves, such as content encouraging self-harm, or in the terrorism cases harmful to innocent third parties). Again, the volume of recommendations is simply too large to be perfectly policed. As such, without immunity, platforms would be paralyzed in their ability to run recommendation algorithms if they faced potential liability for every choice – precisely the result that Section 230 seeks to avoid.

None of which is to say that Section 230 should be read to automatically immunize *all* algorithmic choices. Certainly if a platform *deliberately* designed their algorithms to serve up illegal or harmful content, that would pose a very different situation – and there is no doubt that there exist some niche platforms who are conscious bad actors and who should not be able to shield their deliberate choices through Section 230. In fact, that sort of design choice would seem to fall within the *Lemmon* exception to Section 230 immunity.

But to eliminate any doubt, it is probably a good idea, as Professors Danielle Keats Citron and Mary Anne Frank have proposed, to amend Section 230 to make this point clear.[84] But for most mainstream platforms, so long as they can demonstrate that their algorithms were designed based on neutral criteria and were not intended to favor illegal or harmful content (even if, on occasion, they end up doing so), Section 230 should protect their choices.

Finally, what about AI? Recall that in *NetChoice*, Justice Barrett suggested that turning over content moderation to AI might argue against First Amendment protection, since no human being is any longer making choices about what content to permit/block and favor/disfavor (unlike with traditional algorithms, whose creation involves such human choices). I frankly am doubtful if Justice Barrett's First Amendment doubts are justified, since the First Amendment protects *speech*, not *speakers*.[85] But regardless of First Amendment questions, I think it would be utterly strange to suggest that Section 230 immunities rely on the technology being used to run a platform. Nothing in the text of the statute suggests such a limitation. Furthermore, if Section 230 immunity had been tied to specific technology, it would have quickly become obsolete as the message boards and discussion forums of the 1990s evolved into the modern internet. Tying such protections (or for that matter regulations – more on this in Chapter 8) to specific technologies is a terrible policy choice, given how quickly internet technology changes. Section 230 was originally, and wisely, written in much broader and more flexible terms, and we should continue to read it in that light to protect *all* new technologies that facilitate platforms for third-party content.

---

[84] Citron and Franks, *supra* n. 31, at 70–71.
[85] I would note that this view is supported by the text of the First Amendment, which simply says "Congress shall make no law … abridging the freedom of speech," without regard to the source of that speech. My position in this regard is also rooted in a broader view that the Bill of Rights as a whole was designed not to protect the rights of individuals but rather to provide structural protections against government overreach. *See* ASHUTOSH BHAGWAT, THE MYTH OF RIGHTS (2010).

7

Privacy, Big Data, and Free Speech

The collection and processing of data is a necessary and inevitable aspect of operating a social media platform. Leaving aside business models (on which more later), it is simply impossible to run a platform without access to user data. Given the sheer volume of content on any popular platform (e.g., Facebook, Instagram, Twitter/X, YouTube, TikTok), platform operators have to make constant choices about what content to serve up or recommend to users. And unless they make those choices randomly (a truly horrific thought), those choices are necessarily made for users based on what the platform knows about individual users' interests, preferences, and life experiences (i.e., based on user data). In other words, the collection, storage, and processing of user data is an integral part of how platforms create a good – indeed, even tolerable – user experience. For that reason, no serious commentator or regulator proposes banning the collection and processing of user data.

In addition, for most social media platforms, their current business model necessarily requires the collection and processing of data. The reason for this, as noted in Chapter 3, is that for the major platforms, targeted advertising is their primary source of revenue. Take Meta, the owner of Facebook and Instagram. In required regulatory filings with the US Securities and Exchange Commission, Meta reported revenue of almost $135 billion in 2023; and as Meta itself acknowledges, "[s]ubstantially all of our revenue is currently generated from advertising on Facebook and Instagram" (reading the fiscal report suggests that 99 percent of Meta revenues are ad-based).[1] While precise comparative numbers are difficult to obtain regarding Twitter/X (because Twitter/X is no longer publicly traded, after Elon Musk's purchase of the company), press reports suggest that 70–75 percent of Twitter/X's 2023 revenue of

---

[1] *Form 10-K, Meta Platforms, Inc.* 60–61 (2024), https://d18rn0p25nwr6d.cloudfront.net/CIK-0001326801/c7318154-f6ae-4866-89fa-f0c589f2ee3d.pdf.

approximately $3.4 billion was from advertising sales. And, it should be noted, advertising revenues at Twitter/X appear to have declined around 40 percent from 2022 to 2023, in the wake of Musk's takeover.[2] Even YouTube, which earns substantial revenues from subscription services such as YouTube Music, YouTube Premium, and YouTube TV, earned over twice as much ($31.5 billion)[3] from ad sales in 2023 than it earned from subscription services in which users pay for content ($15 billion).[4] And finally, while TikTok's comparable revenue numbers are hard to nail down (because TikTok is privately owned by ByteDance, a Chinese company), analysts appear to agree that the vast majority of TikTok's approximately $16 billion in US revenue in 2023 was derived from advertising.[5]

All of which is to say that targeted advertising is the revenue mainstay of the social media business, and a highly profitable mainstay at that. But effective targeted advertising of course requires user data. Just as user data tells platforms what content to serve up to individual users, so too the same data allows them to predict which advertisements are going to be most enticing to individual users, given their consumer preferences. This in turn means that user data permits the platform to match potential advertisers to their most potentially lucrative audience – something that is not possible to the same extent with traditional print and broadcast advertising. The enormous numbers quoted on the previous paragraph reflect this simple fact – the product that platforms sell to advertisers is extraordinarily valuable.

On the flip side, restricting the collection and/or use of data for targeted advertising has potentially perverse effects. The less user data that platforms have access to, the less precise their targeting, and so the less valuable the online advertising they sell is to advertisers – a point that Meta itself acknowledges in its regulatory filings.[6] But given that the costs of operating a social media platform are largely fixed, if platforms have to charge less for individual ads (because they provide less value to the ad buyer), they necessarily will

---

[2] Ashley Belanger, *Elon Musk's X Ad Revenue Reportedly Fell $1.5B This Year Amid Boycotts*, ARSTECHNICA (Dec. 13, 2023), https://arstechnica.com/tech-policy/2023/12/stop-comparing-xs-dismal-ad-sales-to-twitters-past-success-x-exec-says/.

[3] *Form 10-K, Alphabet, Inc.* 35 (2024), https://abc.xyz/assets/43/44/675b83d7455885c4615d848d52a4/goog-10-k-2023.pdf.

[4] Todd Spangler, *YouTube and Google Subscription Services Hit $15 Billion in 2023 Revenue*, VARIETY (Jan. 30, 2024), https://variety.com/2024/digital/news/youtube-google-subscription-services-annual-revenue-1235892210/.

[5] *TikTok's US Revenues Hit $16bn as Washington Threatens Ban*, FINANCIAL TIMES (March 15, 2024), www.ft.com/content/275bd036-8bc2-4308-a5c9-d288325b91a9.

[6] *Form 10-K, Meta Platforms, Inc, supra* n. 1, at 61–62.

have to sell a greater volume of advertising. But that, of course, degrades the quality of the service the platforms are providing, and so the user experience.

Finally, if we prohibited targeted advertising altogether, as the European Union (EU) has done with respect to minors under the age of eighteen in its recent Digital Services Act (DSA),[7] this realistically leaves only one business model open to platforms, which is to charge users for their services (after all, *someone* has to pay for those servers and coders and content moderators). But in fact, common sense suggests that paying for services is *not* what most users want.

Until recently, that this was the case was mainly speculation, albeit speculation consistent with common knowledge of human nature. But there is now an ongoing empirical experiment regarding whether users would rather watch advertising than pay for their social media accounts. In November of 2023, in response to increasingly strict EU regulations of data practices (including in the DSA and in its companion the Digital Markets Act), Meta began to offer, only in Europe, a paid, ad-free subscription to Facebook or Instagram. The price was €9.99 per month for a basic subscription, or €12.99 to use the Apple or Android App[8] (which at the August 2024 exchange rate is about $10.90 and $14.10). Furthermore, in response to complaints from European regulators, Meta later offered to halve the price for these services.[9] As of this writing (fall 2024), good data is not yet available about how many Europeans have switched to the ad-free model, but that no doubt will change. However, in the summer of 2024 European regulators (somewhat strangely) formally charged that this paid service option itself violated European law,[10] suggesting that the regulators themselves do not see even a fairly cheap monthly fee as an alternative to Meta's current advertising/user-data-based model.

So, the collection and processing of user data by social media platforms is inevitable, and in some sense desirable. But at the same time, as discussed in detail in Chapter 3, Big Data creates some serious social problems and

---

[7] *Regulation (EU) 2022/2065 of the European Parliament and of the Council of 19 October 2022 (Digital Services Act)* Art. 28(2), https://eur-lex.europa.eu/eli/reg/2022/2065/oj; European Commission, Directorate-General for Communications Networks, Content and Technology, *The Digital Services Act (DSA) Explained – Measures to Protect Children and Young People Online* (2023), https://data.europa.eu/doi/10.2759/576008.
[8] Facebook Help Center, *Subscription for No Ads*, www.facebook.com/help/262038446684066.
[9] Andrew Hutchinson, *Meta Offers to Halve the Price of Its Ad-Free Subscription Package in the EU*, SOCIAL MEDIA TODAY (March 19, 2024), www.socialmediatoday.com/news/meta-offers-to-halve-the-price-ad-free-subscription-package-in-eu/710782/.
[10] Kelvin Chan, *European Union Says Meta Breaking Digital Rules with Paid Ad-Free Option for Facebook and Instagram*, PBS NEWS (July 1, 2024), www.pbs.org/newshour/world/european-union-says-meta-breaking-digital-rules-with-paid-ad-free-option-for-facebook-and-instagram.

concerns which, unlike many of the overblown fears noted in Chapters 1 and 2, appear to have a solid empirical foundation. And therein lies the conundrum that this chapter examines: We have good reasons to regulate social media platforms' data practices, but such regulation itself has the potential to harm not only the platforms but also their users and society at large. And, as we shall see, data privacy also sometimes raises serious free speech concerns. How to resolve these tensions is extremely difficult to figure out; but it is a problem that cannot be avoided.

7.1 DATA PRIVACY IN ACTION: THE GENERAL DATA PROTECTION REGULATION (GDPR) AND CALIFORNIA CONSUMER PRIVACY ACT (CCPA)

Given the many legitimate and serious privacy concerns raised by the day-to-day operations of social media platforms, it is unsurprising that many jurisdictions (though not the US Congress) have adopted privacy regulations directed at technology companies, including social media. Most importantly, long before the EU enacted the DSA, in May 2018 the EU's GDPR came into effect.[11] As Professors Meg Leta Jones and Margot Kaminski discuss, while the GDPR has been described in the United States as a law focused on consumer consent, this is in fact not entirely accurate.[12] Rather than being a traditional data privacy law on the American model (which does typically focus primarily on consent), the GDPR regulates *data* and data processing.[13]

The core of the GDPR, contained in Article 6, is a rule providing that holders of personal data may process it *only* for one of six listed reasons – all other processing is illegal.[14] And this restriction applies to all holders of data, not just the original collector or the firm with which the subject of the data has a relationship (contractual or otherwise).[15] Furthermore, while consent is indeed the first justification for data processing listed in Article 6, it is far from the only one. To the contrary, Jones and Kaminski argue that the sixth justification – that the "processing is necessary for the purposes of the legitimate interests pursued by the controller or by a third party"[16] – is the one that most

---

[11] General Data Protection Regulation 2016/679, 2016 O.J. (L 119), https://gdpr-info.eu/ (henceforth "GDPR").
[12] Meg Leta Jones and Margot E. Kaminski, *An American's Guide to the GDPR*, 98 DENVER L. REV. 93, 95 (2021).
[13] *Ibid.* at 106–08.
[14] GDPR, *supra* note 11, Art. 6(1); Jones and Kaminski, *supra* note 12, at 108.
[15] Jones and Kaminski, *supra* note 12, at 107.
[16] GDPR, *supra* note 11, Art. 6(1)(f).

firms are likely to rely upon, at least in part because consent requirements in the GDPR are far more onerous than under the typical American privacy law.[17] Finally, while the "legitimate interests" provision would appear to permit extensive data processing by tech firms in the course of selling advertising or other business processes, it is important to note that the ability to process data under this justification may be "overridden by the interests of fundamental rights and freedoms of the data subject,"[18] creating substantial uncertainty and leaving lots of scope for regulatory restrictions on data processing.

In addition to restricting data processing, the GDPR also grants important rights to the individual subjects of personal data. While a full description of those rights is not possible here, important elements include extensive rights of detailed notification regarding data collection, storage, and processing;[19] a right to access stored and/or processed data;[20] a right to correct inaccurate data;[21] and a right to object to continued processing of data by government entities or private entities under the "legitimate interest" justification discussed earlier, though, importantly, the right to object is *not* absolute and can be outweighed by "compelling legitimate grounds for the processing."[22] Most famously, the GDPR also codifies the "right to be forgotten,"[23] which had been recognized earlier by the Court of Justice of the European Union (CJEU), the top court in the EU, in a case called *Google Spain*.[24] This provision effectively permits data subjects to demand the erasure of data no longer needed for processing – though as with many GDPR "rights," this one is limited and can be overridden by, inter alia, "exercising the freedom of expression and information."[25]

There is little doubt that the GDPR, through these and many other provisions, establishes one of the most comprehensive data regulation regimes in the world. And because of the huge size of the European market, there are strong indications that firms, including social media platforms, subject to the GDPR have chosen to follow its basic provisions worldwide simply to

---

[17] See Jones and Kaminski, *supra* note 12, at 108–09.
[18] GDPR, *supra* note 11, Art. 6(1)(f).
[19] Ibid. Arts. 13, 14.
[20] Ibid. Art. 15.
[21] Ibid. Art. 16.
[22] Ibid. Art. 21.
[23] Ibid. Art. 17.
[24] Case C-131/12, Google Spain SL v. Agencia Española de Protección de Datos, 2014 E.C.R. 317 ("*Google Spain*"). For an excellent discussion of the *Google Spain* decision and its problems, see Robert C. Post, *Data Privacy and Dignitary Privacy: Google Spain, the Right to Be Forgotten, and the Construction of the Public Sphere*, 67 DUKE L.J. 981 (2018).
[25] GDPR, *supra* note 11, Art. 17(3)(a).

avoid the costs of following diverse rules – the so-called Brussels Effect.[26] The GDPR also creates important personal rights that, if invoked, could return substantial power to individual data subjects. There is no question that these provisions, in combination, have forced firms to change their data practices in significant ways, most importantly by obtaining more frequent and prominent user consent. Furthermore, as a result of a huge GDPR-based fine imposed on Meta in 2023, the GDPR is likely to impact firms' ability to engage in cross-border data transfers.[27] It should be noted, however, that there is absolutely no evidence that the GDPR has substantially restricted or interfered with the fundamental operations and data practices of the major tech companies since it became effective in May of 2018.

Aside from the GDPR, probably the most important privacy protection statute of recent years is the CCPA, which was inspired by the GDPR though it is more limited in scope. The CCPA was first enacted in 2018, with an effective date of January 1, 2020; but in 2020 California voters enacted the California Privacy Rights Act (CPRA), which significantly amended the CCPA and created the CCPA in its current form.[28] The original CCPA's primary provisions give California consumers the right to request information about a firm's data collection, retention, and transfer practices,[29] a qualified right to have personal data deleted,[30] and a right to opt out of the sale of personal information.[31] The CPRA added to this a right to have data holders correct inaccurate data,[32] and a right to limit the use and disclosure of especially sensitive data such as financial information, geolocation data, and genetic data.[33] Since the adoption of the CCPA, nineteen other states (as of summer 2024) have also adopted data privacy laws, many of which are modeled on the CCPA and contain many of the same restrictions.[34]

Even as amended, the CCPA (and its imitators) do not contain the sorts of broad restrictions on data processing, or extensive consumer rights, contained

---

[26] ANU BRADFORD, THE BRUSSELS EFFECT: HOW THE EUROPEAN UNION RULES THE WORLD (2021).

[27] Adam Satariano, *Meta Fined $1.3 Billion for Violating E.U. Data Privacy Rules*, N.Y. TIMES (May 22, 2023), www.nytimes.com/2023/05/22/business/meta-facebook-eu-privacy-fine.html.

[28] CAL. CIV. CODE §§ 1798.100–178.99-100. For a good, short summary of the CCPA, *see California Consumer Privacy Act (CCPA)*, Office of the Attorney General, State of California Department of Justice, https://oag.ca.gov/privacy/ccpa#.

[29] CAL. CIV. CODE §§ 1798.110, 1798.115.

[30] CAL. CIV. CODE § 1798.105.

[31] CAL. CIV. CODE § 1798.120.

[32] CAL. CIV. CODE § 1798.106.

[33] CAL. CIV. CODE § 1798.121. Sensitive data is defined in CAL. CIV. CODE § 1798.140(ae).

[34] *UD Data Privacy Guide*, WHITE & CASE (July 2, 2024), www.whitecase.com/insight-our-thinking/us-data-privacy-guide.

in the GDPR. But these laws, the CCPA most prominently (because of California's sheer size and the fact that it is home to most of the major American tech giants), have forced firms, including social media platforms, to provide consumers with access to their data and a means to delete or correct it.[35] And by incorporating a right to have data deleted, the CCPA and its progeny have arguably imported into the United States a version, albeit a watered down one, of the EU's "right to be forgotten."

7.2 TWO KINDS OF PRIVACY

Before getting into the merits of the GDPR, CCPA, and their brethren, it is useful to take a step back and consider what exactly it is that these laws are trying to accomplish. The obvious answer is that they seek to protect the privacy of individuals. But what exactly is "privacy?" In a deeply insightful article about the CJEU's *Google Spain* decision, which as noted earlier first created a Europe-wide right to be forgotten (which was later incorporated into the GDPR), Yale law professor (and former dean) Robert Post convincingly argues that the concept of privacy is widely misunderstood. In particular, he argues that in *Google Spain* the CJEU conflated two distinct forms of privacy.[36] And he further demonstrates that the CJEU's mistake, which has been carried over into Article 17 of the GDPR, raises serious questions about the scope and legitimacy of the right to be forgotten.

To understand Post's argument, one must deconstruct it a bit. First, let us consider the two forms of privacy he identifies. One form of privacy, the primary concern of the GDPR as well as its predecessor law that was invoked in *Google Spain*, is a right to control how one's personal data is stored and processed by bureaucratic entitles that collect such data, including large corporations such as Google and the major social media platforms. This particular kind of privacy does not have much to do with the *kind* of personal data being stored – it applies equally to innocuous information, such as one's phone number, and highly personal information like medical records. The primary goal in protecting this form of privacy, which we might call "data privacy," is an instrumental one, of ensuring that bureaucratic entities do not cumulate large hoards of data about individuals without need or reason.[37]

The other form of privacy Post identifies is entirely different. It is a deeply personal interest on the part of human beings in not having intensely personal

---

[35] *See, e.g., How Can You Delete Your Information?*, FACEBOOK PRIVACY CENTER, www.facebook.com/privacy/dialog/delete-your-information/.
[36] Post, *supra* n. 24.
[37] *Ibid.* at 993–94, 1000–01.

information disclosed to the world. This form of privacy is dignitary in nature and turns entirely on the form of "data" at issue. Indeed, the deep question raised by this form of privacy, which we can call "dignitary privacy," is what kinds of things *are* so deeply personal that it is offensive and should be unlawful to publicly disclose such facts (which we presume are true) about other people. Dignitary privacy, it should be noted, is *not* the focus of modern data privacy statutes but rather is protected by other forms of law, including in the United States primarily by tort law (in particular, the tort of public disclosure of private fact).[38]

It is difficult in this limited space to do full justice to Post's subtle argument, but in short, he argues that in *Google Spain* the CJEU failed to recognize the existence of these two distinct forms of privacy and so ended up with an incoherent analysis. The *Google Spain* case was brought by a Spanish lawyer who was tied to an embarrassing financial episode many years in the past, the fact of which appeared in a Spanish newspaper. He claimed that one of the first links that appeared in a Google search of his name was to the online archives of that newspaper (which had been digitalized well after the original events). This, he said, caused him severe reputational harm, even though given the passage of time the original episode was now irrelevant. The CJEU accepted the lawyer's argument that linking to this archive violated EU privacy laws, because it constituted the processing of personal data in a way that was "irrelevant or no longer relevant." Therefore, the Court held, Google had a legal obligation to block links to the newspaper archive when the lawyer's name was searched. Notably, however, the Court held that the Spanish newspaper itself was *not* required to remove the relevant content from its online archive.[39]

Post convincingly argues that this reasoning is fundamentally flawed. The basic problem was that the main legal provisions that the CJEU invoked to justify its result was the GDPR's legal predecessor, which like the GDPR focused on data privacy, *not* dignitary privacy. As a result, the Court concluded that Google's legal error was in processing *any* out-of-date personal data in this way, regardless of whether it was highly private or embarrassing.[40] But this is obviously nonsense. Surely the *Google Spain* plaintiff would not have complained if a search of his name linked to a thirty-year-old marriage notice, or to an article about his high school athletic prowess. It was the *embarrassing* nature of the information that was crucial to his case, a point the Court simply ignored or missed.

---

[38] *Ibid.* at 991 and n.36.
[39] *Ibid.* at 995–98.
[40] *Ibid.* at 997–98 (citing *Google Spain*, para. 94).

More fundamentally, Post argues that the CJEU made a categorical error. Its reasoning regarding data privacy would make sense as applied to a database held by, say, a grocery store tracking customer purchases. It might even make sense as applied to Google's own collection, storage, and processing of data about its users (mainly for the purpose of selling targeted advertising). But to apply it to Google's search feature makes no sense. The whole purpose and very function of a search engine is to link to any and all information – which means that such "processing" can *never* be "irrelevant or no longer relevant." More profoundly, Post argues that in the modern world, Google plays a role similar to that played by newspapers in creating a public sphere of information within which public opinion can form, and so democratic politics can operate. And given that fact, it was particularly nonsensical for the CJEU to order Google to stop linking to the relevant newspaper article but permit the newspaper itself to keep the article accessible to the public – because after all, it was the newspaper that was hosting the offending content, not Google.[41]

None of which is to say, and Post does not claim, that disclosure of embarrassing and out-of-date facts can never pose privacy concerns. It certainly might, and while under US law it is almost impossible to win a tort claim under circumstances such as those in *Google Spain* because of the First Amendment, the same need not be true in Europe. But what Post is saying is that if such privacy concerns are to be addressed, it was profoundly mistaken to focus on Google rather than the underlying newspaper archive.

What is the implication of these arguments for social media platforms? To begin with, a sharp distinction needs to be made (as the CJEU failed to do) between such platforms' collection and processing of their users' data, and their hosting functions in disseminating user posts which might well contain personal data/information. The former activities, collecting user data and using it to engage in targeted advertising, fall squarely within the world of data privacy, and so are appropriate subjects of laws such as the GDPR and CCPA (which is not to say that those laws do not have their own issues, on which more later). But when platforms host user content, very different considerations arise.

This is because, even more than search engines like Google, modern social media platforms are the locus of public discourse and so the locus within which public opinion is formed. Therefore, for the same reasons that applying data privacy principles to a Google search is incoherent, so even more so with social media platforms in their hosting capacity. Such platforms are about facilitating *discourse*, and it is deeply problematic for any governmental actors,

---

[41] Ibid. at 1063.

whether EU regulators or US judges, to impose significant restraints on the subjects of that discourse, or to force platforms to police it for them. There are surely times when individual posters can be held liable for invasions of dignitary privacy – posting nonconsensual pornography being an obvious example. It may even make sense, as discussed in the next chapter, to narrow Section 230 slightly to impose obligations on platforms to police such awful content, in extreme and well-defined circumstances. But imposing wholesale obligations on platforms to protect privacy on their platforms makes little sense, even in the face of strong and legitimate dignitary privacy interests.

7.3 DATA PRIVACY AND PLATFORMS

Let us now consider the core of the privacy-based attacks on social media, which target not the hosting function but the tendency of social media companies to collect, store, and process enormous amounts of user data. To begin with, it should be reiterated that such data practices lie at the heart of the business models of most modern platforms. They are, in essence, what permits the platforms both to provide services at all and to provide them without charging users. Any data regulation that significantly interferes with those activities or business models almost certainly does more harm than good and is also likely to prove extremely unpopular with the social media-using public (which is to say, most of the public). As a consequence, even under the GDPR and CCPA, social media platforms continue to engage in their core data processing, either under consent theories or under the GDPR's "legitimate interest" exception discussed earlier.

On the other hand, there is no question that laws like the GDPR and CCPA have forced firms, including social media platforms, to take substantial steps to ensure transparency and data integrity. In most respects, this is undoubtedly a positive outcome. But it too has a significant downside: Such data protection steps are expensive. Obviously, few will shed tears over behemoths such as Facebook/Meta and YouTube/Google having to expend some of their seemingly limitless funds on data protection. It must be recognized, however, that expensive regulatory obligations inevitably act as barriers to entry, preventing startups and small firms from entering into these markets because they cannot afford the same levels of protections. And yet, aside from privacy, one of the prime complaints about the tech giants is their market power. Adopting regulatory regimes that accentuate that market power seems questionable policy.

One way to mitigate this concern might be to exempt small firms from data protection rules; but that is also somewhat problematic. For one thing, insofar as avoiding data regulation would reduce smaller platforms' costs, it might permit them to provide a more seamless experience. But if so, this would have the perverse effect of incentivizing consumers to migrate to platforms that do not protect their data. And furthermore, regimes that exempt small actors from burdensome regulations have the (also perverse) consequence of discouraging them from growing beyond a certain point. But of course that also helps to entrench incumbent market power. Smaller platforms are less valuable to users than large platforms because the latter give access to larger audiences, a phenomenon called "network effects" in the economic literature.[42]

None of which is to say that protections for data privacy are a mistake. They clearly are not, and given the emerging consensus about the need for data protection (demonstrated by extensive regulatory steps taken around the United States and the world), we can expect regulatory initiatives to continue. But it is to emphasize that all regulation, even such seemingly innocuous steps as data transparency and protection rules, comes with cost. And sometimes regulation can have unexpected and potentially severe unintended consequences, as illustrated by a CJEU decision aggressively reading the GDPR to impose strict limits on data transfers between the EU and the United States, which potentially puts at risk $7.1 *trillion* dollars of transatlantic economic interactions.[43]

What this suggests is that, as with all regulatory initiatives in the complex and fraught space of new technologies, it is crucial that regulators remember to adopt a posture of humility. One aspect of the GDPR that is of particular concern in this respect is its flat ban (in Article 6) on all data processing, except for six specified reasons. Admittedly, many of the reasons are stated in relatively broad terms (notably the exception for pursuing the "legitimate interests" of the data processor), but there is still a degree of arrogance in assuming that regulators can predict the universe of possible, legitimate uses of data. Combine this with the fact that the GDPR explicitly states that the right to engage in data processing to pursue "legitimate interests" can be "overridden by the interests or fundamental rights and freedoms of the data subject," without specifying what those "rights and freedoms" are,[44] and one realizes that the GDPR introduces an enormous amount of uncertainty regarding permissibility of data processing. In a world of rapidly changing technology,

---

[42] *What Is the Network Effect?*, WHARTON ONLINE, WHARTON SCHOOL OF BUSINESS, UNIVERSITY OF PENNSYLVANIA (Jan. 17, 2023), https://online.wharton.upenn.edu/blog/what-is-the-network-effect/.

[43] Monika Zalnieriute, *Data Transfers after Schrems II: The EU-US Disagreements over Data Privacy and national Security*, 55 VAND. J. TRANSNAT'L L. 1 (2022).

[44] GDPR, *supra* note 11, Art. 6(1)(f).

including notably the extraordinary recent growth of artificial intelligence, this seems precisely the wrong way to engage in regulation.

7.4 DATA IS SPEECH

Beyond the rather complex and technical issues discussed earlier, moreover, data regulations raise a more fundamental concern that should not be lost sight of. Restrictions on the use and dissemination of data are, in practice, restrictions on speech. In a law review article published some years ago, law professor Jane Bambauer posed the question, "is data speech?"[45] And her unequivocal conclusion was "yes," that data is indeed speech. Furthermore, in its leading opinion addressing regulation of data, a six-Justice majority of the US Supreme Court strongly endorsed (albeit in nonbinding language) the proposition that "information [i.e., data] is speech."[46] What this means is that at least in the United States, laws and regulations aimed at data practices implicate the First Amendment. What practical limitations does this impose on the ability of states (and eventually, presumably, Congress) to adopt data privacy legislation?

One implication seems clear: It would almost certainly be unconstitutional for the United States or any individual US state to adopt the strong form of a "right to be forgotten" established in the EU in the *Google Spain* case and the GDPR. The reason is that enforcement of the right to be forgotten is, in plain English, a direct restriction on speech. It forbids someone – in *Google Spain*, Google – from sharing information (i.e., speaking) because the information at issue is private, and so its disclosure causes dignitary harm. In the EU, with its relatively weak protections for speech vis-à-vis privacy and other social interests, this may be permissible (though it should be noted that even the GDPR recognizes that free speech principles will sometimes trump the right to be forgotten[47]). But in the United States, under the First Amendment as interpreted by the US Supreme Court, it probably is not.

Admittedly, the Court has never adopted a definitive rule regarding how to reconcile free speech and privacy concerns; but in a series of cases from the 1970s and 1980s, culminating in a decision from 2001 involving information obtained via wiretapping, the Court has consistently held that the right of the

---

[45] Jane Bambauer, *Is Data Speech?*, 66 STAN. L. REV. 57 (2014).
[46] Sorrell v. IMS Health, Inc., 564 U.S. 552, 570 (2011). I have argued elsewhere that this is clearly correct analysis under current law. Ashutosh Bhagwat, Sorrell v. IMS Health: *Details, Detailing and the Death of Privacy*, 36 VERMONT L. REV. 855, 867 (2012).
[47] GDPR, *supra* note 11, Art. 17(3)(a).

press to publish private information trumps the privacy rights of individuals.[48] And while the US Supreme Court has never directly ruled on facts analogous to *Google Spain*, the California Supreme Court has. In a case from 2004 in which an individual sued for invasion of privacy when a television documentary disclosed his thirteen-year-old criminal conviction, that court held, relying on the US Supreme Court cases just mentioned, that the First Amendment flatly prohibited imposing liability for publishing information available in public records.[49] And notably, in doing so the California court overruled a previous decision, predating the key Supreme Court cases, permitting an invasion of privacy claim on similar facts.[50]

Aside from the right to be forgotten, the limitations that the First Amendment places on privacy regulation are less clear. It has been generally assumed that existing, pre-internet laws prohibiting the disclosure of sensitive information such as medical or financial records must be constitutional, even though such laws literally restrict "speech" based on its content (something which in other situations is presumptively unconstitutional). It must be admitted, however, that precisely why, as a technical legal matter, this is so remains unresolved. But nonetheless it seems likely that future courts will uphold laws prohibiting tech companies, including social media platforms, from disclosing user data to the public. Such data may not be as sensitive as, say, medical records, but data regarding what one posts, what one searches, etc., are surely still private matters.

It should be emphasized, however, that while as a predictive matter it is likely that courts will uphold prohibitions on personal data disclosure, First Amendment law in this area remains extremely unsettled. As such, the actual fate of laws regulating data disclosure remains uncertain. Furthermore, even if courts generally uphold such laws by analogy to historical privacy legislation, much more difficult questions arise when the disclosures being prohibited or punished involve information about public figures, especially public officials and other political figures. In those situations, the societal interest in having access to the information rises sharply, especially with respect to government officials and political candidates given the obvious relevance of such information to the democratic process. At the same time, there is an argument to be

---

[48] Cox Broadcasting Corp. v. Cohn, 420 U.S. 469 (1975) (disclosure of name of rape victim); Smith v. Daily Mail Pub. Co., 443 U.S. 97 (1979) (disclosure of name of juvenile defendant); The Florida Star v. B.J.F., 491 U.S. 524 (1989) (disclosure of name of rape victim); Bartnicki v. Vopper, 532 U.S. 514 (2001) (disclosure of contents of illegally intercepted cell phone conversation).
[49] Gates v. Discovery Communications, Inc., 34 Cal.4th 679, 101 P.3d 552 (2004).
[50] Ibid. at 563 n.9 (*overruling* Briscoe v. Reader's Digest Association, Inc., 4 Cal.3d 529 (1971)).

made that public officials and politicians, by voluntarily entering the political arena, have consented to a reduced right of privacy. This is not to say that even politicians have *no* reasonable expectations of privacy; of course they do, just reduced ones. As a result, whether in practice courts grant First Amendment protection to otherwise illegal disclosures of private information about public officials and political candidates is likely to turn on a case-by-case weighing of privacy rights against the social interest in public disclosure.

The transparency rights granted in the GDPR, CCPA, and other laws raise fewer serious First Amendment concerns. Requiring firms to disclose their data collection and storage practices, while technically a form of "compelled speech," seem likely to be upheld as routine commercial disclosures.[51] Similarly, granting individuals/users the right to access data about them held by firms and to seek correction of inaccurate data,[52] also do not seem to burden free speech in any tangible way.

What raises more difficult questions, however, is the right to erasure of data granted by both the GDPR and CCPA,[53] even as applied to data privacy (its application to dignitary privacy, as discussed earlier, is almost certainly unconstitutional). Requiring a firm to erase data that it is storing is not a literal restriction on speech (unlike a ban on disclosure). Nonetheless, requiring the erasure of data/deletion of information obviously makes it impossible for that data/information to be shared in the future. In that sense, such laws are parallel to prohibitions on making recordings of government officials such as police officers acting in the course of their duties, which have regularly been found to be unconstitutional.[54] Both types of laws have the direct and intended effect of disabling future speech. As such, there can be no doubt that laws requiring the deletion of data will *sometimes* violate the First Amendment.

Unfortunately, current First Amendment law does not provide clear answers to the question of when data erasure requirements are, or are not, permissible. Focusing on the impact of data erasure requirements on social media platforms (which are, after all, the subject of this book), there is an argument to be made that the First Amendment impact of such requirements is minimal. After all, as discussed in Chapter 3, the major platforms rarely if ever intentionally disclose user information, either publicly or to potential competitors in the advertising market, for business reasons. Of course, any deletion of user data has some impact on platforms' ability to sell targeted advertising, but such an indirect and minor impact on speech is unlikely to

---

[51] Zauderer v. Office of Disciplinary Counsel of Supreme Court of Ohio, 471 U.S. 626 (1985).
[52] GDPR, *supra* note 11, Arts. 15, 16.
[53] GPDR. Art. 17; CAL. CIV. CODE § 1798.105.
[54] Ashutosh Bhagwat, *Producing Speech*, 56 WM. & MARY L. REV. 1029, 1038–44 (2015).

be found to trump users' legitimate data privacy interests. So, while data erasure requirements undoubtedly would, under certain circumstances, violate the First Amendment, their application to social media platforms is unlikely to do so unless the platform can make the unusual showing that the relevant data was intended, in the future, to be an integral part of some form of public communication by the platform.

In short, while the First Amendment does impose limits on some forms of privacy protection, such as protections for dignitary privacy, run of the mill data privacy provisions generally should survive constitutional scrutiny. And this is especially so as applied to social media platforms, because they are not themselves significant producers of content that is created by using and accessing data.

7.5 THINK OF THE CHILDREN

One final topic that requires some special attention is privacy protections for children, meaning minors under the age of eighteen. Children obviously raise special privacy concerns because of both their vulnerability to exploitation of various forms and their reduced ability to make decisions for themselves. The GDPR recognizes the latter point, for example, by providing that for children under the age of sixteen, consent to data processing must be provided by a parent or guardian.[55] But consent is only the tip of the privacy iceberg when it comes to children.

To begin with, it should be noted that when we refer to "children" or "minors," in the context of the major social media forms we are primarily talking about teenagers between the ages of thirteen and seventeen, because platforms such as Facebook, Instagram, and Twitter/X do not permit children under the age of thirteen from opening accounts.[56] Furthermore, in the United States, federal law prohibits the online collection of data regarding children under the age of thirteen without parental consent, making other privacy protections somewhat moot for that age group (since parental consent is prohibitively expensive to obtain in most situations).[57]

---

[55] GDPR, *supra* note 11, Art. 8(1).

[56] *Facebook Terms of Service* ¶ 3(1), www.facebook.com/terms.php; *Instagram Terms of Use*, https://help.instagram.com/581066165581870; *X Terms of Service* ¶ 1, https://x.com/en/tos. TikTok and YouTube are concededly different because they do not place age limits, and while they assert that minors under eighteen must have parental consent to use their services, there is no indication that this requirement is enforced.

[57] *Children's Online Privacy Protection Act*, 15 U.S.C. § 6502; *Children's Online Privacy Protection Rule*, 16 C.F.R. § 312.

Admittedly, even for services that have a thirteen-year-old age cut off, enforcement of this requirement has been uneven because platforms do not typically verify the age of users when they create accounts. In response to this concern (and others), in 2022 California adopted a statute, the California Age-Appropriate Design Code Act (CAADCA), which broadly regulates data practices for minors under the age of eighteen.[58] Among other things, the CAADCA requires online providers to estimate the age of potential child users, and adjust its services and default privacy protections accordingly. Strikingly, however, in late 2023 a federal district court in San Jose, California (in a case titled *NetChoice v. Bonta*) enjoined enforcement of much of the California statute. Regarding the age verification provision in particular, the court held that it violated the First Amendment because given the great burden that age verification requirements impose on online providers, the impact of this requirement would be to limit both children's *and* adults' access to some online content (we will return to other aspects of the CAADCA and this decision later).[59] The status and future of age verification requirements are thus very much in flux.

Turning now to specific data privacy policies aiming to protect children, let us start with targeted advertising. As noted at the beginning of this chapter, targeted advertising is the bedrock of social media platforms' business models, the thing which makes it possible for platforms to not charge users. At the same time, targeted advertising directed at children raises special concerns, because of their greater perceived vulnerability to manipulation. The EU's response to this, as noted earlier, has been to prohibit targeted advertising directed at minors, in its DSA.[60] This provision of the DSA, which has been implemented by the major platforms, has not proven terribly controversial. It should be noted, however, that the prohibition does have a secondary impact, of disincentivizing platforms from providing services specially directed at minors, since those services cannot be monetized under this rule.[61] This may well be a reasonable price to pay in order to protect children from manipulation, but it is a tradeoff nonetheless that should be recognized.

There is no such parallel prohibition on targeted advertising for minors under US law at a federal level. California's CAADCA, however, does have a provision that prohibited online businesses from profiling a child by

---

[58] CAL. CIV. CODE §§ 1798.99.28–1798.99.40.
[59] *NetChoice, LLC v. Bonta*, 692 F.Supp.3d 924, 945–46, 950–52 (N.D. Cal. 2023) ("*Bonta*").
[60] See *supra* n. 7 and accompanying text.
[61] Platforms can be expected to continue to provide access to their general services to teenagers, because the marginal costs of doing so are trivial and teenagers will someday soon become adult customers.

default, which in effect prohibited targeted advertising directed at children.[62] As with that law's age verification requirements, however, the *NetChoice v. Bonta* court also held that this provision violated the First Amendment.[63] Furthermore, that decision was almost certainly correct. The US Supreme Court has made it clear that the First Amendment provides strong protections for speech directed at children.[64] Furthermore, the modern Supreme Court has substantially ratcheted up the amount of constitutional protection given to commercial advertising.[65] The combination of these trends makes any flat restriction on advertising to children highly vulnerable, as the *Bonta* court recognized.

Another area of child privacy protections where regulators have been active is data collection and storage. In the EU, as noted earlier, the GDPR requires parental consent before processing the data of children under the age of sixteen if consent is the justification for that processing – and processing is defined to include collection and storage of data.[66] While this is not an absolute bar to collecting children's data, it is a significant impediment. In the United States, federal law flatly bans collecting data for children under the age of thirteen without parental consent, which is generally not plausible to obtain. Finally, California's CAADCA also contains a broad prohibition stating that online providers may not "collect, sell, share, or retain any personal information" about minors under the age of eighteen, except for some narrow, specified purposes (in light of the federal prohibition, the CAADCA's restriction is only relevant to children between thirteen and seventeen years of age).[67]

Perhaps because of its limited application (only to teenagers), this provision too was struck down by the *NetChoice v. Bonta* court based on the conclusion that the inevitable impact of a restriction on data collection was to make it impossible to provide targeted content to teenagers. The court pointed out that such targeted content can be beneficial for minors, especially teenagers who are members of vulnerable subpopulations.[68] It is hard to imagine, however, that a court would reach the same conclusion regarding data collection targeting younger children, which remains effectively prohibited by federal law, given young children's greater need for privacy and the lesser value to them of targeted content.

[62] CAL. CIV. CODE § 1798.99.31(b)(2).
[63] *Bonta*, 692 F.Supp.3d at 955–56.
[64] Brown v. Entertainment Merchants Assn., 564 U.S. 786 (2011).
[65] Lorillard Tobacco Co. v. Reilly, 533 U.S. 525 (2001); Sorrell v. IMS Health Inc., 564 U.S. 552 (2011).
[66] GDPR, *supra* note 11, Arts. 4(2), 8.
[67] CAL. CIV. CODE § 1798.99.31(b)(3).
[68] *Bonta*, 692 F.Supp.3d at 956–57.

Finally, let us consider special limits on public disclosure of children's data. As noted earlier, prohibitions on disclosure of data are, on their face, direct restrictions on speech, and indeed content-based restrictions, which under current US constitutional doctrine are presumptively invalid. On the other hand, there is a long history of regulating the disclosure of highly sensitive information such as medical histories and financial details, whose constitutionality has not in the past been seriously questioned (at least as to data regarding nonpublic figures). But, it must also be acknowledged, the law in this area is seriously underdeveloped, especially in light of the Supreme Court's strong suggestion that data is speech.

With respect to data regarding *children*, however, it is very hard to believe that restrictions on disclosure would face any serious constitutional scrutiny. The reason, of course, is that children surely have a significantly heightened right and expectation of privacy, given their vulnerability. Furthermore, it is difficult to imagine a situation in which there would be a strong social interest in enabling public access to private facts regarding minors. After all, even famous minors such as child actors or British royals cannot seriously be said to have voluntarily consented to reduced privacy rights in the same way as adults who voluntarily enter the public sphere; even famous minors remain vulnerable to exploitation and long term emotional harms in a way that is categorically different from adults. So at least with respect to data disclosure laws, children probably are special and can legitimately be granted elevated protections.

7.6 PRIVACY AND HUMILITY

For all of these reasons, privacy regulation directed at social media platforms is often addressing a legitimate and serious problem and should not face the same skepticism as the many blatantly ideological attempts to regulate social media discussed in previous chapters. At the same time, especially in the United States, rights of free expression place some significant limits on legislative attempts to protect privacy. And furthermore, in the privacy arena no less than anywhere else, laws and regulations targeting rapidly evolving technologies can easily run up against the law of unintended consequences. As such, regulators should take care not to adopt excessively broad laws (as arguably the EU's GDPR is, in some respects); and more importantly, regulators should stand ready to reconsider their initiatives if unexpected and negative consequences of their actions emerge.

8

Some Ways Forward

To this point, this book has been in many ways an extended disquisition on why many contemporary critiques of social media are flawed or exaggerated, and why many reform proposals directed at social media are misguided. But this book is not meant to be a plea for either complacence or inaction. After all, to say that the war on social media consists to a significant degree of hyperbole and evidence-free innuendo is *not* to say that social media does not create any social harms worthy of a regulatory response.

8.1 FIRST, DO NO HARM: PERVERSE INCENTIVES AND CONSTANT CHANGE

Having acknowledged the existence of harms associated with social media, I would nonetheless argue that the default assumption should be against rather than, as the European Union (EU) increasingly appears to believe, for regulations directed specifically at social media (or for that matter other new technologies). In other words, would-be regulators of new technologies should adopt the principle of medical ethics attributed (somewhat incorrectly) to the ancient Greek physician Hippocrates: *primum non nocere*, or "First, do no harm." And while the relevance of this principle for modern medicine is highly debatable,[1] it made all sorts of sense in premodern times, when medical interventions were incredibly dangerous (especially because of the risk of infection, in a pre-antibiotics age) and rooted in deep ignorance about the basic science of human health. So it is with social media today.

Digging deeper, the reasons why it makes sense to adopt the "do no harm" principle for social media are straightforward. Foremost is simply that social

---

[1] Robert H. Shmerling, MD, *First Do No Harm*, HARVARD HEALTH BLOG (June 22, 2020), www.health.harvard.edu/blog/first-do-no-harm-201510138421.

8.1 First, Do No Harm: Perverse Incentives and Constant Change 165

media is *media*, and regulations of social media are regulations of speech. Furthermore, as the US Supreme Court has recognized, social media is today the primary locus for broad discussions of public issues.[2] But in the United States under its First Amendment, the presumption has always been against government intervention in public discourse. Indeed, the same should be true in any free and democratic society committed to open debate. Why that is so follows from first principles. Free Speech is widely accepted as an essential element of any democratic system of government; and at least in the United States the primary reason why the First Amendment protects expressive freedoms is to advance democratic self-governance.[3] From this follows an important, if controversial, principle: Government, and government regulation in particular, is always and foremost the gravest threat to freedom of expression. This is true for two separate reasons.

First, unlike private actors, government actors have systematically perverse incentives when regulating public discourse. Elected officials, of course, wish to stay in power, and unelected officials need to maintain the support of elected officials to sustain their authority. But the greatest threat to retaining power is public discourse about elected officials' conduct in office, which can reveal their errors, weaknesses, and malfeasance, and so turn voters against them. As such, government regulators are *always* motivated to reshape or suppress public discourse, especially discourse about the government itself. Of course, not all officials act on these perverse motivations; but nonetheless, perhaps the primary purpose of constitutional protections for free expression is to create barriers to such manipulation of discourse.

It should be noted in this regard that while, as Chapter 1 recounts, numerous (mainly conservative) critics of social media accuse platforms of similar censorial motives, this does not make much sense. In fact, at heart the goal of social media firms is to *maximize* speech, because that is in some sense the product they are providing. To be more precise, platforms host speech to attract users, and then make money by selling access to those users to advertisers. Platforms cannot adopt aggressive rules restricting content because their financial goal is to maximize users; and to maximize users they need to maximize the speech that attracts them. And from the point of view of the platform, it is entirely irrelevant if the speech they host is favorable to the government, unfavorable to the government, or has nothing to do with government – the more the merrier. Indeed, even content which is unpopular with the majority

---

[2] Packingham v. North Carolina, 582 U.S. 98, 104 (2017).
[3] I explore these themes in detail in ASHUTOSH BHAGWAT, OUR DEMOCRATIC FIRST AMENDMENT (2020).

of users typically is of interest to some elements of the population, and so, to maximize users, platforms are incentivized to permit that speech. Only when speech is so unpopular with a significant percentage of users that it is likely to scare them away will it benefit platforms to suppress it.

Second, and more fundamentally, for all the wealth and power that owners of social media platforms such as Mark Zuckerberg and Elon Musk possess, governments continue to enjoy a monopoly on legal violence. While tech moguls can ban certain words, and even ideas, from their platforms (for example, as of this writing Elon Musk has apparently banned the terms "cis" and "cisgender" from Twitter/X[4]), they cannot arrest you, lock you up, physically harm you, or even take your property against your will. In contrast, violations of legal regimes such as Germany's NetzDG, as well as India's IT Act and implementing rules (both discussed in Chapter 6), subject platforms to sometimes whopping fines, as well as the potential imprisonment of platform employees. NetzDG, for example, authorizes fines of up to *50 million euros*,[5] and Section 69A(3) of the Indian IT Act of 2000 authorizes imprisonment for up to *seven years* for violations of that section.[6] This kind of coercive authority can silence and deter speech in ways that simply cannot be matched by the inconvenience of having a post blocked, or even being deplatformed, by Facebook or Twitter/X.

Furthermore, even though powerful platforms are sometimes loosely described as "monopolies," they certainly do not possess the monopolistic control mechanisms enjoyed by the state. Elon Musk may try to ban the term "cis" on Twitter/X, but other platforms do not. And even if the very large platforms all ban particular expression such as hate speech, alternative platforms such as Telegram remain available.[7] State power, on the other hand, is pervasive and omnipresent. When Germany bans Nazi propaganda via its NetzDG law, such speech is entirely excluded from the county. Consider in this regard the fact that in early September of 2024 the supreme court of Brazil completely banned the platform Twitter/X from the country (affirming a previous decision by a single justice), because of the platform's failure to comply

---

[4] Siladitya Ray, *Musk Says "Cisgender" and "Cis" Are Now "Slurs" on Twitter*, FORBES (June 21, 2023), www.forbes.com/sites/siladityaray/2023/06/21/musk-says-cisgender-and-cis-are-now-slurs-on-twitter/.

[5] *Germany Starts Enforcing Hate Speech Law*, BBC (Jan. 1, 2018), www.bbc.com/news/technology-42510868.

[6] Information Technology Act, 2000.

[7] Though apparently not without legal consequences, at least in Europe. *See* Aurelien Breeden, *What We Know about the Telegram Founder's Arrest*, N.Y. TIMES (Aug. 27, 2024), www.nytimes.com/2024/08/27/business/telegram-pavel-durov-arrest-explained.html (discussing arrest and charging in France of Telegram founder Pavel Durov based on illegal activity on Telegram).

with Brazilian law regarding illegal content.[8] Presumably other social media platforms will take heed and follow Brazilian law. No social media firm or owner, even Mark Zuckerberg (the effective owner of Facebook, Instagram, WhatsApp, and Threads), has that kind of power.

In short, both because of government's perverse motivations and because of its monopoly on legal violence, it is sensible to approach government regulation of social media with an attitude of heightened skepticism. But there is another, quite separate reason for such skepticism (and a presumption against regulation), analogous to premodern medicine: ignorance and unpredictability. And this in turn is tied to a phenomenon deeply associated with the internet and social media, which is constant change.

Let us begin with the fact that, as technologies go, social media itself is relatively new. Facebook did not become available to the general public until 2006,[9] the same year that Twitter/X was founded[10] and YouTube was purchased by Google (YouTube was founded the previous year).[11] Instagram was not launched until 2010 (and not purchased by Facebook/Meta until 2012).[12] And none of these platforms obtained their ubiquitous presence in society until smart phones gained mass usage in the early 2010s (the first iPhone was launched in 2007[13]). So modern attempts to regulate these platforms such as the EU's General Data Protection Regulation (GDPR) (which was written in 2016 and became effective in 2018)[14] began barely a decade after the primary modern social media platforms came into existence. To give a comparison, while the telephone was invented in the 1870s, the US Congress did not regulate it until 1910 and did not adopt an extensive telecommunications statute until 1934.[15]

---

[8] Tom Phillips, *Brazil's Supreme Court Upholds Ban on Elon Musk's X over "Illegal Conduct,"* THE GUARDIAN (Sept. 2, 2024), www.theguardian.com/technology/article/2024/sep/02/brazils-supreme-court-upholds-x-ban-over-conduct.

[9] Sarah Phillips, *A Brief History of Facebook*, THE GUARDIAN (July 25, 2007), www.theguardian.com/technology/2007/jul/25/media.newmedia.

[10] Jonathan Vanian, *Twitter Is Now Owned by Elon Musk: Here's a Brief History from the App's Founding in 2006 to the Present*, CNBC (Oct. 29, 2022), www.cnbc.com/2022/10/29/a-brief-history-of-twitter-from-its-founding-in-2006-to-musk-takeover.html.

[11] *Google Buys YouTube for $1.65 Billion*, NBC NEWS (Oct. 9, 2006), www.nbcnews.com/id/wbna15196982.

[12] Allison Eldridge, *Instagram*, BRITANNICA MONEY (Sept. 2, 2024), www.britannica.com/money/Instagram.

[13] APPLE, www.apple.com/newsroom/2007/01/09Apple-Reinvents-the-Phone-with-iPhone/.

[14] General Data Protection Regulation 2016/679, 2016 O.J. (L 119), https://eur-lex.europa.eu/eli/reg/2016/679/oj (henceforth "GDPR").

[15] Tim Wu, *A Brief History of American Telecommunications Regulation*, 5 OXFORD INTERNATIONAL ENCYCLOPEDIA OF LEGAL HISTORY 95 (2009), https://scholarship.law.columbia.edu/faculty_scholarship/1461.

But even more significantly than the relative youth of the technology, what is notable about the social media ecosphere is that it remains subject to constant change and flux. Consider that in 2016, when (primarily as a result of the Brexit and US presidential elections) close attention began to be paid to social media's societal consequences, it seemed clear that the largest of those platforms, Facebook, was destined to rise relentlessly. Yet in the United States, the percentage of adults who use Facebook has been almost flat since 2016, and among teenagers Facebook is *far* less popular than other platforms such as TikTok and Instagram.[16] Given its demographic challenges, therefore, the future of Facebook remains very murky.

TikTok presents an even more extreme example of flux. In 2016 TikTok was unknown. Yet TikTok has, in a few years, famously become by far the most popular platform among teenage and young adult users, in the United States and around the world. But TikTok's story continues to evolve. As of this writing (in the fall of 2024), there is a good chance that TikTok will be completely ejected from the United States pursuant to a congressional statute adopted in April of 2024, which will require TikTok to either separate from its Chinese parent, ByteDance, or stop operating in the United States.[17] And even if ByteDance does sell its stake in TikTok, the resulting platform will undoubtedly change with new ownership. Furthermore, TikTok has been banned in India, the world's most populous nation, since 2020.[18] So is TikTok, with its young user base, the future and so worthy of regulatory attention, or is it becoming irrelevant?

Or consider Twitter/X. Because so much political dialogue traditionally occurred on that platform, it was of special concern to would-be regulators (with all of their perverse incentives). President Trump, in particular, used Twitter/X as an official vehicle for policymaking during his first term as President, going so far as to fire his Secretary of Defense via Twitter/X.[19] It was almost certainly Twitter/X's deplatforming of Trump in January of 2021 that led Florida and Texas to enact the social media laws discussed in Chapter 1. Yet since Elon Musk's purchase and takeover of Twitter/X in October of

---

[16] Katherine Schaeffer, *5 Facts about How Americans Use Facebook, Two Decades after Its Launch*, PEW RESEARCH CENTER (Feb. 2, 2024), www.pewresearch.org/short-reads/2024/02/02/5-facts-about-how-americans-use-facebook-two-decades-after-its-launch/.

[17] Bobby Allyn, *President Biden Signs Law to Ban TikTok Nationwide Unless It Is Sold*, NPR (April 24, 2024), www.npr.org/2024/04/24/1246663779/biden-ban-tiktok-us.

[18] Alex Travelli and Suhasini Raj, *What Happened When India Pulled the Plug on TikTok*, N.Y. TIMES (March 22, 2024), www.nytimes.com/2024/03/22/business/tiktok-india-ban.html.

[19] Guy Snodgrass, *Trump Fires Secretary of Defense Mark Esper Via Tweet*, FORBES (Nov. 9, 2020), www.forbes.com/sites/guysnodgrass/2020/11/09/trump-fires-secretary-of-defense-mark-esper-via-tweet/.

2022, most of the conservative concerns and grievances directed at Twitter/X have become entirely moot. Indeed, it is now progressives who are moaning about Twitter/X, given Musk's public right-wing turn, which he is increasingly extending to his management of Twitter/X (recall his banning the words "cis" and "cisgender"). Furthermore, given Twitter/X's enormous financial difficulties in the wake of the Musk takeover, here too the present and the future are grossly uncertain.

Finally, there are many other, continuing evolutions that make it extremely difficult to predict the near, and especially more distant future of social media. Even Facebook, the granddaddy of the current platforms (in terms of age and user base), is constantly tweaking the algorithms that control its Feed, moving from personal to more commercial and political, and then sometimes back to more personal content. It has also come to emphasize reels over posts in its panic over the rise of TikTok (which may perhaps reverse if TikTok goes away). And most famously, Facebook has been extraordinarily inconsistent regarding its willingness to police false information, especially in the wake of the 2016 US election, and even more so the COVID-19 pandemic and lockdowns. In 2020, Mark Zuckerberg famously announced on air that "Facebook or internet platforms in general" should not be "arbiters of truth."[20] Yet it is now public knowledge (which Zuckerberg has acknowledged) that the following year Facebook, under heavy public and private pressure, cooperated extensively with the Biden Administration's efforts to suppress COVID and vaccine mis- and disinformation – something that Zuckerberg later said he regretted doing.[21]

One could go on at length in this vein, but the bottom line is clear: Social media is far from a mature technology and continues to demonstrate constant and fundamental change. But this fact alone creates serious problems for would-be regulators. Regulation, by its nature, is designed to address ongoing and future societal harms connected to the subject of regulation. Indeed, given the slow pace at which laws and regulations are adopted and implemented, in truth the main concern must be future, not present, harm. But in the face of such constant and fundamental change, how can regulators possibly predict what specific harms will be associated, several years down the line, with social media platforms? They of course cannot, making effective regulation

---

[20] Salvador Rodriguez, *Mark Zuckerberg Says Social Networks Should Not Be Fact-Checking Political Speech*, CNBC (May 28, 2020), www.cnbc.com/2020/05/28/zuckerberg-facebook-twitter-should-not-fact-check-political-speech.html.

[21] Gnaneshwar Rajan and Nandita Bose, *Zuckerberg Says Biden Administration Pressured Meta to Censor COVID-19 Content*, REUTERS (Aug. 27, 2024), www.reuters.com/technology/zuckerberg-says-biden-administration-pressured-meta-censor-covid-19-content-2024-08-27/; Murthy v. Missouri, 144 S. Ct. 1972 (2024).

exceedingly hard to draft. One should thus be highly skeptical of social media regulation, and of regulators who claim to be able to predict the future.

Furthermore, it is not just that regulation has a high chance of failing; it can also have perverse effects. Regulation almost always imposes compliance costs, which ultimately will be borne by platform customers, whether users or advertisers. Those costs may well be justified if they are associated with benefits/harm preventions; but absent such benefits, regulation is hard to defend from the perspective of social welfare. In addition, regulation inevitably raises barriers to entry, especially for smaller, start-up potential entrants. But, given that excess concentration is (legitimately) one of the more serious criticisms leveled at the social media sphere, making it harder for entrants to challenge Big Tech incumbents is seriously misguided, unless there are strong, countervailing reason to do so. It may be easier for regulators to deal with only a handful of dominant platforms, but, for we-the-users, choice is better.

All of which is to say, regulation imposes social costs, which must be justified by social benefits. But in the face of change and uncertainty, it is hard to be sure that regulations will, over any reasonable time horizon, produce such benefits. And that is why skepticism and a presumption against new regulation targeting social media make sense.

8.2 ENFORCING EXISTING LAWS

That said, a presumption against new regulation targeting social media does *not* mean that social media should be a law-free zone. Most obviously (though the obviousness of this is sometimes lost), social media companies should be, and are, subject to long-standing, general legal rules. The rules and restrictions I speak of are broad and universal, are not focused on any particular industry or technology, and have stood the test of time. And they address broad societal concerns. As such, there is absolutely no reason why social media firms should get some sort of an exemption or pass from rules that everyone else must follow.

That social media firms must follow the law should be obvious, and in some respects it is entirely uncontested. Of course Meta, Twitter/X, Alphabet, and TikTok must pay their employees at least minimum wage, provide them with safe work environments, and permit non-exempt staff to unionize if they desire. And of course their headquarters must comply with local building codes and zoning laws. One could go on. No one seriously contests this point, but it is important to highlight it. The difficulty arises when such laws interfere with how platforms operate, at which point this consensus appears to vanish.

Take antitrust. The social media industry (and Big Tech more generally) is famously highly concentrated, and so seemingly rife for antitrust scrutiny. Yet for years, antitrust regulators (inexplicably) took a largely hands-off approach, presumably because of concerns about throttling a new and exciting technology. Thus when, early in its existence, Facebook went on a buying spree, purchasing Instagram (a direct competitor) in 2012, and then WhatsApp (seen as a potential competitor) in 2014, the deals were waived through with almost no regulatory scrutiny. It is entirely possible that part of the reason for this was that, at the time, regulators did not fully understand the nature of the social media industry, since on the surface it would seem as if these companies were simply giving away their services for free. But if so, that naivete is surely a thing of the past as we now understand that platforms' true customers are advertisers – users are merely an input into their business model. None of which is to say that Facebook's acquisitions *did* violate antitrust law; but they should not have gotten the free pass that they apparently did at the time. And, it should be added, the same can be said of Google's acquisition of YouTube in 2006 – search and online videos may seem like different industries, but both firms are in the business of selling online advertising and so should have been seen as competitors.

Nor is the failure to scrutinize mergers the only area where regulators may have failed to apply antitrust principles to platforms. Consider, for example, Meta's tendency to introduce new platforms or features to challenge and undermine rivals, such as Instagram stories for Snapchat and Threads for Twitter/X. Such conduct in and of itself does not raise any antitrust (or other) concerns; to the contrary, it probably represents healthy competition. But if Meta were to use its dominance on one platform to leverage competitive advantages into other forms of social media, that *would* be potentially problematic. This is not to say that Meta *has* engaged in such anticompetitive conduct; but certainly, greater attention to such possibilities than regulators have to date given seems in order.

In recent years, fortunately, a bipartisan consensus appears to have been reached among regulators that antitrust law should apply to Big Tech just as to any other industry. Regarding social media platforms in particular, in 2020 (during the first Trump Administration) the Federal Trade Commission (FTC) filed a lawsuit seeking to reverse Facebook's acquisition of Instagram and WhatsApp, potentially requiring Meta to divest itself of both platforms. The Biden Administration FTC has continued the lawsuit, which as of this writing (Fall 2024) is still ongoing.[22] Seen in light of other recently launched lawsuits targeting Google, Amazon, and Apple, these developments suggest

---

[22] Cecelia Kang, *A Facebook Antitrust Suit Can Move Forward, a Judge Says, in a Win for the F.T.C.*, N.Y. TIMES (Jan. 11, 2022), www.nytimes.com/2022/01/11/technology/facebook-antitrust-ftc.html.

that Big Tech's days of freedom from antitrust scrutiny are over. And that is a good thing.

Another body of law that has obvious relevance to the operation of social media platforms is contract law. The basic premise of contract law is blindingly simple: When parties enter into a legally binding agreement, they are responsible for sticking to the terms of that agreement. When social media platforms offer services to users under certain terms and conditions, including content moderation standards, they and the users are entering into a contract. It may seem as if that is not true because platforms do not charge users (i.e., in technical legal terms that there is no "consideration" from users for the services), but that is not actually the case. The "deal" with respect to social media is that platforms offer services in exchange for their users' data and eyeballs, which platforms in turn use to generate advertising revenues.

Why does this matter? Because contracts are *mutually* binding. Just as platforms are entitled to block content or users that violate their terms of service, just so platforms have a legal obligation to users to themselves follow those terms. If they fail to do so, platforms can and should be held legally liable. Admittedly, it is bit unclear what exactly the legal remedy should be when a platform acts contrary to its own terms of service (money damages seem an odd fit, given that users do not pay platforms); but one can imagine inventive jurists finding *some* means to incentivize platforms to play by their own rules, including perhaps judicial injunctions (which are not a standard remedy in breach of contract cases).

Furthermore, the law imposes various restrictions on what terms may be included in contracts. For example, contractual terms may not be "unconscionable," meaning grossly unfair in how the term is imposed on one party and in its substantive effect. Given platforms' essentially unlimited power to set terms of use, the first element is surely satisfied, meaning that courts can and should be entitled to set aside grossly unfair terms of service, at the behest of users or regulators. Similarly, contract law, as well as related consumer protection statutes, provide tools to police misleading terms of service adopted by platforms, in the same way that other industries are forbidden from deceiving customers. And one could go on. The main point is that plain old contract law, perhaps as foundational and un-innovative a body of law as there is, can be a source of many important constraints on platforms.

Another basic and long-standing body of law that can and should, when appropriate, be applied against platforms is tort law. Of course, Section 230 precludes tort liability for third-party content on platforms (on which more later) or for good faith content moderation decisions. But as discussed in detail in Chapter 6, Section 230 does *not* shield platforms from liability for harm caused by design features built into the platforms. This is why the case based on Snapchat's "Speed Filter" could proceed despite Section 230. And this is also why a federal judge in Oakland has permitted parts of a lawsuit brought by school districts against major platforms to proceed (both cases are discussed in Chapter 6).

Also on the topic of tort law, and as also discussed in Chapter 6, serious uncertainty exists about whether Section 230 shields platforms from liability for harm caused by their recommendation algorithms. Some courts (including the judge in the Oakland school district litigation) have said that it does provide such immunity. But other courts have disagreed. In particular, in an important opinion issued in August of 2024, the United States Court of Appeals for the Third Circuit (which covers the mid-Atlantic states), so held.[23] This extremely disturbing case involved a video on TikTok depicting the "Blackout Challenge," which encouraged users to try and make themselves pass out. TikTok's algorithm recommended this video to a 10-year-old child, who ended up dying when she attempted to perform the challenge. The court, reversing a lower court decision, permitted a lawsuit brought by the girl's mother to proceed insofar as it was based on TikTok's recommendation algorithm rather than the content itself. And interestingly, in reaching this conclusion the Third Circuit majority relied heavily on the fact that in its *NetChoice* decision (discussed in detail in Chapter 4), the Supreme Court held that content curation by platforms was protected by the First Amendment. That, the Third Circuit concluded, meant that recommendations were *not* the same as the underlying third-party content, and so fell outside Section 230.

In other words, courts are currently working through many issues regarding how long-standing legal principles, including antitrust, contract, and tort law, apply to modern platforms. And while some questions, such as Section 230's application to recommendation algorithms, remain very much in flux, others, such as the obligation on platforms, just like everyone else, to follow general legal rules, are not. But regardless of how specific issues are resolved, what is very clear is that the space in which social media platforms operate is very much *not* a "law-free" zone.

Finally, if antitrust, contract, and tort law are obvious sources of rules governing platforms, there also exist some other, non-obvious but potentially important legal restrictions. One of those, surprisingly, may be family law. In a very interesting paper, law professor Katharine Silbaugh and her then

---

[23] Anderson v. TikTok, Inc., 116 F.4th 180 (3rd Cir. 2024); David French, *The Viral Blackout Challenge is Killing Young People. Courts Are Finally Taking It Seriously*, N.Y. Times (Sept. 5, 2024), www.nytimes.com/2024/09/05/opinion/tiktok-blackout-challenge-anderson.html.

student Adi Caplan-Bicker argue that family law provides a completely overlooked tool to combat children's exposure to harmful content on social media platforms.[24]

To simplify a complex and thoughtful argument, Silbaugh and Caplan-Baker argue that instead of directly targeting online content that regulators view as harmful, which the First Amendment and Section 230 generally do not permit, regulators should enact consent-based laws which empower parents to opt their children in or out of social media platforms but do not focus on specific types of content. Most intriguingly, they propose creating a central "Parental Decision-Making Registry," on which parents could register their preferences regarding their children's social media access, at a device level. Such a registry could permit parents to simply opt their children out of social media, in which case platforms would be required to comply. But they could also opt into less restrictive limitations, such as a social media curfew. And most importantly, Sibaugh and Caplan-Baker argue that such restrictions, so long as they were content-neutral, are consistent with current First Amendment law.

There is a basic insight underlying this clever proposal. It is largely none of the government's business what types of legal content are accessed by individuals, including minors (especially teenagers). And even when a law is designed to enhance parental authority rather than flatly ban access to specific content by minors, it is presumptively impermissible for the government to single out specific content for regulation. This was the basic, and correct, lesson of an important Supreme Court case invalidating a California law restricting the sale of violent video games to minors.[25] On the other hand, it is a fundamental principle of family law, going back untold centuries, that it is very much the business of parents to control their children's upbringing, including their education and their exposure to different perspectives and information.[26] Indeed, in two decisions from the 1920s that are still followed, the Supreme Court held that parents had a constitutional *right* to control their children's education.[27] And that right surely extends to children's access to information in a non-school setting, including on social media platforms.

---

[24] Katharine Silbaugh and Adi Caplan-Bricker, *Regulating Social Media through Family Law*, 15 U.C. IRVINE L. REV. 1 (2024).

[25] Brown v. Entertainment Merchants Ass'n, 564 U.S. 786 (2011).

[26] I made a similar argument regarding sexually explicit content in the pre-social media era. Ashutosh Bhagwat, *What If I Want My Kids to Watch Pornography?: Protecting Children from "Indecent" Speech*, 11 WM. & MARY BILL OF RT.S J. 671 (2003).

[27] Meyer v. Nebraska, 262 U.S. 390 (1923) (striking down law prohibiting the teaching of modern languages other than English); Pierce v. Society of Sisters, 268 U.S. 510 (1925) (striking down law requiring students to attend public, not private, schools).

Family law is thus a striking instance of a long-standing body of law which can inform, and advance, legitimate restrictions on platforms. And because parental rights are so fundamental to our society (and have constitutional status), they do not always have to yield to the First Amendment. Rather, family law principles must be reconciled with legal protections, such as First Amendment rights, that platforms enjoy. Of course, this does not mean that parental wishes always should prevail. Family law itself requires that parents and guardians exercise their rights consistent with the basic well-being of children. So, for example, parents using their rights to harm LGBTQ minors by cutting off their access to online support communities would raise serious concerns. And I personally have doubts about the wisdom, and perhaps the constitutionality, of permitting parents to fully control social media access for older minors, say above the age of 16, who are on the verge of adulthood. But all that said, family law remains an important potential source of regulatory authority over platforms, in the same way that family law permits the state to empower parental control over other aspects of their children's upbringing.

There are thus many ways in which the application of existing law, or the creation of regulatory regimes built on existing legal regimes such as family law, can address some of the concerns raised by social media platforms without violating the principles of skepticism and presumption against new regulation that began this chapter. Unlike entirely new regulatory initiatives such as the EU's Digital Services Act (discussed extensively in Chapter 6), the application of general, established law to social media platforms does not rest on limited knowledge, nor is it vulnerable to changing technologies and business models. We have been enforcing contracts, imposing tort liability, and protecting parental authority for centuries if not millennia, and we have been enforcing antitrust law for well over a century. Applying such existing principles to platforms thus represents continuity, not legal experimentation.

8.3 SECTION 230 REFORM

Furthermore, while there should be a strong presumption against new laws specifically targeting social media platforms, that presumption is not absolute. There are certain forms of egregious harm associated with platforms, especially platforms that specialize in hosting harmful content, that are sufficiently pervasive, and that we are sufficiently familiar with, that it is probably time to address them. And, to address them effectively, it is probably time to consider amending, albeit in limited ways, that bastion of internet freedom, Section 230.

Recall from Chapter 6 that Section 230 has two primary provisions. The first, Section 230(c)(1), as interpreted by courts, shields platforms completely from liability for third-party content that they host. The second, Section 230(c)(2)(A), grants platforms the right to engage in good faith content moderation without risking liability. Between them, the two provisions of Section 230 effectively give platforms an almost free hand to host, or refuse to host, whatever content they choose. And while regularly criticized as a free pass, or a get-out-of-jail-free card, most commentators would acknowledge that Section 230 has enabled the creation and growth of the modern internet, including social media platforms.

But as law professor and MacArthur fellow Danielle Keats Citron points out, Section 230 has a dark side. Because Section 230 shields *all* platforms from liability, essentially without condition, it protects platforms who seek out, and specialize in hosting, deeply harmful content such as nonconsensual intimate images (including revenge porn), deepfake videos (often sexually explicit ones depicting actual individuals), and violent threats.[28] And while Section 230 of course does not protect the users who post such materials, they are often anonymous or difficult to locate, and so in practice unaccountable. Meanwhile, the owners of such platforms profit off the harm that their users impose on powerless victims. The problem, in simple terms, is that while Section 230 *permits* platforms to moderate harmful content, it does not require them to do so even if the content is defamatory or otherwise illegal (such as explicit deepfakes and threats).

It should be noted that Section 230 already acknowledges this problem, to some extent, and carves out some situations where immunity is not assured. In particular, from its origin, Section 230 exempted from its immunity shield any content in violation of federal criminal law, including obscenity and child pornography, and content in violation of intellectual property (IP) protections.[29] In addition, in 2018 in the "Allow States and Victims to Fight Online Sex Trafficking Act" (FOSTA) statute, Congress exempted from Section 230 immunity civil and state criminal laws relating to sex trafficking.[30] These exemptions, especially the IP one, make it clear that narrow Section 230 carve-outs, designed to address serous social problems, need not spell the death of the internet, contrary to some hyperbolic claims.

On the other hand, it must be conceded that actual experience with these carve-outs, especially the IP and FOSTA ones, has been mixed at best. With

---

[28] Danielle Keats Citron, *How to Fix Section 230*, 103 B.U. L. REV. 713, 718 (2023).
[29] 47 U.S.C. § 230(e)(1) and (2).
[30] 47 U.S.C. § 230(e)(5); Citron, *supra* n. 28, at 722.

8.3 Section 230 Reform

IP, the main (and highly predictable) problem that has emerged is excessive takedowns. The way in which the Section 230 IP exception and the 1998 Digital Millennium Copyright Act (DMCA) operate in tandem is that platforms receive notices from IP holders claiming that content that they are hosting violates IP law. If platforms then fail to take down infringing content, they face liability. In principle, of course, platforms could conduct an independent investigation to determine if the targeted content is in fact infringing (and leave up non-infringing content). But in practice their safest bet is to take down any content which might conceivably be found to violate IP rights. And that is exactly what we see happening, as the Electronic Frontier Foundation has documented.[31]

The story with FOSTA is more complex. As Professor Citron recounts, FOSTA was passed with the entirely admirable goal of helping victims of sex trafficking, by preventing platforms from enabling trafficking (and profiting from it). Unfortunately, that is not what has happened. Instead, concerns about liability under FOSTA incentivized platforms of all sorts to proactively ban any content even distantly related to sex work (note the parallel to IP), which has caused enormous harm to consensual sex workers by depriving them of safe places to connect to clients and to share information among themselves.[32] At the same time, FOSTA does not appear to have had any significant impact on the extent of actual sex trafficking, for complex reasons.[33]

The experience with FOSTA should give us pause in contemplating Section 230 reform. But Citron persuasively argues that many of FOSTA's problems are a product of vague language and bad drafting, which can be avoided if reform efforts are written carefully and narrowly.

As a starting point, under such a careful approach, there are simply no grounds for changing Section 230(c)(2)(A)'s protections for good faith content moderation by platforms.[34] There is no evidence that current content moderation practices are the source of systematic harm (despite the conservative claims discussed in Chapter 1), and in any event as Chapter 4 notes, in the *NetChoice* cases the Supreme Court correctly held that platforms have a First Amendment right to engage in content moderation.

Section 230(c)(1), however, is a different story. As Professor Citron recounts in detail, Section 230 has permitted bad actors to create literally thousands of websites (she counts 9,500 in 2020) dedicated to extremely harmful content, mainly nonconsensual intimate images. Indeed, Section 230 incentivizes

---

[31] Electronic Frontier Foundation, *Takedown Hall of Shame*, www.eff.org/takedowns.
[32] Citron, *supra* n. 28, at 738–40.
[33] Ibid. at 740–42.
[34] Ibid. at 746–50.

websites that are banned in other countries because of privacy violations to set up shop in the United States, where Section 230 and limited jurisdiction shield them from foreign enforcement efforts.[35] Citron's proposed solution is to enact a new and narrow exemption from Section 230(c)(1) immunity for platforms that "purposefully or deliberately solicit, encourage, or keep up material that they know or have reason to believe constitutes stalking, harassment, or intimate privacy violations," the latter term being defined as essentially nonconsensual nude or sexual images.[36] This proposal by and large fits the criteria of being extremely narrow, carefully defined, and limited to consciously bad actors.

The only part of this proposal that raises concerns for me is the phrase "reason to believe." It is included presumably because of the difficulty of proving that a platform knows that particular content falls within the carve-out. But because the resulting legal rule is somewhat amorphous (how much do you have to know, to have "reason to believe"?), it clearly incentivizes some prophylactic takedowns in response to insincere complaints – exactly the same problem associated with the IP and FOSTA Section 230 carve-outs. On the other hand, because the content covered by this proposed carve-out is so carefully and narrowly defined, as compared to the DMCA and FOSTA, a small amount of over-zealous content moderation may well be worth the price of protecting millions of innocent victims. At a minimum, Congress should give serious attention to such a proposal.

Citron's other proposal is to impose a "duty of care" on all platforms, which would condition Section 230(c)(1) immunity on platforms being able to demonstrate that they have taken "reasonable steps to address intimate privacy violations, cyber stalking, or cyber harassment,"[37] including creating mechanisms for victims to report such harmful content, and for platforms to investigate and ultimately take down offending material.[38] In the summer of 2024, US Representatives Jake Auchincloss (Democrat of Massachusetts) and Ashley Hinson (Republican of Iowa) jointly introduced legislation in Congress, the *Intimate Privacy Protection Act*, that would implement Citron's proposal, but adding, to the list of targeted content, pornographic deepfakes.[39] The benefit

---

[35] Ibid. at 728–30.
[36] Ibid. at 750–51.
[37] Ibid. at 753.
[38] Ibid. at 756.
[39] Release: Auchincloss Introduces Bipartisan Bill to Tackle Rise in Non-Consensual Deepfakes on Social Media Platforms, https://auchincloss.house.gov/media/press-releases/release-auchincloss-introduces-bipartisan-bill-to-tackle-rise-in-non-consensualdeepfakes-on-social-media-platforms.

of this approach is that it provides platforms who want to be good actors with a safe harbor – as long as they take reasonable and defined steps to identify and take down content invading intimate privacy, they will not be held liable for the occasional, and inevitable, mistakes. This can create a comfort level which reduces (though does not eliminate) the risk of excessive takedowns. And again, because the harmful content being targeted is carefully and narrowly defined, any harms associated with unnecessary takedowns would be very limited. Congress should give serious consideration to the Auchincloss/Hinson measure.

Professor Citron's article and the proposed legislation based on it address one set of very specific and serious issues: intimate privacy violations, stalking, and harassment. The sheer scale of this problem (which almost always victimizes women and girls) justifies legal reform, so long as it is undertaken carefully. It is tempting to move from this to propose a whole series of other carve-outs for other troubling content. But absent strong proof of a widespread and extremely serious problem, of the sort that Professor Citron and others have gathered,[40] I would resist that temptation.

It is important to remember that, for all of the reasons discussed in Chapter 6, Section 230 is very, very important. It enables platforms to operate and users to reach broad audiences. If we carve up Section 230 too much, converting it into Swiss cheese, at some point the effect will be the same as repealing Section 230 altogether. Imposing potential liability for a wide variety of user content will cause platforms to either simply abandon third-party content, or to engage in such aggressive content moderation as to silence enormous amounts of protected and harmless speech. In other words, weakening Section 230 too much will effectively end the *social* aspect of social media platforms, which is its capacity to permit millions, if not billions, of users to freely share content. And that would be a very unfortunate outcome.

8.4 PROCEDURAL RIGHTS FOR USERS

One important, difficult, and contentious question is whether regulators can and should grant users procedural rights vis-à-vis social media platforms. By procedural rights, I mean in general some sort of a legally enforceable right to notice from platforms, along with some explanation, when platforms take negative action against a user such as blocking or deemphasizing user content, as well as some right to internal review/appeal of the negative decision. On its

---

[40] Danielle Keats Citron, *Sexual Privacy*, 128 YALE L.J. 1870, 1909–28 (2019); Mary Anne Franks, "Revenge Porn" Reform: A View from the Front Lines, 69 FLA. L. REV. 1251, 1261–77 (2017).

face, procedural rights seem fair and reasonable, given platform power over their users. But on closer examination, procedural rights raise extraordinarily complex issues.

The arguments in favor of procedural rights seem simple enough, and parallel the broader arguments in favor of due process in the judicial system. The first and most obvious is, of course, that process enhances accuracy. Requiring a statement of reasons guards against arbitrary or ill-considered actions, and internal review provides a check against platform errors in content moderation – something that even Mark Zuckerberg has conceded are extremely frequent.[41] Of course no level of process can assure that no errors occur; but the idea that procedural rights reduce the likelihood of error is the basis of our entire legal system (and in the Anglo-American tradition can be traced back to Magna Carta).

In addition to reducing error, procedural rights also advance some more fundamental, dignitary values. In particular, granting individuals procedural protections and the right to participate in decisions about themselves gives them a sense of being taken seriously, and treated fairly, quite independently of whether the process reaches the "right" result, or if the individual prevails.[42] These dignitary interests provide an independent reason, in addition to accuracy, to grant procedural rights to users, though in some sense both of these interests fall within the general rubric of "fairness."

Given the strong values advanced by procedure, one might think that giving users robust procedural protections is an obviously justified step. But there are important countervailing arguments. Indeed, at some point those arguments have constitutional dimensions because granting procedural rights to users can significantly burden platforms' own editorial rights. In Chapter 4 we saw that in the *NetChoice* cases, the Supreme Court recognized that platforms enjoyed a First Amendment right to control the content that they host or refuse to host, analogizing to cases that recognized such rights for earlier media including newspapers and cable television operators. But consider newspapers in this context. Imagine if a regulator or legislature required newspapers, when they decline to print a letter to the editor submitted by a reader, to provide the reader with a voluminous explanation for the rejection. As a practical matter, this would place an enormous burden on newspapers, and indeed would lead many of them to stop publishing letters from the public. For that reason, such a requirement would surely be found to violate newspapers' First Amendment editorial rights.

---

[41] See *supra* ch. 6, n. 52 and accompanying text.
[42] See Jerry Mashaw, *Administrative Due Process: The Quest for a Dignitary Theory*, 61 B.U. L. REV. 885 (1981).

Exactly the same argument can be extended to social media platforms. Indeed, because of the sheer scale at which platform content moderation occurs, providing detailed explanations for moderation decisions could potentially be sufficiently burdensome to effectively force platforms to eliminate content moderation. Facebook, for example, is reported to review three million flagged items of content on a daily basis.[43] And YouTube stated to the Fifth Circuit in the *NetChoice* litigation that it removed over a billion comments over a three-month period in 2020.[44] Newspaper editorial decisions are by comparison child's play. So even given the availability of automation to platforms, at some point the burden of explanation and review would become unsustainable.

Even aside from the burdensomeness of disclosure-and-review requirements, there is at least an argument to be made that requiring disclosure of the reasoning behind editorial decision-making is inherently unconstitutional. Indeed, with respect to newspapers and other traditional media, the argument is a powerful one. In a case arising out of a defamation claim against a magazine and a television broadcaster, the US Supreme Court stated that a "law that subjects the editorial process to private or official examination merely to satisfy curiosity or to serve some general end as the public interest … would not survive constitutional scrutiny as the First Amendment is presently construed."[45] Admittedly, the Court then went on to permit discovery into the editorial process as part of resolving a specific defamation claim; but the Court's broader language strongly suggests that an across-the-board requirement to explain editorial decisions, if addressed to traditional media, would be found unconstitutional.[46]

Whether to extend this logic to social media platforms, however, poses a difficult question. On the one hand, as the Supreme Court recognized in *NetChoice*, platforms enjoy the same sorts of editorial rights as traditional media, including presumably the right to make editorial choices for contradictory, no, or inconsistent reasons (the Eleventh Circuit suggested as much in its *NetChoice* decision[47]). But it must be acknowledged that social media

---

[43] John Koetsier, *Report: Facebook Makes 300,000 Content Moderation Mistakes Every Day*, FORBES (June 9, 2020), www.forbes.com/sites/johnkoetsier/2020/06/09/300000-facebook-content-moderation-mistakes-daily-report-says/.

[44] NetChoice, L.L.C. v. Paxton, 49 F.4th 439, 487 (5th Cir. 2022), *vacated and remanded* Moody v. NetChoice, LLC, 144 S. Ct. 2383 (2024).

[45] Hebert v. Lando, 441 U.S. 153, 174 (1979).

[46] The Fifth Circuit found otherwise in the *NetChoice* litigation, in the course of upholding a part of Texas's HB 20 which imposed an explanation-and-review requirement on platforms. *NetChoice v. Paxton*, 49 F.4th at 487–88. But the Fifth Circuit's reasoning in that case was so thoroughly debunked by the Supreme Court on appeal that it need not be taken seriously.

[47] NetChoice, LLC v. Attorney General, Florida, 34 F.4th 1196, 1222 (11th Cir. 2022), *vacated and remanded* Moody v. NetChoice, LLC, 144 S. Ct. 2383 (2024).

platforms are different from other, traditional media. Their almost complete reliance on third-party content itself distinguishes them from traditional media such as newspapers, magazines, and broadcasters (though not from cable television operators). And their relatively *laissez faire* attitude, permitting most content to go up while moderating a relatively small fraction, helps create an expectation on the part of users that they will be hosted, unlike with letters to newspaper editors. Furthermore, for many individuals and small businesses, access to social media plays a far more central role in their lives and livelihood than being published in a newspaper.

Another distinction between platforms and newspapers is that platforms *already* in most instances *voluntarily* provide some forms of explanation and review to users. Meta, for example, states that when it identifies content that violates Facebook Community Standards or Instagram Community Guidelines, "Meta will remove it. We'll also notify you so you can understand why we removed the content and how to avoid posting violating content in the future."[48] It also states that if content is removed, "we offer appeals for the vast majority of violation types on Facebook and Instagram."[49] And furthermore Meta, admittedly uniquely among platforms, offers the possibility of a further appeal of a unfavorable content decision to its Oversight Board.[50] Of course not all platforms provide as extensive user protections as Meta (and not all platforms engage in such extensive content moderation); but Meta's experience does suggest that granting users some procedural protections is consistent with robust content moderation.

All of these factors help to distinguish platforms from traditional media, and so cut in favor of recognizing *some* user rights with respect to platforms. On the other hand, the concerns about the burdensomeness of elaborate procedural obligations, and their likely negative impact on content moderation, cut in the opposite direction. How to balance these competing considerations is, quite frankly, a conundrum, and it turns significantly on very practical considerations about just how burdensome specific procedural rights would be – information that is only available to the platforms themselves (if even that). Furthermore, there is an argument to be made that business considerations alone (meaning retaining users) may well sufficiently incentivize platforms to protect users, so no state intervention is necessary. And there is also a very real

---

[48] Meta Transparency Center, *Taking Down Violating Content* (Feb. 22, 2023), https://transparency.meta.com/enforcement/taking-action/taking-down-violating-content/.

[49] Meta Transparency Center, *Appealed Content: What Can Be Appealed* (Nov. 18, 2022), https://transparency.meta.com/policies/improving/appealed-content-metric/.

[50] Meta Transparency Center, *How to Appeal to the Oversight Board* (April 3, 2024), https://transparency.meta.com/oversight/appealing-to-oversight-board/.

concern that when regulators *do* impose procedural obligations on platforms, as Texas did in HB 20, the true motivation may well be to hamstring platform moderation practices rather than to benefit users. These arguments raise serious doubts about the wisdom of any regulatory imposition of procedural obligations on platforms.

On balance, however, I am inclined to think that some regulatory intervention here may be justified and will not be unduly burdensome. Articles 20 and 21 of the EU's Digital Services Act (DSA), which as noted earlier was enacted in 2022 and is now in effect, grants precisely such rights to platform users, including a right to an internal appeal and a right to appeal further to an out-of-court dispute settlement entity designated by member nations.[51] This suggests that granting at least a right of internal appeal may well be a manageable burden, so long as elaborate explanations are not demanded of platforms. On the other hand, I do worry that the further right to external review, and potential judicial review, that the DSA envisions might impose very significant burdens, especially on smaller platforms, and so might be inadvisable (the EU is famously insensitive to such concerns, making it a rather poor role model for regulators). But I see no fundamental objection to a federal statute in the United States requiring platforms to create an internal review system for content moderation and deplatforming decisions, recognizing that some smaller platforms may be able to successfully challenge the application of such a law to them, on the grounds that it is excessively burdensome.

Procedural rights, in short, is another area where *some* regulatory initiatives may well be justified, simply in the name of fairness. But as always in this sensitive area, regulators must be sure to carefully thread the needle between protecting users and burdening platforms. And as always, courts must be available as a backstop to block excessively burdensome regulation.

8.5 DATA PRIVACY

The last area of possible regulatory reform that I will touch on is, unsurprisingly, data privacy. This is an area, as discussed in Chapter 7, in which there has been significant regulatory movement in recent years, including the EU's GDPR and California's Consumer Privacy Act (CCPA), as well as similar statutes in other states. In the United States, however, there has been no significant progress toward *national* privacy legislation, despite growing bipartisan

---

[51] *Regulation (EU) 2022/2065 of the European Parliament and of the Council of 19 October 2022 on a Single Market for Digital Services and amending Directive 2000/31/EC (Digital Services Act)* Arts. 20 and 21, https://eur-lex.europa.eu/eli/reg/2022/2065/oj.

calls for such legislation and the obvious benefits (for both individuals and platforms) of a uniform nationwide regulatory regime. There is a strong argument that the time has come to close that regulatory gap. And it should be noted that any privacy legislation should be targeted not at social media platforms' data practices specifically but rather at all online data collection and processing.

The basic contours of needed federal privacy regulation seem relatively clear. First and foremost, it is entirely legitimate to require holders of personal data to take reasonable steps to prevent inadvertent disclosures and hacks. Given that the harms of data disclosures fall primarily on data subjects, but the power to prevent disclosures lies with data holders, the latter obviously have insufficient incentives to guard against inadvertent disclosures or hacks. The law can legitimately seek to correct this imbalance.

In addition, at a minimum, as with essentially all extant privacy laws, federal legislation must give the subjects of data collection some basic rights, including the right to be informed regarding how their data is collected, stored, and used; a right to access their personal data; and a right to have incorrect data be corrected. In addition, such legislation should probably include a right to object to the transfer or sale of especially sensitive data. These rights parallel the rights granted in the GDPR, CCPA, and other similar (sometimes copycat) state and national legislation around the world. And they are essential if data subjects are to be able to protect themselves from privacy violations and other misuse of sometimes highly personal information.

Why these rights are needed is straightforward. Basic notice about data practices are essential because otherwise users/data subjects have no ability to exercise their other data rights, or to choose to simply decline to use the relevant service, if the service providers' data practices seem too intrusive. The right to access personal data is similarly necessary to make other rights, including the right to correct inaccurate data, meaningful. Furthermore, being able to determine/confirm the content of the data collected by any particular entity also has obvious relevance in determining whether to consent to further transfer of the data. After all, my personal interest in keeping my work email and phone number (both freely available on the internet) private is far less pressing than it is, say, for medical or financial data, or even data regarding buying and web browsing habits.

Being able to correct inaccurate data is also fundamental to meaningful data privacy. While some data inaccuracies (say having a data subject's phone number wrong) can be fairly harmless, and indeed sometimes beneficial (fewer spam calls and texts), others can be effectively defamatory. Thus if a database inaccurately reports that one has filed for bankruptcy (as happened in a leading US Supreme Court defamation case[52]), this can have serious economic and social repercussions. Similarly, albeit less seriously, inaccurate data about purchasing habits can result in being inundated with irritating and pointless advertising. Furthermore, it is hard to conceive of why a data holder would have any legitimate interest in maintaining inaccurate data. Of course, data correction rights do impose some costs on data holders; but the European and California experiences suggest that the costs are quite manageable (in part because such rights are rarely exercised, as discussed further later).

Finally, we come to what is potentially a more controversial right: the ability to opt out of data transfers and sales. This right implicates a more profound legal/ethical question, which is who "owns" personal data, the subject of the data or the data holder. The EU clearly views data subjects, if not as "owners" of data, as having fundamental rights to exercise control over their data – that is indeed what the first two findings in the preface to the official text of the GDPR, as well as Art. 1 of the GDPR, state.[53]

But at least in the US legal tradition, the truth of this proposition is not evident. After all, personal data that data holders collect was generally freely shared by data subjects, usually in exchange for valuable services (including such things as discounts at grocery stores[54]). And personal data is notoriously an article of commerce – reports suggest that the global data brokerage market will be worth close to $400 billion in 2024.[55] Normally in the US legal system we assume that when a valuable commodity (which data is) is exchanged for services, title to the commodity moves to the recipient. And unlike in the European tradition, US law is much more resistant to amorphous rights of personality which limit traditional property rights.

The preceding discussion would suggest that a right to object to data transfers and sales is in tension with existing property and contract law principles. But there are countervailing considerations. Most obviously, there are some specific types of highly personal data, such as financial and medical information, that even in the United States are already heavily regulated, because of the obvious harms associated with disclosure. That seems entirely appropriate, for the same reasons that we regulate the sale and distribution of other

---

[52] Dun & Bradstreet, Inc. v. Greenmoss Builders, Inc., 472 U.S. 749 (1985).
[53] GDPR, *supra* n. 14, Findings (1) and (2), Art. 1.
[54] Devan Burris, *How Grocery Stores Are Becoming Data Brokers*, CNBC (Dec. 10, 2023), www.cnbc.com/2023/12/10/how-grocery-stores-are-becoming-data-brokers.html.
[55] Knowledge Sourcing Intelligence, *Global Data Broker Market Size, Share, Opportunities, and Trends by Data Type (Consumer Data, Business Data), by End-User (BFSI, Retail, Automotive, Construction, Others) and by Geography – Forecasts from 2025 to 2030* (Dec. 2024), www.knowledge-sourcing.com/report/global-data-broker-market.

harmful items. And with respect to such highly sensitive data, data holders are surely on implicit notice (and if and when legislation is enacted, explicit notice) when they collect and store the data that their ability to use or transfer that data is likely to be restricted.

All of this raises some doubts about the flat right granted by GDPR and CCPA to data subjects to completely opt out of data sharing and sales.[56] Such an unrestricted right enacts an across-the-board preference for data subjects over the arguably legitimate interests of data holders. But if data subjects (in the case of platforms, users) have obtained valuable benefits in exchange for sharing their data, it is not clear why such a flat preference is justified. Admittedly, there is an argument to be made that, when users share data, they do so knowing that the data will be used for commercial purposes (primarily to sell targeted advertising) but do not necessarily consent to the transfer or sale of non-anonymized data. So the question is a close one. My own inclination would be to limit the right to opt out of data sharing and sales to particularly sensitive data, as the CCPA does with respect to data use;[57] but certainly other reasonable people might support the kind of flat opt-out right that the EU and California currently grant.

In short, there is plenty of room for legitimate data privacy regulations, and a pressing need for national data privacy legislation in the United States. But that said, there are also important limits on what data privacy laws should seek to accomplish. Consider opt-out rights. There are, as just acknowledged, legitimate arguments in favor of the EU's and CCPA's grants of rights to opt out of data sharing and sales. But the GDPR goes beyond permitting an opt-out from data transfers. In addition, the GDPR expressly grants data subjects the right to stop processing for the purposes of direct marketing unless they have explicitly consented to such processing[58] – and the GDPR also grants the right to withdraw consent "at any time."[59] But there is obvious tension between these rights and the original bargain under which the data subject shared their personal information, knowing that it would be processed in exchange for specific services. Essentially, an unlimited opt-out right grants users a free lunch. Certainly, users have a right to insist that processing is limited to the uses that the user/data subject originally consented to. But the right to opt out of a bargain after having received (and presumably continuing to receive, in many instances) the benefits that were bargained for is an odd form of "fairness."

---

[56] GDPR, *supra* n. 14, Art. 7; CAL. CIV. CODE § 1798.120.
[57] CAL. CIV. CODE § 1798.121.
[58] GDPR, *supra* n. 14, Art. 21(2) and (3).
[59] GDPR, *supra* n. 14, Art. 7(3).

Similar objections can also be raised to the rights to data deletion/erasure, also granted by both the GDPR and CCPA.[60] But in addition to benefit-of-the-bargain arguments, this so-called right to be forgotten also threatens basic principles of free expression. Data is information, and information undergirds public discourse. And while much personal data has little relevance to public discourse, that may not be true regarding personal information about prominent individuals, especially historical information such as past criminal convictions or other misconduct. Most obviously, such information is highly relevant to judge the fitness for office of high elected and appointed government officials. For that reason, any right to data deletion should be phrased carefully and narrowly, to ensure that data subject to deletion is not of the sort that could have relevance to current or future public discourse. Neither the GDPR nor the CCPA have any such limitations.

Admittedly, both of those regulations qualify the right of data deletion, saying that it does not apply insofar as the data is necessary, in the GDPR's words, "for exercising the right of freedom of expression and information."[61] But it is hard to know what this vacuous qualification means, especially given that in many European legal systems privacy rights, even for prominent individuals, are regularly found to trump free speech rights. Moreover, it is hard to know in advance what information *will* be relevant to public discourse. For example, one could easily imagine an individual contemplating running for local elective office arranging to have negative information about themselves deleted prior to announcing the run, thereby shielding themselves from legitimate scrutiny. Data deletion is thus an area where regulators need to tread extremely carefully – which to date they have not done.

Underlying all of these concerns about the reach of data privacy laws is a broader point: There is a fundamental tension between data privacy and the business models of the major platforms (as well as related services such as search). That business model is based on an exchange of personal data for free services – services, it should be noted, that no one is obliged to use. Data privacy advocates sometimes seem to believe that this business model is illegitimate and should be abandoned. But then they bear the burden, which they have not even attempted to meet, of coming up with an alternative model for the provision of services such as social media and search. Absent a pay-for-use model, which it is hard to believe most users would prefer, the vision seems to be that rich Big Tech giants will simply hand these services out for free,

---

[60] GDPR, *supra* n. 14, Art. 17; CAL. CIV. CODE § 1798.105.
[61] GDPR, *supra* n. 14, Art. 17(3)(a). The CCPA similarly exempts data necessary to "Exercise free speech." CAL. CIV. CODE § 1798.105(d)(4).

indefinitely. But that is a fantasy. Someone has to pay the substantial costs of providing online services, and in the long term if the advertising-based model is undermined by law, that someone is going to be users.

One final caveat is necessary here regarding data privacy regulation: efficacy. Data privacy statutes such as the GDPR and CCPA grant data subjects broad rights to control their data, including accessing their personal data, deleting data, and opting out of the sharing and sale of data. But most of those protections are effective only if data subjects affirmatively assert their rights (the major exception is the GDPR's restrictions on data processing, which are in the main self-executing). So, do data subjects assert their rights? Because if they do not, privacy laws (at least in their current incarnation) are not doing much good. And on that point, a recent study's results are not encouraging.

The study was conducted by Ella Corren, then a doctoral candidate at the University of California, Berkeley School of Law. Corren took advantage of the fact that regulations issued by the California Attorney General in 2020 to implement the CCPA require large firms (defined as those that process the data of more than 10 million consumers in California a year) to file reports laying out how many data control requests they received, and how they acted on those requests.[62] Corren used these filings to compile a database of data control requests received by 137 firms in the year 2020, and 121 firms in 2021.[63] The database focuses on three data control rights: the right to know (meaning to access one's personal information), the right to delete such personal information, and the right to opt out of the transfer or sale of personal data.[64]

The results are somewhat stunning. In 2020 the vast majority of firms – 75 percent – reported fewer than 10,000 requests annually invoking *any* of these rights, which translates to fewer than 0.1 percent of these firms' data subjects. Indeed, the majority of firms report fewer than 1,000 requests, and 88 percent of firms report less than 100,000 requests, translating to at most 1 percent of data subjects. The number of requests in 2021 was slightly higher, but even in that year 73 percent of firms reported fewer than 10,000 requests for the most-invoked right (and 89 percent of firms reported fewer than 100,000 requests).[65] In short, what Corren learned was that for the vast majority (90 percent) of firms, 99 percent of their data subjects make no data requests; that for three-quarters of firms 99.9 percent of their data subjects make no requests; and for a solid majority of firms almost no data subjects make requests.

---

[62] Ella Corren, *Gaining or Losing Control? An Empirical Study of the Real Use of Data Control Rights and Policy Implications*, 109 IOWA L. REV. 2017, 2023 (2024).
[63] Ibid. at 2033.
[64] Ibid. at 2023.
[65] Ibid. at 2035–36.

Digging slightly deeper into the data, one finds that the most-invoked of the three rights Corren included in her study is the right to opt out of data sales, by a small but significant margin. This is unsurprising because the right to opt out is the only one firms are required to highlight on their website, via a prominent "Do Not Sell My Personal Information" link.[66] In addition, it makes intuitive sense that this is the right that data subjects would care most about, because having one's data proliferate on the internet is obviously more threatening to privacy than having a single firm hold personal data. It should be noted, however, that for the major social media platforms this is also the least relevant right because, as noted in Chapter 3, they do not sell their users' data.

What are we to make of these findings, and what implications do they have for privacy regulation? It might be that regulators need to ensure that data holders provide consumers with prominent notice of all of their data control rights, including easy mechanisms for invoking them, as is true with opt-out rights. But it should be noted that even with respect to opt-out rights, 88–89 percent of firms report receiving fewer than 100,000 annual requests, meaning that fewer than 1 percent of their users invoke them. So while prominent notice might contribute to *some* greater uptake of data control rights, the impact appears to be small.

In truth, then, the main lesson of this study *might* be that people simply do not care all that much about data privacy. Admittedly, that is not what people say, but it does appear to be their revealed preference. If this is true (a contentious question), that cuts strongly against regulations which would undermine targeted advertising-driven business models for platforms, because the impact of such government action would be to take away from users something they care about (free services) in exchange for providing them something they do not much care about (data privacy).

The other possible lesson, however, is that while users might well care about data privacy, they do not want to bear the burden of protecting their own privacy. People are busy, life is hectic, and the instinct of even users who do value data privacy is to quickly click through consent buttons. Indeed, many prominent privacy scholars have made precisely this point, arguing that data control/consent laws are not a particularly effective way to protect data privacy.[67] Exploring that voluminous literature on how more effective privacy regulations might work is beyond the scope of this chapter and book. But one

---

[66] *Ibid.* at 2043–45.
[67] *See, e.g.*, Daniel J. Solove, *The Limitations of Privacy Rights*, 98 NOTRE DAME L. REV. 975 (2023); Ari Ezra Waldman, *Privacy's Rights Trap*, 117 NW. U. L. REV. ONLINE 88 (2022); Woodrow Hartzog, *The Inadequate, Invaluable Fair Information Practices*, 76 MD. L. REV. 952 (2017).

clear and striking lesson to take from all of this is that data control regimes, which are by far the most popular forms of data privacy regulation across the globe, appear to be quite ineffective, which raises serious questions about whether they are worth the costs of enactment, compliance, and enforcement.

* * * * * *

There is, in short, plenty of room for careful, targeted new regulation of social media platforms to address specific, empirically confirmed social issues. In this chapter, I have sought to highlight some possible regulatory initiatives that seem currently justified, without purporting to address the entire universe of possible government actions. But, it should be emphasized, even when action does seem necessary, an attitude of caution and skepticism regarding how to proceed remains in order, given how young social media platforms are and how quickly they continue to evolve.

Conclusion

Embracing the Unknown

Social media platforms have revolutionized the ways in which people in the United States and around the world communicate, engage with public affairs, and even organize their relationships with others. Yet social media is a very new technology. Most of the major extant platforms (Facebook, Twitter/X, YouTube) did not become available to the general public until around 2006, Instagram was founded in 2010, and TikTok did not become available internationally until 2017. Furthermore, even the early platforms were relatively niche interests until the widespread adoption of smartphones, starting around 2010 (the first iPhone was released in 2007). Yet in 2016 social media, including Russian interference via social media, was said to play a potentially significant role in the US presidential election. And by 2020, both US presidential candidates were calling for regulation of social media. Very rarely, if ever before in human history, has a new technology been adopted so quickly and widely, and had such a rapid impact on society worldwide.

Given the rapid adoption and impact of social media, it is perhaps unsurprising that so many critics find the growth of social media disorienting or even threatening. After all, change, especially rapid social and technological change, is often unsettling. In the case of social media, the primary way in which this reaction has manifested itself is through a torrent of criticism from across the political spectrum. This book has argued, however, that much of this criticism is unwarranted or exaggerated, and lacks an empirical basis.

Criticisms of social media from the political right generally come down to an argument that platforms are silencing too much speech. In particular, many conservative politicians and commentators have alleged a systematic bias on the part of platforms against conservative viewpoints. As we saw, however, empirical studies simply do not support these charges, and in any event the evolution of the most important platform for political discourse, Twitter/X, since its purchase by Elon Musk makes these claims highly dubious going forward.

In contrast to conservatives, progressive attacks on social media generally express a desire for platforms to silence more speech than they do, especially hate speech and disinformation. Yet these critiques too are not entirely coherent. After all, the major platforms *do* have policies against hate speech – indeed, it is the enforcement of these policies that triggers many of the conservative attacks on social media. Progressive criticisms thus ultimately come down to complaints that platforms are imperfect in their efforts to block harmful speech. Yet the dream of perfectly effective content moderation is a fantasy, and certainly left-wing critics have utterly failed to articulate how they think it could be achieved.

Furthermore, just as many of the politically motivated attacks on social media lack a solid grounding, so too most of the proposals to regulate or reform social media platforms are, as we have seen, deeply problematic and often blatantly unconstitutional. Many would-be regulators, from across the political spectrum, approach social media regulation as if it were equivalent to regulating consumer products or prescription medications. But social media is *media*, meaning it is a platform for speech and public discourse. And in the US constitutional tradition, anchored in the First Amendment, there is a strong presumption against governmental intervention in public discourse. At a minimum, would-be regulators must bear the burden of proving the need for, and efficacy of, proposed regulation. And in the social media sphere, that burden has generally not been met.

None of which is to say that all regulations directed at social media are without merit. There can be little doubt that given how much social media has accelerated the spread of information, it has to some extent exacerbated existing, troublesome social problems and divisions. Some of the criticisms of social media from across the political spectrum, in particular about privacy and about the impact of social media on children, certainly have a basis (though it should be said that, especially regarding the impact of social media on children, the attacks are often exaggerated and lacking in empirical support).

Regardless of the strength or weakness of specific critiques of social media, some things are clear. First and foremost, as discussed in the last chapter of this book, it is high time that social media firms be held to account when they violate existing, generally applicable legal principles. This includes obvious sources of constraint such as antitrust laws and the common law of torts. But it also includes some well-established bodies of law, including family law, which have not been thought to apply to social media platforms, arguably incorrectly.

In addition, there are some new and narrow regulatory proposals directed specifically at social media or new technology that are worth considering.

This includes some narrowly focused forms of Section 230 reform, badly needed (especially in the United States) privacy regulations, and laws protecting minors from online harms by empowering parents. Social media is not, and should not in any way be, a law-free zone.

Ultimately, however, much of the current war on social media is rooted in hysteria. And it is an historically familiar form of hysteria, which has regularly been triggered by revolutionary new communications technologies, from the printing press to motion pictures to video games. In 1909, for example, in the infancy of the motion picture industry, the New York Times published an article suggestively titled "Moving Pictures as Helps to Crime."[1] And perhaps as a result of such overblown fears (to put it gently), when the US Supreme Court was first faced with efforts to censor the new industry, it held that motion pictures were not constitutionally protected "speech."[2] We should not repeat the errors of our past.

Furthermore, any such efforts would be futile. Just as Henry VIII of England could not tame the printing press by imposing press licensing, modern day would-be Henrys cannot put the social media genie back in the bottle. The fast spread of information and the democratization of speech are here to stay, and no government has the power to turn back the clock on these developments. Nor should they try.

It is time to acknowledge that we live in a new era. The age of Gatekeepers carefully controlling what the public sees and hears is over. So too is the age of elites and experts monopolizing public discourse. And while members of the traditional media, as well as politicians, have understandably fixated on the negative impacts of these changes – they are, after all, the ones disempowered by them – the rest of us need not be so pessimistic. After all, for all our current growing pains, the democratization of public discourse enabled by the internet, and especially social media, should be seen as a *good* thing. In perhaps the most famous passage ever written about the First Amendment, US Supreme Court Justice Louis Brandeis opined that "the greatest menace to freedom is an inert people [and] public discussion is a political duty."[3] But there is nothing more likely to encourage inertia, and dissuade political participation, than excluding the *public* from public discourse. Social media has proven to be a revolutionary tool in reengaging the broader public in political discussions, sometimes for the worse, but often for the better. In our rush to rein in social media, we should not forget this basic point.

---

[1] *Moving Pictures as Helps to Crime: Exhibitions That Excel the Old-Time Dime Novel in Suggestiveness Watched by the Police*, N.Y. TIMES (Feb. 21, 1909), https://timesmachine.nytimes.com/timesmachine/1909/02/21/106117731.html?pageNumber=40.

[2] Mutual Film Corp. v. Industrial Commission of Ohio, 236 U.S. 230, 241–45 (1915).

[3] Whitney v. California, 274 U.S. 357, 375 (1927) (Brandeis, J., concurring).

Nor does it make sense to instinctively fear disruptive new technologies, as those who wield social and political power tend to do. The printing press brought religious wars to Europe, but it also ultimately brought a scientific revolution, mass literacy, and an explosion of the arts. Who knows what a new, truly interconnected world, in which every person can potentially have a global voice, will bring. Perhaps it will resemble Aldous Huxley's dystopia;[4] but perhaps it will instead give birth to new, positive social revolutions. In the face of that uncertainty, it behooves us not to risk strangling that new world in the cradle because of fear of the unknown.

---

[4] ALDOUS HUXLEY, BRAVE NEW WORLD (1932).

Index

Abbott, Greg, 1, 14–15
addiction issues, social media as influence on, 41–47
adolescents, social media influences on, 41–47
  body image issues, 45–46, 50
  legislative regulations regarding, 42
  mental health issues, 43–45
advertising revenue
  data privacy for children and, 161–62
  hate speech content as influence on, 109–10
  for Meta, 146–48
  for TikTok, 147
  for Twitter, 146–48
  for YouTube, 147
The Age of Surveillance Capitalism (Zuboff), 51
algorithms. *See* platform algorithms
Alito, Samuel (Justice), 23, 63, 72, 77–79
anchorman/network reporters, as gatekeepers, 99. *See also specific people*
antisemitism, 19
Apple, data privacy issues and, 53–54
Auchincloss, Jake, 178

Bache, Benjamin Franklin, 101
Baker, Gerard, 17
Baldwin, Adam, 34–35
Balkin, Jack, 57
Bambauer, Jane, 40, 114, 157
Bannon, Steve, 9–10, 34–35
  data privacy and, 51
Barrett, Amy Coney (Justice), 142, 145
Bezos, Jeff, 57–58
Biden, Hunter, 107
Biden, Joseph, 11–12. *See also* 2020 presidential election
  COVID-19 policies, 31
  on Section 230, 124

Big Data, 51–54
  surveillance capitalism, 52–53, 57–58
  targeted advertising with, 53–54
Big Tech, 13–14. *See also* social media
  data privacy and, 51
body image issues, social media as influence on, 3–4
  among adolescent girls, 45–46, 50
  progressive response to, 41–47
Boy Scouts of America v. Dale, 78–79
Brandeis, Louis (Justice), 108, 193
Breitbart, 34–35
broadcast media. *See also specific news organizations*
  anchorman/network reporters as gatekeepers in, 99
  Federal Communications Commission and establishment of, 98–99
  Fairness Doctrine, 22–23, 101–3
  news organization rules under, 22–23
  as institutional gatekeepers, 98–100
  radio, 98
  television news broadcasters, 98–100
ByteDance, 58–59, 168

California Age-Appropriate Design Code Act (CAADCA), U.S., 161–62
California Consumer Privacy Act (CCPA), U.S., 51–52, 149–52, 158–60, 183–84
  data transfer and sales under, 186–88
  regulatory scope of, 151–52
Cambridge Analytica scandal, 9–10, 51
Candeub, Adam, 69–70, 122
capitalism, surveillance, 52–53, 57–58
Carlson, Tucker, 104
Catholic Church, Index of Prohibited Books, 4–5
CCPA. *See* California Consumer Privacy Act (CCPA), U.S.

195

censorship, social media and
  through deplatforming, 9
  after January 6th Capitol attacks, 9
  misinformation and, during COVID-19
    pandemic, 11–12
  prohibition of hate speech, 18–19
  Twitter Files, 16–19
children. *See also* adolescents, social media
    influences on
  data privacy for, 160–63
    under General Data Protection
      Regulation, 162
    NetChoice v. Bonta, 161–62
    public disclosure limits, 163
    targeted advertising, 161–62
China
  data privacy issues and, 55
  TikTok as spying platform for, 58–59
Citron, Danielle Keats, 33–34, 127–28, 145,
    176–79
CJEU. *See* Court of Justice of the European
    Union (CJEU)
Clinton, Bill, 2, 27
Clinton, Hilary, 27. *See also* 2016 presidential
    election
  use of social media by, 9
CNN, 21–22
common carriage status
  Alito on, 77–79
  in English common law, 64–67
  Federal Communications Act of 1934, 64
  historical scope of, 64–67
  holding out approach to, 66
  Interstate Commerce Act of 1887, 64
  public interest issues and, 68–69
  during technological revolutions, 64–65
  for telecommunications companies, 74
  Thomas on, 65–66, 68–70, 72, 77–79, 87
common carriers, social media platforms as
  conceptual approach to, 62–63
  in court cases, 62–63, 65–66, 72
    constitutional issues in, 71
    NARUC I/II cases, 66, 68
    NetChoice cases, 62–63, 71–83, 85
  critiques of, 86–91
    in Florida, 89–91
    for illegal content, 88
    for lawful-but-awful content, 88–89
    in Texas, 89–91
  definition of, 63–70
  deplatforming of users, 63–64, 67, 76
    regulatory proposals against, 86, 89–90
  editorial rights issues, 70–77, 79–81
    First Amendment protection arguments,
      71–74, 78–80, 82–83, 85
    ideological content and, 77, 83
    transparency requirements, 83
    viewpoint neutrality and, 90

  Facebook and, 67–68
  NetChoice cases, 62–63, 71–81, 85
  regulatory proposals for, 84–86
    against deplatforming of users, 86,
      89–90
    for hate speech, 85–86, 90–91
  terms of service for, 76–77
  TikTok and, 67–68
common law, common carriage status in,
    64–67
Communications Decency Act, U.S.,
    31–32. *See also* Section 230, of
    Communications Decency Act
Conservative Political Action Conference
    (CPAC), 18–19
conservatives, conservative media and. *See
    also* Fox News
  Breitbart, 34–35
  CPAC convention, 18–19
  4Chan, 34–35
  hate speech and, 19
  Musk role in, 24
  Section 230 reforms by, 125–26
  Texas Republican Party, 18–19
  Twitter support of, 20, 24
  "War on Big Tech" and, 15
  "War on Woke" and, 13–15
content moderation, for hate speech
  on Facebook, 96, 110
  incentives for, 115–17
    by government, 115–16
    by private platforms, 116–17
  Zuckerberg's influence on, 96
Corren, Ella, 188–89
Court of Justice of the European Union
    (CJEU), 152–55
COVID-19 pandemic
  during Biden Administration, 31
  Fox News misinformation on, 31
  gatekeepers during
    government as, 92–93, 96
    social media as, 107
  history of, 28
  misinformation through social media,
      10–12
    anti-misinformation policies and, 30
    censorship claims and, 11–12
    claims of social media censorship and,
      11–12
    on Facebook, 19–20
    of false cures, 29–30
    progressives' response to, 28–33
    on Twitter, 19–20
  Section 230 during, 92–93
CPAC. *See* Conservative Political Action
    Conference (CPAC)
Cronkite, Walter, 99, 102
Cruz, Ted, 9–12

Index

data erasure requirements, 160
data integrity, 155–57
data privacy, social media companies and, 155–57. *See also* General Data Protection Regulation (GDPR), EU
  analysis of, 163
  Apple, 53–54
  Big Data and, 51–54
    surveillance capitalism, 52–53, 57–58
    targeted advertising with, 53–54
  Big Tech and, 51
  Cambridge Analytica scandal and, 9–10, 51
  for children, 160–63
    under General Data Protection Regulation, 162
    NetChoice v. Bonta, 161–62
    public disclosure limits, 163
    targeted advertising, 161–62
  China and, 55
    TikTok as spying platform for, 58–59
  conceptual approach to, 51–52
  counter considerations to, 58–61
  data erasure requirements, 160
  data integrity strategies, 155–57
  data transfers and sales and, 185–86
    under California Consumer Privacy Act, 186–88
    under General Data Protection Regulation, 186–88
  dignitary privacy and, 153
  in EU, 54
    in CJEU cases, 152–55
    Google Spain case, 152–55, 157
  Facebook and, 9–10, 51, 160
  free speech and, 157–60
    First Amendment protections for, 158–60
  network effects and, 156
  reform proposals, 183–90
  restriction of access to, 60–61
  risks and threats to, 54–58
    in data storage, 54–55
    financial information, 59–60
    information leaks, 54–55, 59–60
  Russia and, 55
  social manipulation through, 60
  on TikTok, 56, 160
    banning of, 58–59
    as spying platform, 58–59
  transparency strategies, 155–57, 159
  Uber, 55–56
  in U.S., 54
    under California Age-Appropriate Design Code Act, 161–62
    under California Consumer Privacy Act, 51–52, 149–52, 158–60, 183–84
  on YouTube, 160
data transfers and sales, regulation of, 185–86
  under California Consumer Privacy Act, 186–88
  under General Data Protection Regulation, 186–88
deepfakes, 176
  under *Intimate Privacy Protection Act*, 178
deplatforming, of users
  common carriers and, 63–64, 67, 76
  regulatory proposals against, 86, 89–90
  of Trump, D., 9
    First Amendment arguments against, 15
    after January 6th Capitol attacks, 12–13
DeSantis, Ron, 1, 3
  claims of social media bias, 13–14
  political polarization and, 41
  "War on Woke" and, 13–14
Digital Millennium Copyright Act (DMCA), U.S., 136, 177
Digital Services Act (DSA), EU, 137–38, 148, 175
dignitary privacy, 153
disinformation. *See* misinformation, disinformation and
DMCA. *See* Digital Millennium Copyright Act (DMCA), U.S.
doom scrolling, 42
doxing, 33
DSA. *See* Digital Services Act (DSA), EU

The Economist, 42
editorial rights
  for social media, 70–77, 79–81
    First Amendment protection arguments, 71–74, 78–80, 82–83, 85
    ideological content and, 77, 83
    legal implications of, 82–84
    viewpoint neutrality and, 90
  for traditional media, 74–75
election fraud, 2020 presidential election and, 12
Epstein, Richard, 29–30
European Union (EU). *See also* General Data Protection Regulation (GDPR), EU
  data privacy issues in, 54
    in CJEU cases, 152–55
    Google Spain case, 152–55, 157
  Digital Services Act, 137–38, 148, 175

Facebook, 4, 24
  Cambridge Analytica scandal, 9–10, 51
  Community Standards, 17–19
  data privacy issues, 9–10, 51, 160
  hate speech controls, 18–19
    progressive responses to, 35–36
  misinformation on
    claims of political pressure on, 20–21
    during COVID-19 pandemic, 19–21
  prohibition of hate speech on, 18–19

Fairness Doctrine, 22–23, 101
  repeal of, 102–1
FCC. *See* Federal Communications Commission (FCC)
Federal Communications Act of 1934, U.S., 64
Federal Communications Commission (FCC)
  establishment of, 98–99
  Fairness Doctrine and, 22–23, 101
    repeal of, 102–3
  news organization rules under, 22–23
Federal Trade Commission (FTC), 171–72
Fight Online Sex Trafficking Act (FOSTA), U.S. (2018), 176–77
films and cinema
  early negative reactions of, 5
  First Amendment protections for, 5
filter bubbles, 38–41
First Amendment
  data privacy under, 158–60
  editorial rights protections, 71–74, 78–80, 82–83, 85
  government gatekeepers and, 93–95
  hate speech and, 36
  protections for film and cinema, 5
Florida
  common carrier issues in, 89–91
  legislation on social media in, 13–14
FOSTA. *See* Fight Online Sex Trafficking Act (FOSTA), U.S. (2018)
4Chan, 34–35
Fox News, 21–23
  conservative slant of, 22
  COVID-19 misinformation on, 31
  political polarization influenced by, 2, 50
  social media compared to, 23
Franks, Mary Anne, 34–35, 127–28, 145
FTC. *See* Federal Trade Commission (FTC)

Gab, 24, 31
Gaetz, Matt, 18
Gamergate, 33
gatekeepers
  definition of, 92
  for disinformation, 94–95
  government as, 92–96
    during COVID-19 pandemic, 92–93, 96
    First Amendment protections in, 93–95
    under Section 230, 92–95
    for hate speech prohibitions, 94–95
  institutional, 96–104
    anchorman/network reporters as, 99
    collapse of, 102–4
    Murrow–Cronkite Effect, 102, 104
    newspapers, 98, 101
    objectivity of, 100–2
    radio, 98
    television news broadcasters, 98–100
  new technologies as influence on, 102–4
  political polarization influenced by, 104
  social media as, 103–8
    during COVID-19 pandemic, 107
    economic incentives for, 106
    lack of expertise and, 107–8
    lack of training, 106–7
    misinformation and, 107
  traditional media as, 6, 97–99
General Data Protection Regulation (GDPR), EU, 167
  Article 6, 149–50
  data privacy rights under, 149–52, 156–57, 159, 162, 183–84
  data processing under, 150
  data transfer and sales under, 186–88
  regulatory scope of, 150–51
Germany
  hate speech in, 111
    under NetzDG law, 36–37, 112
    progressives' response to, 36–37
  NetzDG law, 36–37, 112, 166
Gianforte, Greg, 58–59
Gillespie, Tarleton, 143
Gingrich, Newt, 2, 41
girls. *See* adolescents
Goldman, Eric, 46–47, 88
Google Spain case, 152–55, 157
Gorsuch, Neil (Justice), 23, 63, 72
Graham, Linsey, 124
Greeley, Horace, 101
Greene, Marjorie Taylor, 18, 41
Grewal, Gurbir S., 36, 93
Gutenberg, Johannes, 4

Haidt, Jonathan, 39, 42, 113–14
harassment. *See* online harassment
Harris, Kamala, 60
hate speech, on social media, 108–12
  antisemitism and, 19
  conservatives and, 19
  on Facebook, 18–19
    for content moderation, 96, 110
    progressives' response to, 35–36
  in Germany, 111
    under NetzDG law, 36–37, 112
    progressives' response to, 36–37
  progressives' response to, 35–38
    Facebook and, 35–36
    First Amendment protections, 36
    in Germany, 36–37
    legislative regulations and, 35–37
  regulation for common carriers, 85–86, 90–91
  on Twitter, 18–19, 109–10

advertising revenue influenced by, 109–10
progressive critics of, 109
in U.S.
First Amendment protections, 36
under Section 230 of Communications Decency Act, 112
in Supreme Court case law, 36
hateful conduct. *See* hate speech, on social media
Haugen, Francine, 45–47
Hawley, Josh, 1, 42–43, 126, 139
Healey, Maura, 52
Hearst, William Randolph, 98, 100
Henry VIII, 4–5
Hinson, Ashley, 178
Hippocrates, 164–65
Hofstadter, Richard J., 49
Holmes, Oliver Wendell (Justice), 108
Hurley v. Irish-American Gay, Lesbian and Bisexual Group of Boston, 78–79
Huxley, Aldous, 194

illegal content, 88
immunity, for speech, under Section 230, 131–40
for content moderation, 122, 133, 135, 138–40, 143–44
relationship to First Amendment, 121–22, 131–34, 139–40, 145
for third-party content, 131–38
Index of Prohibited Books, 4–5
India, 138, 166
Information Technology Act, India (2000), 138, 166
Ingraham, Laura, 75
Instagram, 24
institutional gatekeepers, 96–104. *See also* media, traditional
anchorman/network reporters as, 99
collapse of, 102–4
Murrow–Cronkite Effect, 102, 104
newspapers, 98, 101
objectivity of, 100–2
radio, 98
television news broadcasters, 98–100
Interstate Commerce Act of 1887, U.S., 64
Intimate Privacy Protection Act, U.S., 178

Jackson, Ketanji Brown (Justice), 72
Jackson, Robert (Justice), 69
John Birch Society, 49
Johnson, Lyndon, 99
Jones, Meg Leta, 149
Jordan, Jim, 20–21
journalism, journalists and

Code of Ethics for, 100
as institutional gatekeepers, 98, 101
Society of Professional Journalists, 100

Kagan, Elena (Justice), 72
Kaminski, Margot, 149
Kennedy, Anthony M. (Justice), 7
Kennedy, Robert F., Jr., 104
Klobuchar, Amy, 1, 31–32, 84–85, 92, 126–27

lawful-but-awful content, 88–89
Lawrence, Jennifer, 54
Lemmon v. Snap, 129–30
Levin, Mark, 22
liberal bias
in social media, 2–3, 9
DeSantis on, 13–14
Twitter Files and, 16–19
"War on Woke," 13–14
Limbaugh, Rush, 22
Lujan, Ben Ray, 31–32
Luther, Martin, 4

Maddow, Rachel, 75
Madison, James, 89–90
manipulation. *See* political manipulation, through social media
McCarthy, Joseph, 99
media, traditional. *See also* broadcast media; print media; *specific news organizations*
editorial rights for, 74–75
as gatekeepers, 6, 97–99
social media compared to, 23–25, 182–83
displacement in media sphere by, 103–4
Fox News and, 23
mental health, social media as influence on, progressives' response to, 42–45
for adolescents, 43–45
suicidal ideation and, 43
Meta. *See also* Facebook; Instagram
targeted advertising revenue for, 146–48
Miers, Jess, 88
misinformation, disinformation and
anti-misinformation policies, 30
during COVID-19 pandemic, 10–12
anti-misinformation policies, 30
claims of social media censorship and, 11–12
on Facebook, 19–21
of false cures, 29–30
progressives' response to, 28–33
on Twitter, 19–20
progressives' response to, 48
during COVID-19 pandemic, 28–33
on political manipulation, 26–28
2020 presidential election and, of election fraud, 12

Modi, Narendra, 138
Moody v. NetChoice (NetChoice cases), 62–63, 71–81
MSNBC, 21–22
Murrow, Edward R., 99, 102
Murthy, Vivek, 31, 44–45
Musk, Elon, 3, 15–16, 19–20, 30, 168–69. See also Twitter
  conservative messaging favored by, 24
  global impact and power of, 57–58, 60, 166–67
  Trump, Donald, support of, 57
MySpace, 4

NARUC I/II cases, 66, 68
NetChoice cases, 62–63, 71–81, 85
  Section 230 and, 132–33, 140, 145
NetChoice v. Bonta, 161–62
NetChoice v. Paxton. See NetChoice cases
network effects, data privacy and, 156
NetzDG law, in Germany, 36–37, 112
  Section 230 compared to, 135–36
New York Times v. Sullivan, 131–33
newspapers, as institutional gatekeepers, 98, 101
Nunes, Devin, 13
Nunziato, Dawn, 137

Ochs, Adolph, 98, 100
online harassment, 33–35, 108–12
  against African Americans, 33–34
  doxing, 33
  4Chan, 34–35
  through threats of violence, 33–34
  of women, 33–35
    Gamergate, 33
    revenge porn, 33

The Paranoid Style in American Politics (Hofstadter), 49
Parler, 24, 31
Pelosi, Nancy, 1
platform algorithms
  political manipulation through, 114–15
  political polarization influenced by, 40
  TikTok, 173
polarization, political. See also political manipulation, through social media
  Fox News and, 2, 50
  gatekeepers as influence on, 104
  progressives' response to, 38–41
    arguments against social media influence, 40–41
    platform algorithms as influence on, 40
  social media as influence on, 2
political manipulation, through social media, 113–15

political polarization and, 113–15
  platform algorithms, 114–15
of progressives
  through misinformation, 26–28
  by Russian actors, 26–28
  during 2016 presidential election, 26–28
by Russia
  of progressives, 26–28
  in U.S. presidential elections, 113
pornography. See also deepfakes; illegal content
  under Intimate Privacy Protection Act, 178
Post, Robert, 152
presidential elections, in U.S.
  2016 election, 26–28
  2020 election, 12
Prigozhin, Yevgeny, 27
print media. See also journalism, journalists and
  early negative response to, 4–5
  Index of Prohibited Books, 4–5
  newspapers, 98, 101
  origins of, 4–5
privacy. See data privacy, social media companies and
procedural rights, for social media users, 179–83
  for content moderation, 180
  under Digital Services Act, 183
  in NetChoice cases, 180–82
progressives, social media and
  addiction and, 41–47
  body image issues influenced by, 41–47
    among adolescent girls, 45–46, 50
  children and adolescent issues and, 41–47
    body image issues, 45–46, 50
    legislative regulations for, 42
    mental health concerns, 43–45
  disinformation and, 48
  filter bubbles and, 38–41
  hate speech controls and, 35–38
    Facebook and, 35–36
    First Amendment protections, 36
    in Germany, 36–37
    legislative regulations, 35–37
    under NetzDG law, 36–37
  ideological silos and, 38–41
  mental health issues and, 42–45
    for adolescents, 43–45
    suicidal ideation and, 43
  misinformation and disinformation, 48
    during COVID-19 pandemic, 28–33
    political manipulation through, 26–28
  online harassment and, 33–35
    against African Americans, 33–34
    doxing, 33
    revenge porn, 33

through threats of violence, 33–34
   against women, 33–35
political manipulation of
   through misinformation, 26–28
   by Russian actors, 26–28
   during 2016 presidential election, 26–28
political polarization influenced by, 38–41
   arguments against, 40–41
   platform algorithms as influence on, 40
   Section 230 reforms, 126–28
Protestant Reformation, 4
public accommodation laws. *See also* common carriage status
   common carriers and, 78–79
Pulitzer, Joseph, 98, 100
Putin, Vladimir, 27

QAnon conspiracy, 49, 104

radio, as institutional gatekeeper, 98
Rand, David G., 20
Reddit, 24
#*Republic* (Sunstein), 38
Republic.com (Sunstein), 38
revenge porn, 33
Ricks, Morgan, 70
Rogers, Yvonne Gonzales, 130–31
Roosevelt, Franklin Delano, 98
Rubio, Marco, 126, 139
Russia, social media use by
   data privacy issues and, 55
   political manipulation in U.S., 26–28

Salk, Jonas, 102
Scalia, Antonin (Justice), 5
Section 230, of Communications Decency Act
   Barrett's opinions on, 142, 145
   Biden, J., on, 124
   common carriers and, 69–70
      regulatory proposals regarding, 85–86
   conceptual approach to, 118
   during COVID-19 pandemic, 92–93
   criticism of, 118–19, 123–28
   defense of, 123, 131–41
      analysis of, 141, 143
   First Amendment in relation to, 121–22, 131–34, 139–40, 145
   hate speech on social media under, 112
   historical development of, 119–23
   immunity under, 131–40
      for content moderation, 122, 133, 135, 138–40, 143–44
      for third-party content, 131–38
   key provisions of, 120–23
   Lemmon v. Snap and, 129–30
   liability under, 135–36
   limits of, 128–31

NetChoice cases, 132–33, 140, 145
NetzDG law compared to, 135–36
New York Times v. Sullivan and, 131–33
reform proposals for, 118–19, 125–28, 175–79
   by conservatives, 125–26
   by progressives, 126–28
repeal proposals, 125
social media platforms and, 128–30, 173
   protections for algorithms, 141–45
take-down regimes and, 136–38
Thomas objections to, 125
Trump, Donald, on, 124–26, 128
Zeran v. American Online, 120–21
Shapiro, Ben, 22
Singh, Manvir, 47–48
Sitaram, Ganesh, 70
1619 Project, 49
social harms, from social media, 164–70
   do no harm principle, 164–65
social media. *See also* common carriers; of Communications Decency Act; deplatforming of users; Section 230; *specific people; specific topics*
   body image issues influenced by, 3–4
   congressional reaction to, 5
   cost of speech and, 6
   COVID-19 misinformation through, 10–12
      claims of social media censorship and, 11–12
      on Facebook, 19–21
      on Twitter, 19–20
   critics of, 1–2, 7–8
      complaints about liberal bias, 2–3
   data privacy practices, 9–10
   gatekeepers on, 103–8
      during COVID-19 pandemic, 107
      economic incentives for, 106
      lack of expertise and, 107–8
      lack of training, 106–7
      misinformation and, 107
   in Germany, 36–37
   as global revolution, 191–94
   historical context for, 1–8
   MySpace, 4
   offensive material and, 5
   political polarization influenced by, 2
   as primary source of news, 21
   regulation of, 23–24, 170–75
      antitrust scrutiny in, 170–72
      through contracts, 172–73
      under family law, 175
      through state legislation, 13–15
      under tort law, 173
   traditional media compared to, 23–25, 182–83
      displacement in media sphere, 103–4
      Fox News, 23

Society of Professional Journalists, 100
Stein, Jill, 27
suicide, suicidal ideation and, social media influences on, 43
Sunstein, Cass, 38–39
Supreme Court, U.S. *See also specific cases; specific justices*
   common carrier cases, 62–63, 65–66, 72
   NetChoice cases, 62–63, 71–83, 85
   hate speech on social media and, 36
surveillance capitalism, 52–53, 57–58

Taibbi, Matt, 16–17
take-down regimes, 136–38
Telecommunications Act of 1996, U.S., 119
Telegram, 24, 67
Texas
   common carrier issues in, 89–91
   legislation on social media in, 13–14
Thiel, Peter, 3
Thomas, Clarence (Justice), 15, 23, 62–63
   on common carriage status, 65–66, 68–70, 72, 77–79, 87
   objections to Section 230, 125
TikTok, 24
   common carrier issues, 67–68
   data privacy issues and, 56, 160
      banning of TikTok, 58–59
      as spying platform, 58–59
   global expansion of, 168
   platform algorithms for, 173
   targeted advertising revenue for, 147
tort law, 173
traditional media. *See* media, traditional
transparency, data privacy and, 155–57, 159
Trump, Donald. *See also* 2016 presidential election; 2020 presidential election
   deplatforming of, 9
      First Amendment arguments against, 15
      after January 6th Capitol attacks, 12–13
   Musk support of, 57
   political polarization and, 41
   on Section 230, 124–26, 128
   Truth Social, 13, 24, 67–68
   use of social media, 9–13
      COVID-19 misinformation and, 10–12
Trump, Donald, Jr., 13
Truth Social, 13, 24, 67–68

Twain, Mark, 69
Twitter (X), 4, 24
   anti-progressive bias on, 20, 24
   conservative support on platform, 20, 24
   content rules, 17–19
   hate speech on, 18–19, 109–10
      advertising revenue influenced by, 109–10
      progressive critics of, 109
   Musk purchase of, 15–16, 19–20, 30, 168–69
   political dialogue on, 168–69
   prohibition of hateful conduct on, 18–19
   targeted advertising revenue for, 146–48
2016 presidential election, political manipulation during, 26–28
2020 presidential election
   election fraud claims, 12
   misinformation after, 12

Volokh, Eugene, 6, 122

"War on Woke," 13–15
Warner, Mark, 31–32
Warren, Elizabeth, 1, 32, 92, 126–27
Weiss, Bari, 16–17
women, online harassment of, 33–35
   Gamergate, 33
   revenge porn, 33
Wu, Brianna, 33

X. *See* Twitter

Yoo, Christopher, 65–66
YouTube, 24
   data privacy issues and, 160
   targeted advertising revenue for, 147

Zeran v. American Online, 120–21
Zittrain, Jonathan, 57
Zuboff, Shoshana, 51, 57–58
Zuckerberg, Mark, 10, 20–21, 50, 126–27. *See also* Facebook
   common carriage status and, 67–68
   on content moderation, 180
   content moderation decisions by, 96
   global impact and power of, 57–58, 60, 166–67
   political impact of, 21

For EU product safety concerns, contact us at Calle de José Abascal, 56–1°,
28003 Madrid, Spain or eugpsr@cambridge.org.

www.ingramcontent.com/pod-product-compliance
Ingram Content Group UK Ltd.
Pitfield, Milton Keynes, MK11 3LW, UK
UKHW020916211025
464179UK00021B/1377